RESEARCH METHODS FOR HEALTH CARE PRACTICE

RESEARCH METHODS FOR HEALTH CARE PRACTICE

FRANCES GRIFFITHS

Los Angeles | London | New Delhi
Singapore | Washington DC

First published 2009

Apart from any fair dealing for the purposes of research or private study, or criticism or review, as permitted under the Copyright, Designs and Patents Act, 1988, this publication may be reproduced, stored or transmitted in any form, or by any means, only with the prior permission in writing of the publishers, or in the case of reprographic reproduction, in accordance with the terms of licences issued by the Copyright Licensing Agency. Enquiries concerning reproduction outside those terms should be sent to the publishers.

SAGE Publications Ltd
1 Oliver's Yard
55 City Road
London EC1Y 1SP

SAGE Publications Inc.
2455 Teller Road
Thousand Oaks, California 91320

SAGE Publications India Pvt Ltd
B 1/I 1 Mohan Cooperative Industrial Area
Mathura Road, Post Bag 7
New Delhi 110 044

SAGE Publications Asia-Pacific Pte Ltd
33 Pekin Street #02-01
Far East Square
Singapore 048763

Library of Congress Control Number: 2008938923

British Library Cataloguing in Publication data

A catalogue record for this book is available from the British Library

ISBN 978-1-4129-3576-0
ISBN 978-1-4129-3577-7 (pbk)

Typeset by C&M Digitals (P) Ltd, Chennai, India
Printed in Great Britain by CPI Antony Rowe, Chippenham, Wiltshire
Printed on paper from sustainable resources

Mixed Sources
Product group from well-managed
forests and other controlled sources
www.fsc.org Cert no. SGS-COC-2953
© 1996 Forest Stewardship Council
FSC

Contents

List of Figures, Tables and Boxes

Figures

Tables

Boxes

Acknowledgements

This book was made possible by my experience of teaching and learning from students undertaking research projects, many of whom were also working as health professionals. I am also indebted to many colleagues who, over the years and in different places, have shared ideas with me, worked with me, encouraged me, taught me and left me to learn in my own way.

The examples used in the book draw on the research ideas and projects of students and colleagues. I am grateful to the referees and publisher who read a draft of this book, gave helpful feedback and encouraged me to complete it. The unquestioning support of family, friends and colleagues has been vital to the writing of this book.

This book was written while the author was funded by the UK Department of Health through a National Primary Care Career Scientist Award for undertaking research and scholarship on 'Complexity and Healthcare'. The text is the responsibility of the author.

Introduction

I have written this book with a wide audience in mind. Health professionals, those new to research, teachers, research users, managers, students, experienced researchers will all benefit from the detailed guidance. It is illustrated throughout with carefully chosen case examples that will be familiar to health professionals but accessible to everyone.

This book is for you if you are a health professional keen to undertake research that is of direct relevance to health care practice. You have probably got an idea of what you want to investigate, such as something that troubles you in your clinical practice. You may have some other motivation for doing this, perhaps a research degree or dissertation, or perhaps frustration with your clinical work or the health service.

This book is for you if you are unsure how to get started on research. It takes you through each step in great detail, making sure that what you actually research is what you really want to research. It guides you through research that reveals how and why things happen the way they do and gives you results that you can use in health care practice.

You may have some knowledge of research but are confused by the different types of research or cannot see how you could use the various research methods. Maybe you were told that small research studies are a waste of time. This book gives in-depth illustrations and examples of the different approaches to research and the arguments about their usefulness. It explains how different research methods relate to each other and how small research studies can contribute new knowledge about our world.

You may have talked to people doing research who are confident about what they are doing and are clear about the difference between theory and hypothesis, between qualitative and quantitative research, between an interview study and a survey and between a research user and a research participant. If these differences are not so clear to you, then this book is for you as it clarifies these distinctions. It avoids using jargon and provides you with a glossary of words used in research.

This book is also for you if you:

- teach research methods at undergraduate or postgraduate level to health professionals in training or practice. The book provides a structure for working through the issues of developing research, including critical thinking and critical use of research methods.

- are a 'research user' such as an advisor to a research team, a member of a research user group or on a research ethics committee. This book will introduce you to the way researchers think and to research methods that are useful for health care practice. The Glossary also provides non-technical explanations.

- manage a health care service and want to encourage a critical approach to developing an innovative and evidence-based service where research becomes part of everyday clinical practice.

- are an experienced researcher interested in exploring what is distinctive about research for health care practice.

The research process and the structure of the book

The first chapter of this book, 'Research for Health Care Practice', introduces you to research and the various types of research related to health care practice. It explores the basics of research including how we think about the world and what our research can tell us about how it works. The research process as mapped out in Table 0.1 guides you through the different phases of research.

Phase I of the research process is discussed in Chapter 2, 'Getting Started on Your Research'. The steps taken are very similar for all types of health-related research. Each step is important and needs careful thought. Often we have to go through the different steps in this phase several times before we are ready to move

Table 0.1   The research process

Phase	Steps to be taken		
I	Becoming motivated and examining our motivations Critical observation of difference and change Establishing the overall aim of our research Clarifying the frame and focus of our research Developing the research aim, questions and objectives		
II	Examining our preferences for how to approach the research Defining the focus of our research Reviewing literature in preparation for designing research Matching the research approach to the research aim Modelling the research focus	Involving users	Ethical considerations
III	Using existing data or collecting new data Analysing data		

on to the next phase. It may seem that these steps are really preparation for research rather than the research itself, which we often think of as collecting and analysing data. These early steps underpin the whole of our research. Taking time and care on this phase ensures that the rest of the research process goes well.

In phase I and throughout the research process we need to consider the ethical implications of the research. This is discussed in Chapter 3, 'Considering the Ethics of Your Research'.

The perspective of future users of the results of our research can be of great value and is discussed in Chapter 4, 'Involving Users in Your Research'. Users can contribute throughout the research process.

Once we know what we want to research there is a further stage (phase II) of preparation needed, before designing the details of our research. This is discussed in Chapter 5, 'Preparing to Design Research for Health Care Practice'. This phase ensures that we understand as much as possible about what we want to research and are clear about the focus of our research and the best way of approaching it. It is at this point that our decisions will determine the way we collect our data.

Phase III considers the collection and analysis of research data. There are now many sources of data about health and health care that are collected for other purposes. These resources can be used as data for our research and are introduced in Chapter 6, 'Using Existing Data in Research' for Health Care Practice'. Published research can also be used as a source of data for research. Chapter 6 describes how to collect and analyse published research for our own research.

How to collect new data is described in both Chapter 7, 'Collecting and Exploring New Data Using Qualitative Methods' and Chapter 8, 'Collecting and Exploring New Data Using Quantitative Methods'. These chapters complement each other, each covering issues relevant to the other. The chapters describe how to ensure that the data collected is directly relevant to the research and collected in a way that can reveal what is happening in the world.

The term **qualitative** is used in health-related research to distinguish data collection methods such as interviews from **quantitative** data collection methods, which involve counting and measurement. The distinction can be useful in designing data collection; however, both qualitative and quantitative data can be collected within one study and using both approaches can enhance the value of a study. There has been a great deal of debate about the value of qualitative and quantitative research methods. The debate relates, at least in part, to the ways of reasoning with which the methods are associated (discussed in Chapter 1). This book clarifies the value of both types of data in research for health care practice.

Methods of data analysis can be used for data drawn from an existing source and for new data. When using the approach to research described in this book, analysis usually starts very soon after the commencement of data collection, and early results of analysis are used to improve the collection of subsequent data and decisions about further data analysis. This early exploration of data is included in Chapters 7 and 8.

There are many approaches to the analysis of data relevant for health and health care. This book does not attempt to cover them all but rather explores an approach of particular relevance for health care practice. However, the further reading sections at the end of Chapters 7, 8 and 9 direct the reader to books that describe other methods of analysis.

Chapter 9, 'Analysing Data in Research for Health Care Practice' discusses an approach to data analysis where the results can directly feed into health care practice. It uses the well-established principle for data analysis of constant comparison. The chapter emphasises the importance of understanding the whole nature of what the research is about, rather than the details. This approach is accessible by all health care professionals without special expertise, and through this approach insights can be gained of direct relevance for clinical practice. The chapter then explores the potential of further analysis that requires additional expertise but based on constant comparison. This analysis has potential for understanding the tailoring of interventions, in terms of their nature and timing, to individual people in clinical practice.

The position of research for health care practice, and its particular contribution to the wider world of research is summarised in the Conclusion to this book.

This book is written as an introduction to the issues you need to consider for undertaking research within your own practice setting, using examples drawn from the everyday work of health professionals. It will enable you to develop and plan your own research. You may need to read further details of particular aspects of your research, so a brief list of further reading is provided after each chapter. Glossary terms are highlighted in bold at their first appearance in each chapter.

1 Research for Health Care Practice

This chapter tells you what research is and explains why your research is important, introduces you to the basics of research and the various ways of undertaking research.

The research approach described and discussed in this book can be used by anyone involved in health care practice within their own health care setting. The research can contribute to the development of health care practice for the particular time and place it was undertaken as well as adding to the wider body of knowledge about health and health care.

Anyone engaged with health care can use the research approach described in this book. This includes people living with long-term health conditions and community groups. People working as health professionals can incorporate this type of research into their day-to-day work, including those who directly care for patients and those managing or planning services.

Research undertaken as collaboration between people using health care services and local health care professionals is ideal as it brings into the research the perspective of those using health care services. However, health professionals have a key role to play in research for health care practice.

Health professionals are well positioned to take the initiative in research. They are often committed to health care for long periods, sometimes all their working life, so research can continue as part of their health care practice in the long term. They are well placed to notice change; for example, the impact of a new diagnostic or treatment technology, changes in the **population** they serve through migration or change in the local environment. Such changes may be the stimulus for research. Health professionals build up considerable knowledge of their own health care service and the community it serves, including its history, so they can take this into account in their research. They can also continue to observe the impact of change as well as the impact of their own service developments in the long-term.

Research is about the discovery of new knowledge. This includes any study of the natural, social or technical world that increases our understanding of it, and is undertaken in such a way that others can follow how it was done (**transparency**) and assess the robustness of the results. Research is a global collaborative effort. Every research project, including those undertaken in a specific health care setting, can contribute to the development of new knowledge.

Health professionals contribute to the global research effort

Research can be thought of as many spirals of activity extending through time, with cycles of activity changing over time both locally and globally. Health professionals can contribute to research as part of the global research effort in the same way as academics and full-time researchers. The world is constantly changing, so we need to reinvestigate the world because it has changed. Our new knowledge about the world will itself change something about the world and so prompt further research. This could be in our own local context or more widely. New methods of investigating the world lead to further research as they give us the opportunity to find out more. Individual researchers only contribute to one part of the research spiral. For example, inspired by a need identified by a health professional in their research, an engineer may work on a new technology. This technology may be tested by another health professional for use in health care. A social scientist then studies the impact of this new technology on people's experience of illness. Understanding the experience of illness may prompt the engineer to modify the new technology or a health professional to review how the technology is incorporated into health care practice.

Most academic and research disciplines have knowledge and expertise relevant to health care. Being part of this multidisciplinary research effort is exciting and challenging but can also feel overwhelming. There is a danger that we ignore unfamiliar academic and research disciplines and assume that all relevant sources of knowledge and expertise for health care research are within the body of expertise we think of as health science or clinical science. We need to find a balance between drawing on the resources of the wider research community and getting on with investigating the health issues that concern us.

Understanding the range of types of research that relate to health and health care helps us to open our minds to knowledge, ideas and possibilities that we may rarely think about in our daily work in health care. The following examples illustrate the range of types of research relevant to health and how they feed into the research spiral. Each example is a patient we could meet in our clinical practice.

> An 18-year-old man with insulin-dependent diabetes who has failed to attend follow-up at the diabetes clinic. His last blood test indicated poor control of his diabetes.

Insulin is the key to this man's survival. To understand the research that led to the clinical use of insulin we have to look back into history. My aim is not to give you all the details of the history but alert you to the many different types of research that contributed over time to its discovery and use.

> Diabetes has been known since ancient time. Physicians observed each individual patient as a **case study**, describing their symptoms in detail. By comparing each **case** with other cases, they identified the symptoms they had in common as diabetes. In the 18th century, chemistry experiments showed the urine and blood of those with diabetes contained a lot of sugar. In the 19th century, the link was established between the symptoms of diabetes and changes found in the pancreas on dissection of those that had died. Detailed examination of the pancreas revealed the Islets of Langerhans and towards the end of the 19th century, research including animal experiments identified insulin as the key substance. In 1922 the joint work of physiologists and biochemists, with technical help from a pharmaceutical company, led to the isolation of insulin as an extract. This was then tested on a young boy dying of diabetes who survived on continuing insulin injections.

The research disciplines in the front line of this research included clinical research, chemistry, anatomy and pathology, physiology and biochemistry. These were supported by other disciplines including physics and engineering for the development of the microscope and organic chemistry for understanding substances such as proteins.

Once people with diabetes were able to survive on insulin, research continued to refine insulin treatments and to seek to understand the cause of diabetes. **Epidemiology,** the **social sciences** and **behavioural sciences** have also contributed to research on diabetes. Table 1.1 gives examples of research related to diabetes currently undertaken by different research disciplines.

Table 1.1   Examples of the diverse research disciplines that contribute to the health care of people living with diabetes

Research disciplines	Examples of research issues related to diabetes
Genetics	Heredity of diabetes
Biochemistry	Refinements of insulin; new drugs
Engineering	Development of technology, e.g. artificial pancreas
Clinical research	Effect of treatment on short- and long-term health outcome
Psychology	Behavioural interventions to improve diabetes self-care
Epidemiology	Causation of diabetes; population health need assessment
Sociology	Understanding experience of diabetes including self-image; socio-economic influences on illness
Anthropology	How illness is expressed and controlled through social norms and culture
Organisational sciences	Health service organisation and its development
Information sciences	Access and content of health information
Economics	Health care funding, e.g. public/private
Political sciences	Prioritisation of health care; food and drug policy

A man in his fifties who has low mood, insomnia, fits of tearfulness and irritability. He has successfully worked for a company at a local manufacturing plant for 10 years. With the shut-down of the local plant he was made redundant. He has a supportive family.

Research from many disciplines directly or indirectly informs the assessment and management of this patient. Different research disciplines tend to tackle different types of research question. Table 1.2 suggests examples of research questions inspired by encountering the man in the example above and the research discipline most likely to tackle each one. Notice the different focus of the different disciplines including: society, community, organisations, individuals, groups of individuals, physiology, biochemistry and genetics. Note also the different types of question words used: what, where, when, how, why, who. We consider the development of research focus and research questions in Chapter 2.

The research questions in Table 1.2 all feed into an overall research question of interest to health professionals:

Why do people get depressed and why do they get better (or not)?

Table 1.2   Examples of the types of research question different academic and research disciplines may ask in relation to depression

Type of research question	Research discipline
What are the cultural representations of depression? Why do people respond to depression in this way?	Anthropology
What symptoms indicate that an individual is suffering from clinical depression? How effective is a drug/psychological therapy for treating depression?	Clinical research
What is the loss of earning in the country related to depression? How cost-effective is the introduction of a new treatment?	Economics
How many people (who and where) suffer from depression? Why does the number of people with depression in a population change over time? How is the variation linked to the level of unemployment?	Epidemiology
How does the genetic make-up of a person influence their mental health? Where in the human genome are genes that influence mental health?	Genetics
How is mental health portrayed in the media and who/what influences this?	Media studies
How are services for the mentally ill best delivered in a rural setting and why?	Organisational
How does the culture of an organisation influence the health of the work force?	studies
How does a drug change the biochemistry at the neuron synapses? What dose of a drug is safe and effective?	Pharmacology
Why does the biochemistry of the neurone synapses differ in people with and without depression?	Physiology
What are the patterns of thought and behaviour in people with depression and why?	Psychology
What influences the prioritisation (or not) of mental health services for state funding? How does employment law influence the health of workers?	Social policy
Why is depression perceived as an illness? What do those with depression experience and what influences it? What is the influence of social networks on vulnerability to depression and how is this mediated?	Sociology

It is unlikely that one piece of research could answer this overall question, but we build up understanding of depression through many different research projects undertaken in many different disciplines using various research approaches.

Whatever health problem we research, we need to remain open to the possibility that our research may suggest that health professionals don't have a lot to offer but that change is needed in the environment or society. For those of us working as health professionals, keeping an open mind about this can be difficult as it seems to undermine ourselves as health professionals and those who experience illness. However, keeping an open mind is vital for research and does not prevent us continuing to recognise the distress experienced by patients. If our research does suggest that what health professionals do makes little difference, this is an important contribution to the ongoing spiral of research activity. Other researchers will pick up the research issue and investigate it in a different way.

Finding out new knowledge while also improving health care

Research is sometimes considered as something very different from activities such as **evaluation** and **audit** that aim to improve health care. This can lead to health professionals feeling they can do audit and evaluation but cannot do research. However, there is no clear boundary between these activities and health professionals can contribute to both, often at the same time.

In research we aim to step back from studying particular people in a specific place and timeframe to ask what the study can tell us generally about how the world functions. Audit and evaluation are terms used to describe the process of studying a local health care service with the aim of improving that service. For example, an audit of diabetes care may involve the health professionals providing that care identifying people with diabetes who are not having regular check-ups, changing how they provide check-ups with the aim of improving the service, then observing whether those changes have made a difference. Evaluation also looks at the effect of changing how health care is delivered, though this may be undertaken by people not involved in providing the service. The methods of collecting **data** and analysing it may be similar for audit, evaluation and research. One of the key differences is the audience for the results. Generally, audit is for the practitioners in a local health care service, evaluation is for those making decisions about health care service provision, and research is for a wider audience to contribute to increasing knowledge of health and health care overall. However, studies aimed at a local audience can contribute to the development of new understanding more generally.

Box 1.1	Evaluation of waiting times in an emergency department

The manager of a busy hospital emergency department notices that many people attending seem to wait for hours before a decision is made about whether they stay in hospital or go home. This problem has been the focus of much media attention, so the manager knows it is not just a problem for this hospital. The manager cannot sort out the problem for the whole country, but can find out what is happening in his own department and why.

The manager asked those working in the department what they thought caused the long waits, but they all had different views on the issue. He therefore sought advice from colleagues experienced in the evaluation of organisations and decided to measure the length of time patients waited at different points in their progress through the emergency department. He set up a data collection system tracking where patients wait, how long they wait and what they wait for; for example, the length of wait to speak to the reception clerk, the wait to see a doctor, the wait to go to X-ray. Analysis of these patient flows showed that a major delay was the wait for a porter to take patients to X-ray.

With this evidence that the department needs an extra porter he presented the evaluation to the hospital executive board. They were convinced by the results, as they could follow how the data had been collected and that it revealed what really happens in the emergency department.

As the manager had worked out how to collect the data about patient waits without disrupting the everyday work of the department, he was able to collect data again, after the introduction of the extra porter. The evaluation therefore became an ongoing audit.

There are many different ways in which a local study can contribute to the development of new knowledge. Box 1.1 illustrates this using the example of an evaluation of the waiting times for patients in the emergency department of a hospital. The evaluation showed that the emergency department needed an extra porter. If the project were presented at a national conference about emergency care, people might return to their own departments suggesting an increase in the number of porters. Imagine what might happen: in some places an extra porter might reduce patient waiting times, in others it might make no difference because there were different causes of delay, and in some it might increase the patient waiting times as it led to a reduction in porters elsewhere in the hospital. Although the results of an evaluation may not seem to be of use to other people, there are many ways in which its findings can provide useful new knowledge as discussed below.

If the evaluation were presented in some detail, those hearing about it could assess whether their emergency department was similar to the original department, and from this make a judgement as to whether an extra porter would make a difference in their own department. For those of us working in the UK, where national policy has a strong influence on how local services are delivered, it may be possible to find sufficient similarity to be fairly sure the solution will work so it can be directly transferred to a different department (**transferability**). Someone from a very different health care service would need to assess this very carefully as fundamental service issues, such as who is responsible for paying for what, can make a big difference to how a service functions. Of course, the only way of being sure is to try it out and assess what happens. If a number of emergency departments tried out introducing extra porters and observed and reported what happened, by comparing the experiences it might be possible to develop new knowledge about what is happening, and why, in a more general sense (**generalise**). For example, it might help increase understanding of how local social and organisational issues influence the implementation of national policy and guidance. These ideas could be compared with studies already published in research literature.

The lead nurse of an emergency department in a different hospital may decide to repeat the evaluation to see if they get the same results. If the health care service is similar, they may be able to collect and analyse the data in almost exactly the same way as the original study. They are using new knowledge from the original evaluation; that is, the way it was done, both the overall approach and how it was applied in the setting of emergency care.

Another department may want to try a modified approach, using only data collected routinely. To test this out the original department could be asked to re-analyse their data, including only data that would be routinely available (recorded as part of daily clinical activity), to see whether they would come to the same conclusion. If this is not possible, the other department could undertake the modified method themselves and compare their results with the original research. As the departments are not identical it is not possible to make a direct comparison, but the type and quality of data can be compared in order to judge how likely it is that the new data will give a robust result. If there are many gaps in the data, for example, some important delay points could be missed. This is new knowledge for understanding how to evaluate health care organisations.

Ten years on from the original evaluation, the way in which emergency departments are run may have changed because of changes, internal or external to the health care system, that could be local or global. Examples include: change in the funding system; the availability of a different mix of health professional skills; new housing for families or older people nearby; a reduction in road traffic, and so fewer accidents; or changes in society's expectation of services. Although we may know a great deal about how organisations work and how to study organisations, because the time and context are different we may need to repeat the original evaluation to check whether our understanding still applies. This could then lead to new knowledge about health care organisation and how it is influenced by changes in a social context.

The evaluation may provide the opportunity to develop and test new ways of studying the world. For example, the availability of computers means it is now possible to carry out forms of data analysis that were previously very time-consuming or just not possible. Analysis of patient flow through an emergency department can now be studied using a technique called agent-based modelling, which requires a computer to do a huge number of calculations relatively quickly. Using this analysis method it is also possible to demonstrate what is likely to happen if changes are made in the emergency department, such as increasing the number of porters. This type of analysis is continually being improved through testing on data from real-world situations, and so using it contributes new knowledge about the analysis method.

Studies undertaken in a particular health care setting, such as the emergency department described above, have the potential to contribute to the development of new knowledge about the world in many ways. The individual leading the local study may not have the time and resources to develop all the possible ways in which it can contribute to new knowledge, but others can through **collaboration**. The collaboration may be by working directly with other people, or indirectly through making the details of the local study available to others through formal publication or more informally, for example, by making the study report available to a network of interested people or on the Internet. However, the local study can only contribute to the development of new knowledge if it has been undertaken in a thoughtful and systematic way and the study reported in sufficient detail for the reader to really understand what was studied, where and when, how it was studied, why it was studied, who was studied and by whom.

The basics of why we do research and how we do it

If we understand how the world works we are better able to predict what will happen in the world. For those of us working in health care, this may be the ability to predict the course of a disease, the effect of treatment or the impact of a change in the environment on health. If everything about the world we live in were obvious just from us observing it, then we would not need to do research. This is not how it is. There are important aspects of the world and how it functions, both natural and social, that cannot be immediately observed. Natural and social scientists have built up knowledge about how the world works and keep improving on this knowledge. The knowledge we have is only the best truth we have about the world at the moment. Researchers take what is currently known and change it to new knowledge. They do this using:

- their own knowledge about an issue and what other people know about it
- research methods and skills

- a way of reasoning

- special equipment such as microscopes or computers.

If it is obvious how a particular aspect of the world works, then we may not need to undertake research. There are examples from health where the effect of a treatment is so obvious that no further research is needed to demonstrate its effect. Perhaps the most famous example is the dramatic effect when penicillin was first introduced: patients who were expected to die from infections were given penicillin and got better.

What is currently known about an issue and how to study it, including the availability of current knowledge and of special equipment, influences what is researched and how research is undertaken. However, research is also influenced by what is happening in society, including cultural, political and economic factors. Even the research question itself is under these influences. The story of research on tuberculosis illustrates some of these issues (see Box 1.2).

The different ways of reasoning in research and the development of theory

The way we reason in research is the process of thinking about what we observe in the world and what this tells us about how the world works. There are different ways of reasoning used in different types of research. This can cause confusion for us as health professionals because we draw on so many different types of research. Our understanding of how certain aspects of the world works is expressed as **theory**. This is a description of how the world works in a general sense (to the best of our understanding) rather than a description of what is happening in a particular time and place involving particular people. Sometimes the word theory is used to mean our suggestions about how the world works, before we have undertaken research to see if our suggestions are correct. These suggestions about how the world works are our **hypotheses**.

Undertaking research seeks knowledge that is not only about one particular time, place or person but may apply to many people in many places at different times. However, in our research we use data about particular people in particular places at a particular time. A key part of our reasoning in research is moving from the particular to the more general. In this process, known as **abstraction**, we leave out many details about particular people and their context, and use only the details we think are relevant to our research. If we get this wrong we can miss out the very details that are important.

Box 1.2	Research on tuberculosis

Identifying the bacillus that caused tuberculosis

The microscope was a key invention that led to understanding many infectious diseases including tuberculosis. The German microbiologist Robert Koch led the team which confirmed in 1882 that mycobacterium tuberculosis was the bacillus that caused tuberculosis. Koch had a clear definition of what he meant by a micro-organism causing a disease. This included finding the micro-organism in every person suffering from the disease and being able to reproduce the disease in experiments with animals by inoculating it with the micro-organism. Thus, through the use of the microscope Koch and his team isolated one aspect of the world, the bacillus, and then in a controlled environment (his laboratory) experimented to see if the animals inoculated with the bacillus developed tuberculosis.

Social influences on tuberculosis

In Europe in the 18th and 19th centuries tuberculosis was a very common disease but not everyone who came into contact with the tuberculosis bacillus died of tuberculosis. Since the 17th century in the UK, births, marriages and deaths had been recorded. This meant that patterns of disease could be identified. Most of those dying of tuberculosis were the urban poor. This pattern of disease could be identified through the research methods used by epidemiologists who study health and disease of populations.

Historically, the discipline of epidemiology was developing as other social change took place, so by the time it was well established in the 20th century, the plight of the urban poor was changing. The social change was not driven only, or even mainly, by research findings but by other social issues, such as the need for healthy adults in the army and industry.

Demonstrating that streptomycin treats tuberculosis

By 1944 the microbiologist Selman Waksman had isolated the antibiotic streptomycin from fungus which killed the tubercle bacillus. This was tested in humans in the first **randomised controlled trial** carried out with human subjects in 1946. Patients with the disease were identified and randomly allocated to a group receiving the new treatment or a group not receiving it. This random allocation is a way of controlling for other influences on the disease so that we can be sure any improvement in health is due to the new treatment and not to other factors. Waksman found more of the patients receiving streptomycin recovered from tuberculosis than patients who did not receive it. In order to design and analyse the trial, Waksman used **statistics**, a developing research discipline at that time (Porter, 1997).

Theories encapsulate our understanding of why things happen and help us predict what is likely to happen in other places, at other times, to other people. Theory is developed through research, refined through debate and comparison with existing research results and tested with further research. Theory is constantly being challenged and changed, as we understand more through research. Some theory may be very broad in its scope, claiming almost universal relevance, whereas other theory may only explain how the world works in certain types of situations. It is often the latter type of theory that we develop and test in our research as health professionals. However, by drawing together many research studies that suggest local theory, it is possible to develop more broad-ranging theory.

How theories are presented varies, and different research disciplines have different preferences. Many theories are explained through written text, sometimes accompanied by diagrams or models that represent the theory and are designed to aid understanding of the theory (Figure 5.3 is an example of this type of diagram). The use of text and diagrams is common in social, behavioural and health sciences. Other disciplines have very different ways of presenting theory, for example, computer models or mathematical formulae. Whatever form it takes, theory is a way of representing the particular aspect of the world we are studying and how it works. Sometimes theories are known as **models**. The usage of these terms varies and are sometimes interchangeable.

In health care our understanding of the world as expressed through theory draws on research undertaken in different ways using different ways of reasoning. The experimental method is used in a great deal of research related to health and has led to very successful theories about health and disease. To undertake experiments the aspect of the world to be studied is identified and defined, for example a disease or a drug. The experiment tests ideas (hypotheses) about cause, what causes what to happen. For example, in studies of tuberculosis (see Box 1.2), as the tubercle bacillus was found in everyone dying of tuberculosis, Koch reasoned that the bacillus caused tuberculosis in the sense that if the tubercle bacillus was not present a person would not get tuberculosis. In the randomised controlled trial of streptomycin as a treatment for tuberculosis, Waksman reasoned that as more of the people given streptomycin recovered than those who did not receive the drug, in a general sense streptomycin caused the recovery from the disease. This way of reasoning, known as **induction**, is now usually supported by statistical tests that tell us whether our observations could have happened by chance or not. Observing that the tubercle bacillus causes tuberculosis or that streptomycin cures tuberculosis does not tell us how this happens, that is the mechanism underlying the cause and how this might be different in different people, times and places. Induction as a way of reasoning is important within health-related research, but this type of research is not the focus of this book.

Epidemiologists and social scientists often use a similar way of reasoning to experimental research, although they often cannot manipulate the world to isolate a part of it to study. Instead, they identify the aspects of the world to study and develop ideas (hypotheses) about what may be happening. For example, when studying tuberculosis they may suspect that poorer people living in towns are more likely to die of the disease than poor people living in rural areas (see Box 1.2). They then collect data and look to see if the pattern of data supports their hypothesis or not, and use statistical methods to check whether the pattern may be a chance finding or not. This book will introduce you to this type of research approach as it is often used to clarify further research questions. For example, finding that a poor person with the tuberculosis bacillus living in a town is more likely to die than a poor person with the tuberculosis bacillus living in the country does not tell us exactly what is happening to these people, why they die. What is it about living in a town that leads to more deaths, and does this apply to all towns wherever and whenever? To understand the mechanisms underlying their findings, researchers draw on other types of research evidence, such as laboratory research or research using 'thought experiments'.

The way of reasoning which can be thought of as 'thought experiments' involves observing a particular aspect of the world and collecting data and examining it for patterns that may indicate how the world is working at the time and place it is studied. The purpose is to understand the mechanisms by which the world works that we cannot easily see. However, there is no assumption that how the world works in one time and place will be the same at a different time and place. The world may work in a similar way in a similar time and place, but this would need checking. However, from the understanding of how the world works in many different times and places it is possible to develop ideas about how the world works in more general terms, which is known as theory. This process, known as **abduction**, differs from induction described above, as there is no assumption that the mechanisms by which the world works are exactly the same at different times and places, that is, that causes of a particular phenomenon are always the same. For example, understanding that social stigma is an important influence on how people respond to illness (Goffman, 1983) helps us understand this aspect of the world but does not specify that stigma develops in the same way for everyone nor remains the same at different times and places. Researchers often take existing theory and explore how it helps to understand what is happening for a certain group of people at a particular time and place. This research may then help to develop and refine the theory further. This research approach is the main focus of this book. It introduces you to how to undertake studies of people in a particular time and place that increase understanding of what is happening for these people, there and then, but which also contributes to the broader understanding of how the world functions using this way of reasoning.

Within disciplines such as mathematics a different way of reasoning is used which we mention here but is not the focus of this book. Having identified and defined the mathematical problem, the researcher develops what can be thought of as an internal logic to the problem (**deduction**). When the researcher applies mathematical knowledge to understanding the world, one of the other ways of reasoning described above is used.

We undertake research in a particular time and place, collecting data from particular people. However, research also involves taking a step back from the detail to develop theory about how the world works, at least locally, using a way of reasoning that is clear to other people. Other researchers can test our theory elsewhere. The need to step back from the detail of individual people and their context when undertaking research underlies the difficulty of using research evidence in clinical practice. This is particularly so for evidence based on the inductive way of reasoning of experimental research.

Using research evidence in clinical practice

Research evidence is difficult to apply in health care practice because we need to focus on a particular individual within a social context at a particular time in history, whereas research seeks to understand how the world works in a more general sense, not tied to time, place and person. In health care, there will always be this tension between the particular and the general as health care research requires us to move in our thinking from the particular to the general and evidence-based health care requires us to move from the general to the particular (Rosenburg, 1998). Uncertainty of clinical practice is due to the nature of individuals and the nature of research evidence.

Research based in a laboratory considers a person in terms of their biochemistry in order to study one aspect of the person such as diabetes or depression. There is an underlying assumption that there is sufficient similarity between people at the level of biochemistry that such research findings may be applied to most people with diabetes or depression. However, in clinical practice we may find a particular patient with depression does not respond to, for example, a drug affecting the biochemistry of nerve synapses. There are many factors that may inhibit the effect of the drug in a particular individual; a slight difference in their genes or biochemistry, a psychological influence, or factors in their social environment. Such uncertainty applies to any health care intervention.

The uncertainty of whether an intervention that is known to work for most of a group of people (as in a randomised controlled trial) will work for a particular patient is a different type of uncertainty. If results of a trial show that an intervention prevents early death in, for example, 50 out of every 100 patients (**probability** of benefit is one in two), then if the intervention is otherwise fairly safe it is worth trying for all patients. However, as health professionals we cannot guarantee to any one particular patient that they will be one of the 50 to benefit rather than one of the 50 that do not.

There is uncertainty in clinical practice because a health professional does not know enough or because the research has not been done. These are important, but in principal can be overcome. The uncertainty in clinical practice due to the very nature of research evidence is different, as it will always be there (Fox, 2002). This uncertainty is difficult to deal with because it is a difficult concept, particularly for those of us living in a culture where science tends to be portrayed as providing certainty. Health professionals tend to avoid or skim over the issue in clinical practice (Griffiths et al., 2005).

Despite this uncertainty we should continue to use research evidence in our practice. History reminds us of the importance of seeking evidence for whether an intervention works. For example, blood letting was a popular practice from the 2nd century right through to the mid-19th century, although it is very unlikely to have benefited many patients.

Uncertainty due to the nature of research evidence may be less when research is undertaken in a similar setting to our own or with similar patients. For example, evidence about the best way of providing health care to a local population in the UK served by the National Health Service is more likely to be applicable to other populations in the UK than it is to a population in the USA where there is a very different health care system. Similarly, research evidence about the effect of a drug may be more applicable to people who are similar to the population participating in the research than to people who are very different.

Health care professionals who undertake research as part of their daily work can produce research evidence applicable to other similar situations or similar people, but we have to be cautious as we may not be aware of what it is about a particular situation or person that would make a difference to what happens when we attempt to apply the evidence. However, health professionals are well placed to observe what happens, as it happens, and can adapt the way the evidence is applied for the benefit of their patients.

Using our skills of observation and noticing difference and change for research

Health professionals are trained to observe patients and can use this skill in research. Observing and describing what we observe is necessary for all research, although not all researchers undertake this research activity, relying on the observations of others. When we observe and then describe what we observe, we start the process of abstraction, picking out from all the many details of life the aspect we want to study. As our aim is to understand more about how the world works, we need to observe as much as possible about what affects the aspect of life we are interested in. We observe the world with prior knowledge about what we are likely to observe; however, we need to be open to surprise and look for what we don't expect, otherwise we will only see what we expect to see and discover nothing new or, worse, reinforce current erroneous knowledge. This is no different to how we work with patients where we have to constantly check that we are not missing new or unexpected aspects of our patient's story.

When we observe we make **comparisons** noting what is different or what has changed. We may hardly be aware we are doing this, as it is so much part of how we function as humans. Comparison can suggest why there is difference or change, that is, how it has come about. The skill of noticing difference and change is central to research and to health care practice. When assessing a patient we notice what is different about them compared to others or compared to how they were in the past. Noticing difference or change is often what sparks off a new piece of research. We notice something has changed and want to find out why. The process of doing research involves looking out for difference or change and assessing whether there really is a difference or change and how much. The difference or change may suggest the mechanism, or part of the mechanism, by which the change has occurred. We may not be able to establish exactly why something has changed because of the **complexity** of the world but by comparision we can develop theory. Observation of change and constant comparison is central to the research approach (**methodology**) described in this book.

Complexity and research for health care practice

When working in health care practice we become immersed in the health care setting, the local community it serves and the rich variety of patients. Through working in this setting we become accustomed to things not working out quite as we expected and adjust accordingly what we do for a particular patient or situation. We do this because we are working with the complexity of life and the world. Complexity can be a problem for research as it makes it difficult to know what we should focus on in our research. Research on tuberculosis illustrates some of these problems (see Box 1.2).

Although everyone dying of tuberculosis had the tubercle bacillus in their body, if a person was poor in the 19th century they were more likely to die of tuberculosis than if they were rich. There may be many different ways in which this came about, for example, the poor had inadequate nutrition, exposure to environmental pollution, concurrent diseases and needed to do hard physical work. This is an example of how causes of disease may be many and interacting and some may be difficult to identify.

During the 19th century, there were improvements in housing and nutrition for the urban poor at the same time as the methods of studying disease in populations were being developed. The world around the issue under study, in our example tuberculosis, changed while it was being studied. In experimental research where one aspect of the world is isolated, changes in the world during the research have little impact on the results. However, in research for health care practice we cannot isolate ourselves from this constant change.

Since the 19th century, tuberculosis and the tubercle bacillus itself have changed. For example, the presentation of tuberculosis has changed as it has become associated with AIDS and the bacillus has become resistant to some antibiotics. This very specific aspect of the world under study has changed. As we undertake our research we have to consider whether what was being studied at a different time and place is the same as what we are studying here and now. We must also be aware that during our own research what we are studying may change. These issues can be very unsettling as they prompt questions such as:

Is my research about something that is real, that actually exists?

Is it possible to find out what is actually happening in the world?

There have been centuries of debate about the nature of the world (**ontology**) and how we investigate it and understand it (**epistemology**). For those of us working as health professionals we may not want to delve into these debates very much, but it is important that we are aware that there is debate. The way we decide to approach our research is influenced by the way we understand the nature of the world and how it can be investigated.

For those of us working as health professionals within Western scientific culture, our training and the evidence we use in practice is mostly based on the assumption that it is possible to understand the world through scientific endeavour and to identify what causes what, particularly through experiments and what is known as **reductionism**, where we look at the details underlying the focus of our research (for example, the structure of the tubercle bacillus). This approach has been very successful for many health issues, but the limitations of this approach continue to be tested and debated. For many health issues social factors are important, for example poverty, personal relationships and community context. How these social factors cause ill health can be difficult to pin down.

In this book I have assumed that it is possible to identify aspects of the world that are really there, to understand the world, at least to some degree, through our research endeavour and that to some extent this understanding helps us to predict what is likely to happen in the future and how our interventions may change this. This view of what research can achieve has been termed **critical realism**: we assume there is a real world that exists even when we are not aware of it and that we can research it, yet we take care about the assumptions we make, in particular the assumption that we can prove what causes what. The words and phrases 'at least to some degree', 'to some extent', 'likely to' and 'may' are important as we need to be constantly aware of the limitations of what we do in research. However, we only find out more about these limitations by continuing to investigate the world.

The way we develop our research questions and undertake our research is based on the assumptions we make about the world. Although it is unsettling, our research for health care practice is more likely to lead to new knowledge about the world if we continue to question the nature, even the reality, of what we are investigating and keep in mind that what we do discover is probably only a small part of what is actually happening and may also change.

Uncertainty underlies all research. We undertake research to be less uncertain, yet we have to continually be aware of uncertainty and question what may appear certain. This can make it very difficult to know how to go about doing research. Following the research process set out in the Introduction to this book provides a way of checking that, despite all the uncertainty, we are moving forward in our research. As we move through our research it is important to keep notes about our thoughts as well as what we do in a **research diary**, as by looking back over these notes we can see how our understanding of the world has changed. The next chapter guides you from your very first thought about undertaking research through to developing your research aims, questions and objectives.

References

Fox, R.C. (2002) Medical Uncertainty Revisited, in *Gender, Health and Healing: The public/private divide*, G. Bendelow, M. Carpenter, C. Vautier and S. Williams (Editors). London: Routledge. p. 236–53.

Goffman, E. (1983) *Stigma: Notes on the management of spoiled identity*. New York: Prentice-Hall.

Griffiths, F., Green E. and Tsouroufli M. (2005) 'The nature of medical evidence and its inherent uncertainty for the Clinical consultation: the example of midlife women'. *BMJ*, 330: 511–15.

Porter, R. (1997) *The Greatest Benefit to Mankind: A medical history of humanity from antiquity to the present*. London: Harper Collins.

Rosenburg, C. (1998) Holism in Twentieth-Century Medicine, in *Greater than the Parts: holism in biomedicine 1920–1950*. New York: Oxford University Press. p. 335–55.

Further reading

The following reading provides greater depth on some of the issues covered in this chapter. You may also find the references above useful for reading about the history of medical research (Porter, 1977) and the nature of evidence (Rosenburg, 1988; Fox, 2002; Griffiths et al., 2005).

Evaluation and research

Pawson, R. and Tilley, N. (1997) *Realistic Evaluation*. London: Sage.

One of the most important books on evaluation. This book clarifies what is meant by evaluation and how to do it to inform real-world issues. It contributes to the ongoing debate about what is research and what is evaluation, including the question of how we know what we know about the world. However, it also assists you to undertake rigorous evaluation.

Robson, C. (2002) *Real World Research*. Oxford: Blackwell.

An excellent book on research methods for real-world issues written for a broad social science audience including those of us working in health care.

May, C. (2006) 'A rational model for assessing and evaluating complex interventions in health care'. *BMC Health Services Research*, 6: 86.

This is an example of using the results of evaluations of several different, specific health service innovations to develop new understanding of health service organisation more generally. The paper includes a description of how this was done, so provides a useful template for other researchers wanting to draw out more general lessons from many specific, local studies.

Complexity

Holt, T. (2004) *Complexity for Clinicians*. London: Radcliffe Medical Press.

This book provides an accessible introduction to complexity for clinicians and includes examples of clinical issues where complexity science may provide new perspectives.

Cilliers, P. (1998) *Complexity and Postmodernism*. New York: Routledge.

This book takes a more theoretical approach to complexity, placing complexity science within the social theory dominant at the time it was written. It remains one of the best expositions of complexity, though you may not want to read every chapter.

Critical realism

Danermark, B., Ekstrom, M., Jakobsen, L., Karlsson, J.C. (2002) *Explaining Society: Critical Realism in the social sciences*. London: Routledge.

This book provides a comprehensive introduction to the approach to research known as critical realism. The authors explain critical realism very thoroughly and explain how it contrasts to other approaches to research. The attention to detail by the authors makes it a book that takes time to read, but it is well worth reading from cover to cover to gain an understanding of ontology, epistemology, ways of reasoning and theory.

2 Getting Started on Your Research

Getting started on your research can be the most difficult part of the research process. This chapter guides you from your very first thought about undertaking research to developing your research aims, questions and objectives.

As health professionals we are often motivated to undertake research by our experiences in clinical practice. We identify an issue that troubles us and we want to investigate it so we can make it better in some way. In our clinical practice we aim to improve the health of our patients and this same motivation inspires our research. Our research can be very relevant for health care because it tackles issues we have identified in our day-to-day work. The close tie between our clinical practice and our research is important, but equally important is our ability to step back from the issue we have identified, reflect on it, ask questions about it and try and look at it in as many different ways as possible. We can use our familiarity with our clinical setting to advantage in our research as we know a great deal about what happens and why, but we need to notice when we are making assumptions, for example about what people think or do, and ask ourselves whether we have checked these assumptions out. Our enthusiasm for improving health care gives us the energy to carry us through the sometimes difficult research process, but we need to harness it into a questioning approach.

One of our functions as health professionals is to help solve problems, including our patients' health problems and problems of service provision in our local context. When there is an issue that troubles us, we quite naturally start thinking of how to solve it. If the solution is very obvious, we do not need to do research. Considering whether there is an obvious solution or not is important and may involve talking to colleagues and reading about health care policy and practice. If the solution is not obvious, we may want to undertake research. Although we may have some good ideas about how to solve the problem, we need to stop ourselves thinking of solutions and instead try to open our mind to what our research will tell us.

This chapter will help you get started on research by taking you through the process of identifying a research issue, reflecting on it, asking questions about it and thinking about it in different ways. These early steps in our research take time and care but need to be undertaken thoroughly to ensure that our research is successful. The different steps are laid out in sequence through the chapter for clarity (see also Table 0.1), but in reality different stages may be undertaken at the same time. For example, the reflective processes of examining our motivations and clarifying our aims may be undertaken at the same time. The exploratory processes of taking a critical approach to our observation of difference and change and of clarifying the **focus** and **frame** of our research issue could be undertaken at the same time, or at least inform each other.

It may feel that the process of getting started on research seems to go round and round. We reflect on our research issue, then explore it further, then return to reflect on it before continuing. This is how it should be, but there should also be movement forward, like a spiral, as we develop and refine our ideas. Keeping notes of our reflection and exploration in a research diary helps to clarify this forward movement as we can look back and see where we were before.

As we get started on our research as described in this chapter we also need to involve users in our research and consider any ethical issues. These are very important issues and warrant separate chapters (3 and 4). However, considering these issues should be integrated with the process of getting started on your own research.

Examining our motivations for research

Motivation for research in health care practice often comes from our own experience of providing clinical care, not infrequently because of our frustration with the difficulty of providing what we think would be the best possible health care. Our motivation gives us energy for research. However, our first step should be to examine our motivations carefully, as they will shape our future research. This includes considering why we want to do research on this issue at this time and in this place.

To explore the influence of time and place on our desire to undertake research, let us consider the example below.

> A doctor undertaking her specialist training in dermatology. She feels some frustration at seeing so many patients concerned about skin moles that are quite harmless. She thinks there must be some way of reducing the number of people attending the clinic with skin moles that do not need specialist treatment.

Let us pause and consider this issue. Why does it interest this doctor? I have made a list of possible reasons in Box 2.1.

Box 2.1	**Possible motivations for research on patient attendance at dermatology clinic with normal skin moles**

Reasons why a doctor working in a dermatology clinic may be interested in reducing the number of people attending the clinic with normal skin moles could include:

- The doctor is not seeing interesting patients for her training.
- There is a new piece of technology that makes it much easier to know if a skin mole is normal or not.
- She is concerned about the anxiety for patients in going to see a specialist.
- Many patients live a long way from her clinic, making it difficult for them to get there.
- Resources used in seeing patients with normal skin moles could be better spent on treatments of more serious problems.
- She thinks general practitioners should be more selective about whom they refer for specialist advice.

There may be many other reasons for the doctor's interest in this issue and which may shape her research. It is important that the doctor herself is aware of what prompts her interest and that the reasons are clear to the audience for the research. For all of us engaged in research it is good to write down, as honestly as possible, our reasons for being interested in a particular issue. These notes are an important document for our research both at the time of writing and later on. They help us to reflect on our motivations, consider how they will influence our research and how we can open our minds to possibilities that are beyond our immediate motivations. This helps us avoid setting out to prove what we want to prove, or even setting out to prove our own worth as health professionals. Research is about finding out new knowledge, so we need to be receptive to what is new or unexpected.

If we consider the list of motivations in Box 2.1, we can see that they are all tied in with where and when the doctor is working:

- The doctor is in training as a specialist
- A new piece of technology has been developed
- A locality where some patients live at a distance from the clinic
- An established health service with specialist dermatology clinics, where general practitioners act as gate-keepers to specialist services.

The research issue, that of skin moles, cannot be considered outside of a particular context. Where and when an issue becomes the focus of our interest for research both frames it and shapes the issue itself. Thus the context or frame of the 21st century is very different to that of the 19th century. We have different technology for examining skin moles; treatments for skin cancers are different; the epidemiology of skin moles has changed; our health services are very different; skin moles are discussed in our media; fashions in relation to exposure to sunlight are different. For an individual with a skin mole, the experience will be shaped by time and place and the biology of the skin mole itself may well be different from a century earlier. Being clear about the particular time and place of research, how this motivates us in our research and frames and shapes the research is important, both for the researcher in developing clear thinking about what is new knowledge and for the audience of the research to understand why it was done and how the knowledge gained may be useful in other times and places. This careful consideration of the effect on our research of who we are, where, when, how and why we undertake research is known as **reflexivity**. The frame within which we undertake research is discussed further throughout this book.

Underlying our motivation for research is our experience of working in health care and the observations we make in the course of our daily work. We observe and compare. For example, we notice how we provide health care and compare it with how we would like to provide it or how we have seen it done elsewhere. Through observation and comparison we note what is different or what has changed over time and this gives us clues for understanding what is happening and why. Observation and comparison underpin the research described in this book, and is discussed further in the next section.

Observation of difference and change underpins our research

Noticing difference and change gives us clues as to what is happening in the world and why, and underpins research. Throughout the book I will talk about ways we can observe and assess difference and change. This section briefly introduces how we notice difference and change and the ways in which this is talked about in research.

Difference is noted through comparison; for example, comparing two patients, two communities, two hospitals, or comparing what we observe with what we expect to observe. Differences may be noticed at a particular time; for example, differences between two hospitals in a particular year, or what I expect to observe now and what I actually observe now. A comparison may also be undertaken at the same point in a particular **timeframe**; for example, comparing two patients six weeks after completing a treatment, or comparing medical students' skills at the end of their medical training. Although the time as described by clock or calendar will be different for each patient or medical student, the time relative to the identified event (end of treatment or end of medical training) is the same.

If we compare lots of different people or several different hospitals we may find they are all slightly different: there is **diversity**. For example, there is diversity in how people experience medication. If we ask 20 different people how they feel when they take a particular antibiotic we are likely to get 20 different accounts, which may include similar themes such as abdominal pain or a metallic taste in the mouth, but each account will be slightly different. If we ask 20 people to measure their blood glucose after taking a glucose drink, each measurement is likely to be slightly different. This diversity can also be called **variation**. If diversity or variation is assessed focusing on certain aspects of a person, hospital or community, these aspects are known as **variables**. In the examples above the variables are: level of pain, whether they have or do not have a metallic taste, and blood glucose level.

Variation can also refer to change over time, for example, blood glucose levels change over time, hospital activity changes over time. The comparison is between the blood glucose or hospital activity at one point in time and the blood glucose of the same patient or activity of the same hospital at a different point in time.

Difference, diversity, variation or change may suggest what is happening in the world that is not obvious. However, we need to be critical of what we mean by change. Is what we notice really an indication of change in the world? This issue is familiar to us; for example, we ensure that equipment we use for measurement is **standardised** and checked regularly so we know any change is in what we are measuring and not due to a problem with the equipment, such as when measuring weight, blood pressure or blood glucose. This same critical approach to change is used for all observation whether or not measuring equipment is used, and is considered further in the next section.

Taking a critical approach to observation of difference and change

When we notice difference, diversity, variation or change, we need to check whether what we have noticed is because the thing itself has changed or whether how we observe or understand it has changed. Making this distinction may sometimes be easy, but often it needs careful consideration. We also need to be aware that we are more likely to notice a change that impacts on us in some way and may miss other important changes.

An observed difference or change may come about because of change in the meaning of the issue we are interested in or because of a change in what is happening in the world around us.

<table>
<tr><td>Examples of change in meaning underlying observed change in clinical practice</td><td>Box 2.2</td></tr>
</table>

Rectal bleeding

Observation: Increasing number of referrals to specialists of patients with rectal bleeding.

Change in meaning: For the people in the community, rectal bleeding used to be thought of as 'something everyone gets occasionally' but now means 'sign of cancer and always needs checking'.

There may be no change in the number of people developing a disease.

Miscarriage

Observation: Increasing number of women experiencing miscarriage.

Change in meaning: With more sophisticated pregnancy tests, more women are aware of being pregnant earlier and so more are aware of losing a pregnancy.

The number of miscarriages in one sense may not have changed, as we are detecting miscarriages of which we were previously unaware. However, the women experience it as a miscarriage, and so in another sense the number of miscarriages has increased.

Examples of how change in the understanding of issues can lead to observing change in health care practice are given in Box 2.2. To understand the meaning of what we want to study we can read other people's research (see Chapter 6), but it may also be important to check meaning for our own particular research context. This may be undertaken through the involvement of **users** in our research (see Chapter 4) or through undertaking **observation, interviews** or **focus groups** (see Chapter 7).

Difference or change we observe in clinical practice may be due to change in the world around us (see Box 2.3). The research approach discussed in this book enables us as health professionals to clarify what is happening in the world, begin to explore the reasons why, and contribute to the global research effort to understand these health issues. Some reasons for an observed change suggested in Box 2.3 may need very little work to uncover; for example, an increase in the size of the population served by the general practice is something that most practice managers would know about. Other reasons for the change, such as families sharing experiences of health care, may not be obvious to health professionals and may need some investigation. Observing and investigating change may leave us with more questions; for example, finding an increase in incidence of a health problem leaves us with the question why: why do more people suffer hay fever: why is the incidence of leukaemia increasing?

Box 2.3	**Examples of change observed in clinical practice and possible causes**

Hay fever

Observation: Increasing number of people attending general practice about hay fever.

Possible reasons for the observation:

- Increase in number of people developing hay fever in the community (**incidence**).
- Increase in number of people suffering from hay fever in the community (**prevalence**).
- Increase in size of population served by the general practice but same prevalence of hay fever.
- A new treatment is more expensive to buy from the pharmacy than it is if prescribed, but no change in prevalence of hay fever.
- Weather conditions increase pollen count so people who may only suffer mild symptoms most years suffer more severe symptoms and so seek help from their GP.

Leukaemia

Observation: Increase in number of children seeing a general practitioner who have a diagnosis of leukaemia.

Possible reasons for the observation:

- An increase in number of children developing leukaemia in the community (incidence).
- An increase in the number of children living with leukaemia in the community as treatments improve outcome (prevalence).
- An increase in size of the population of children served by the general practice but no increase in prevalence of leukaemia.
- Families where a child has leukaemia may get to know each other in hospital and share experiences of their GPs. This could result in families changing their GP to one they hear is very supportive.

We may perceive difference or change when there is none because of the way our memory tends to select certain experiences. For example, a general practitioner is unlikely to forget looking after families where a child develops leukaemia as it is not very common and can be distressing. If he recalls caring for a number of families where a child has leukaemia, he may wonder if there is an increase in incidence of leukaemia.

A particular GP can, by chance, look after several families in the same locality where a child has leukaemia even though there is no increase in incidence locally and no pattern underlying the observation. This is due to coincidence. Even when there is overall no particular pattern to events or variation, what we call **random variation**, there can appear to be patterns within a particular place or over a short period. Throughout our research we need to check whether what we are observing is such a local pattern. This sometimes can be tricky and may need careful statistical assessment.

Noticing difference, diversity, variation and change, and checking the nature of what we notice, is a vital first step in research. At the start of this section I refer to 'the thing itself', that is what we are particularly interested in, and whether it has changed (Boxes 2.2 and 2.3 discuss the examples of rectal bleeding, miscarriage, hay fever and leukaemia). As discussed in Chapter 1, the research approach considered in this book assumes it is, at least to some degree, possible to identify and define the aspects of the world that we are interested in, that they are really there, although accepting that their nature may change even as we undertake our research.

In the next section we consider the aim of our research and in the section following we learn how to explore our research issue.

Establishing the overall aim of our research

We often have some idea of what we want to achieve through undertaking research, such as improving the experience of health care for our patients or reducing the variation in health outcome among our patients. Writing down our **aim** is important as it obliges us to make clear what we hope to achieve, and forms an important document for our research, just as writing down our motivations is important. The aim of our research is often much broader than what we can achieve with one research project. Take for example the nurse described in Box 2.4. His aim, to improve the provision of information for people with renal failure, could lead to several research projects; for example, identifying the information needs of patients, analysing communication between health professionals and patients, and evaluating the impact of a new way of providing information. Some of us may be able to undertake a whole programme of research involving many projects, but mostly we undertake just one project contributing to a wider aim, and leave the other aspects of the research to others (see Chapter 1). Even though we may only contribute part of the research needed to achieve our aim, we need to be clear about our aim, for those that read about our research need to understand this. When I write a research proposal I often describe the overall aim for the research, then specify the aim for the particular project.

Within our aim we describe the research issue in which we are interested. For the nurse described in Box 2.4, this is information and renal failure. It may seem straightforward to then develop the **research question**. However, before that, further exploration is needed to ensure that the issue is what we really want to investigate. To do this we unpack or explode the issue, as described in the next section, to clarify the focus of our research and the frame for the research.

Box 2.4	**Getting started on research to improve the provision of information for people living with renal failure**

Health care professional role: Nurse working with people living with renal failure.

Motivation: Improving experience of health care for patients; increasing patient self-reliance; reducing patient reliance on health care professionals.

Observation of difference or change: Many patients and their families understand very little about renal failure, but when he takes time to give them information and explain about it they are more able to manage their treatments.

Overall aim: To improve the provision of information for people living with renal failure.

Research issue: Information and renal failure.

Clarifying the focus and frame of our research

When working as health professionals we are used to rapidly focusing in on problems in order to solve them. When getting started on research we may feel we know exactly what we want to research and want to get on with it. However, it is important to explore the issue to check that when we do our research it is focused on the issue we really want to investigate. We do this by pulling the issue apart, or exploding it. I describe it as 'exploding the issue' as when going through this process, it can feel as though our precious research idea has been blown apart, that it is no longer something contained and manageable but something that has exploded into unmanageable fragments. This can be uncomfortable, but research is uncomfortable as it involves constantly challenging ourselves, particularly our habitual patterns of thinking. To undertake robust research we need to work with this discomfort, as it is all part of the process of exploration. I will take you through some examples of exploding research issues to clarify the focus and frame of the research.

We start with the example from Box 2.4. The research issue is information and renal failure. Let us consider the different perspective on this issue, first by asking questions such as who needs information, how does information spread between people and what are the various sources of information? Box 2.5 is a brainstorm on these questions; it may not cover every possible perspective, but brainstorming in this way opens our minds to the many different perspectives on the research issue.

Brainstorm answers to questions that help identify the many different perspectives on information and renal failure	**Box 2.5**

Who may have a need for information about renal failure?

- People living with renal failure.
- Families of people living with renal failure, including those living with them in their households as well as those living elsewhere.
- Friends, neighbours, work colleagues and others who encounter people living with renal failure in their daily lives.
- Employing organisations, trades unions and other work-related groups, particularly about implications for the work context.

How is information spread about renal failure?

- Stories people tell each other in families and other social contexts.
- The media (newspapers, TV, radio and the Internet).
- Experts such as professionals, professional groups, expert patients, advocacy groups.

What are the sources of information about renal failure?

- Patient experience and the experience of those that engage with them.
- Health care professionals such as doctors, nurses, dieticians, psychologists and pharmacists.
- Complementary and alternative therapy practitioners.
- Researchers in hospitals, universities, pharmaceutical companies, health technology companies.

We also need to consider diversity in relation to the research issue. For example, each person living with renal failure will have a view on what they want to know and what they want other people to know. They will encounter many different health professionals, each with their own expertise and opinion. Different people will have different severity of renal failure and need different treatments. Availability of treatments may vary according to the health care system.

In Box 2.5 we have identified a range of people, organisations and aspects of life which have some link with the issue of renal failure and information. Figure 2.1 charts the different perspectives we identified. The links indicate connections I made during the brainstorm. For example, thinking about work colleagues led me to note down 'employing organisations'. Writing out such a chart can be useful in exploding the research issue.

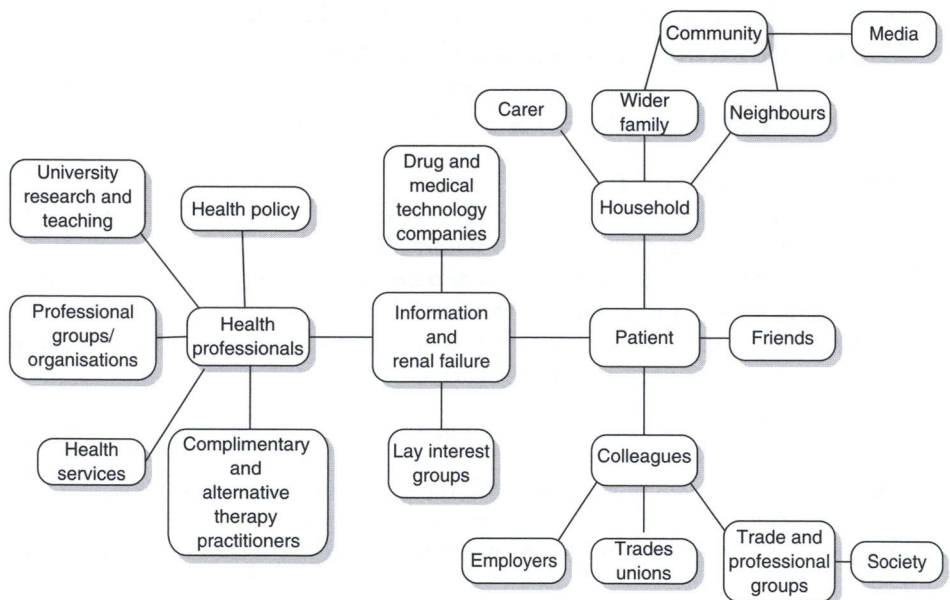

Figure 2.1   Charting the different perspectives on the research issue: information and renal failure

To continue with the example, after exploding the research issue, the nurse can decide on what to focus and what to leave for others to research. He may want to research information needs and preferences of patients. He may not want to study the media or health professionals but keep them in the background. This background forms the frames for the focus of the research, just as a picture is framed by the picture frame, the wall where it is hanging, the room and the building it is in. The frame affects how we perceive and understand the focus. Rather than focusing on patients, the nurse may decide to focus on how renal failure is represented in the media, as patients have mentioned what they have read and heard and how this has led to misunderstandings. Alternatively, the researcher may focus on what doctors and nurses who are not specialists in renal failure know about the condition, in order to help design an educational package for their continuing professional development.

Deciding on his focus helps the nurse identify who would be able to advise him about his research. For example, for a focus on patient information needs and preferences, he may discuss the research with a social scientist with experience of research on understanding patient perceptions of health and health information. To study media representations of renal failure, he would seek advice from an academic in media studies and to study health professional knowledge in order to develop an educational package he would seek help from an educationalist.

Getting started on research exploring the use of e-mail for follow-up consultations in general practice	**Box 2.6**
Health professional role: Manager of a general medical practice. *Motivation*: For follow-up consultations in general practice increase patient convenience and reduce doctor time. *Observation of difference or change*: Reports of use of e-mail for consultations in family medicine in North America. *Overall aim*: To improve the efficiency of general practice, particularly for those needing follow-up for chronic health conditions. *Research issue:* Follow-up consultations and e-mail.	

Another example of a research issue, described in Box 2.6, is about health care organisation rather than direct patient care. To stimulate her thinking, the manager can explode the research issue by asking who may have something to say about e-mail follow up. Some answers are presented in Box 2.7 but these do not cover every possibility.

The manager may also think about wider social issues, such as the potential exclusion of those unable to use e-mail and how e-mail follow-up may change expectations of access to health care.

By exploding the issue we are able to make explicit decisions about what our research will focus on and what forms the frame or background of the research. For the same issue, the focus and frame may be different at different times or places. For example, social policy on confidentiality and the archiving of clinical records may currently all form part of the frame for this research issue. However, in the past these were the focus of research.

Box 2.7	**Brainstorm answers to a question that helps identify the many different perspectives on e-mail follow-up**

Who may have something to say about e-mail follow up?

People who would have immediate contact with e-mail follow-up:

- Doctors, nurses
- Patients
- Those who live with the patient or care for the patient in relation to their health (family, friends, neighbours, people employed to care for them).
- Those responsible for looking after the information technology, for the practice and for the patient (if it is not the patient themselves).
- Practice receptionists and practice manager.

Organisations providing:

- information technology for health care.
- education and training of health care professionals, particularly in communication skills.
- Health policy makers – resources implications, confidentiality and record keeping.

The practice manager may decide she wants to focus on the doctors' perspective on using e-mail to follow up patients. This may be fine, but she needs to be very clear about why she is focusing on the doctors and not patients, and why she is setting aside wider social issues such as inequalities of access. Thinking this through may lead her to conclude that her research should include the patient perspective. However, she may then find there is research in the literature on this, so she can remain focused on the doctors framed by the patient perspective.

Through this process of exploding our research issue, blowing it apart to see the different perspectives on the issue and how it relates to other aspects of life, we are able to clarify the focus of our research and identify what frames our research. Now we are clear what it is we are really interested in, we can start to formulate our research question. However, getting started on our research involves reviewing what we are doing several times each in a slightly different way, so we will return to considering the focus of our research in later chapters of this book.

Developing the research aim, questions and objectives

Developing the research question is often considered the first task in undertaking research. It certainly comes in the early stages of research but, as indicated in this chapter and Chapters 3, 4 and 5, there is a great deal of thinking, exploring issues, reading and consulting with others that takes place first. Before developing our research question we need to be clear about the overall aim for our research and the particular aspect of our research issue that we want to research (described above). We can then clarify the aim for our research project and the research question.

From our experience of working as health professionals, we may find it easier to clarify our project aim before turning it into a question as we are used to planning ahead for a specific purpose, for example, making a treatment plan. The nurse working with people living with renal failure (introduced in Box 2.4) has the aim of improving the provision of information for his patients. Through the process of exploding the research issue described above, he decides to focus on the patient perspective (see Box 2.8). His aim is to understand their information needs and preferences.

Developing the research aim for the issue of information and renal failure	**Box 2.8**

Health care professional role: Nurse working with people living with renal failure.

Motivation: Improving experience of health care for patients; increasing patient self-reliance; reducing patient reliance on health care professionals.

Observation of difference or change: Many patients and their families understand very little about renal failure, but when he takes time to give them information and explain about it they are more able to manage their treatments.

Overall aim: To improve the provision of information for people living with renal failure.

Research issue: Information and renal failure.

Research focus: Patients living with renal failure.

Research aim: To understand the information needs and preferences of patients living with renal failure.

Moving from aim to question requires adding question words: what, where, when, how, why, who. It may involve more than one question. A useful exercise is to consider using all six question words and phase as many questions as possible even if they seem to be similar. Examples are given in Box 2.9. If we imagine having a conversation about information with a patient living with renal failure, the conversation may well range over many or all of these questions. However, we need to be clear which questions are priority for the research project and which, although interesting, are not currently our priority. This is important, as we need to ensure that we collect all the data to answer our priority questions and not get distracted by other questions. The data we collect may well give us hints about the answers to other questions but not be sufficient to provide a robust answer. Our decision about which questions have priority influences our whole project, from data collection through to analysis and dissemination of our results. Taking time to explore all the questions that could be asked and considering our priorities is of great benefit later in our research.

Box 2.9	**Potential research questions for the research aim of understanding the information needs and preferences of people living with renal failure**

What are the information needs of people with renal failure?
What effect does receiving information have on the patient?
What information do people living with renal failure pass on to their families/carers?
What influences peoples' information needs and preferences?
Where, when, how is information already available?
Where, when and how would people prefer information to be conveyed?
When is information needed (e.g. time after diagnosis, stage of illness, timing in relation to treatment)?
How much information is needed and how fast?
How do they use information to manage their illness?
How do information needs and preferences change over time?
Why is the information needed?
Why do patients use and/or trust some information sources and not others?
Who conveys information and to whom?

Let us continue by considering the example of the practice manager introduced in Box 2.6, who has decided to focus her research on the doctors' perspective on e-mail consultations. Her aim is to understand the potential for e-mail follow-up consultations from the perspective of doctors. A list of potential questions for her research is presented in Box 2.10.

Potential research questions for the research aim of understanding the potential for e-mail follow-up consultations from the perspective of doctors	Box 2.10

What questions do doctors ask in follow-up consultations?
What questions do patients ask in follow-up consultations?
What is the standard of skill in using e-mail among the doctors?
What are the doctors' attitudes to e-mail consultation?
Where would doctors be when undertaking the e-mail consultations, and would the technology available work in different locations?
When would e-mail consultations be scheduled for the doctor?
How many appointments in a week are for following-up patients?
How many of these appointments require a clinical examination?
Why are some doctors keen on e-mail consultation and not others?
Who do doctors consider suitable for e-mail follow up and why?

Reviewing her potential research questions, the practice manager may decide that she needs to start with the ones that will provide her with a description of what happens now in follow-up consultations so she can then consider how much of this activity could take place by e-mail (see research questions in Box 2.11). Although interested in doctors' attitudes, opinions and skills, she is putting this to one side for now and focusing on describing what they do in follow up consultations, what actually happens. We explore further how to decide on which research questions to give priority in Chapter 5.

When we write a plan for our research, it is normal practice to write a set of **objectives**. This is straightforward if we have clear research questions as they directly reflect the questions as shown in Box 2.11.

Development of research: an iterative process

Most of us need many attempts at deciding on our priorities and refining our research questions before they are clear. This is quite normal and it is good practice to revisit each stage of the process of developing research questions, including going back to examine our motivations and assumptions, re-examining the different perspectives on an issue and the many different questions that can be asked. This process of moving forward then going back to an earlier step to move forwar our research questions again is known as **iteration.** We continue to refine our research questions as we continue the preparation for our research by reading research literature and considering the range of research approaches we could use. These issues are discussed in Chapter 5 on preparation for designing research. The next two chapters consider the ethics of your research (Chapter 3) and involving users in your research (Chapter 4). These are important for getting started on your research and are also revisited many times during the iterative process of developing research.

Box 2.11	**Developing the research aim, questions and objectives for research exploring the use of e-mail for follow-up consultations in general practice**

Health professional role: Manager of a general medical practice.

Motivation: For follow-up consultations in general practice, increase patient convenience and reduce doctor time.

Observation of difference or change: Reports of use of e-mail for consultations in family medicine in North America.

Overall aim: To improve the efficiency of general practice, particularly for those needing follow-up for chronic health conditions.

Research issue: Follow-up consultations and e-mail.

Research focus: Doctor's perspective on e-mail for follow-up consultations.

Research aim: To understand the potential for e-mail follow-up consultations from the doctor's perspective.

Research questions

How many appointments in a week are for following up patients?

How many of these appointments require a clinical examination?

What questions do doctors ask in follow-up consultations?

What questions do patients ask in follow-up consultations?

Research objectives:

- To estimate the number of follow-up appointments per week.
- To estimate the number of follow-up appointments per week when a clinical examination is performed.
- To describe the type of questions asked by doctors in follow-up consultations.
- To describe the type of questions asked by patients in follow-up consultations.

Further reading

Read examples of research which relate to your area of interest and for each example note and reflect on the following:

- Health professional role(s) of research team members
- Motivation for research
- Observation of difference or change that underpins the research
- Overall aim to which the research project contributes
- Research issue
- Research focus
- Research aim
- Research questions
- Research objectives

3　Considering the Ethics of Your Research

There are well-established ethical principals for research involving people. This chapter explores how these principals apply in research for health care practice, including the ethics of involving vulnerable groups in research.

For any research involving people there are well-established **ethical** principals: balancing the risk of harm with potential benefit, ensuring **consent** and protecting **confidentiality**. These principals are explained in guidance for researchers available from a number of sources (see Resources at the end of this chapter) and should be read before embarking on research and used as reference throughout the research process. This chapter discusses these principals as they apply to research we undertake as health professionals in our own health care context. Although the principals are the same for all research with people, there are issues over which we have to be particularly cautious when we are studying our own patients or health care service.

The chapter explores each ethical principal in turn, starting with balancing the risk of harm with potential benefit. The potential benefit is the likely gain in new knowledge from our research and its use to improve health. The risk of harm can range from worsening the health and wellbeing of patients through to inconvenience of taking people's time unnecessarily. When people are asked to participate in research they should give consent only after being fully informed about the research. If we work as a health professional in the same place as we are doing the research, we need to take particular care over this. Data provided to us in the course of research should remain confidential and if published the anonymity of participants should be preserved. This may seem straightforward, but our ability to preserve anonymity when research is done in one locality depends on the research issue and the form of the data.

For undertaking research involving people, many countries have formal processes for gaining **ethical approval**. These vary from country to country (Hearnshaw, 2004). In the UK, the National Health Service has its own research ethics system (see Resources), and universities also have systems in place for ethical approval. When planning to undertake research, you should find out about the current local requirements for ethical approval and adhere to them.

Balancing the risk of harm with potential benefit

Although we may be very keen to undertake research on a particular issue, we need to ask ourselves:

Do we need to do this research?

Do we need to involve people in this research?

Do we need to involve these people in this research?

We will consider each of these questions for our local research.

Do we need to do this research?

This is a difficult question to ask when we are enthusiastic about doing some research, but asking it can be very fruitful as it can help us refine our research issue, aims and questions (see Chapter 2) while also exploring the ethical dimension of our research. We will discuss this using the example in Box 3.1 of a nurse working with young people living with diabetes.

Getting started on research to understand why young people living with diabetes fail to attend clinic appointments	**Box 3.1**

Health professional role: Nurse specialising in diabetes.

Motivation: Improving the wellbeing and life expectancy of young people living with diabetes, including reducing admissions to hospital due to diabetes being out of control by providing better health care through the diabetes clinic.

Observation of difference or change: Compared to children and older adults, more young people miss their appointments at the diabetes clinic.

Overall aim: To improve the control of diabetes among young people.

Research issue: Young people, diabetes.

Research focus: Clinic for young people living with diabetes.

Research aim: To understand why young people living with diabetes do not attend the clinic.

Research question: Why do young people living with diabetes fail to attend their clinic appointments?

To answer the research question, we are likely to need to ask the young people about attending the clinic. However, before planning this, we need to consider what else we should do before taking up their time. As the research focus is the clinic, this is where we should start. We don't need to ask the young people why they don't attend to find out that clinic appointments get sent out too late or are cancelled at the last minute. We can also uncover poor professional practice, such as poor communication skills, which may put young people off attending. By attending to the quality of service provided at the clinic we may find that our original research question becomes irrelevant.

However, if we find young people are still not attending for appointments, we may want to pursue our research question. The next step is to find out what is known more generally about the research issue. This will include reading **research literature** about providing diabetes care for young people and about young people and health more generally, as young people with other health concerns or chronic illness may experience similar issues. If there is a lot of literature on the topic we may find that our research project turns into a review of the literature (see Chapter 6).

Even a **literature review** has an ethical dimension. It should be done using the best available methods and to a high standard as a poorly done literature review can result in misleading conclusions and recommendations. If as health professionals we are not sure of how to do a literature review well, we have a responsibility to ask for training, help and guidance. This is no different from undertaking a new clinical procedure. It could be that the answer to our question 'Do we need to do this research?' is 'No, but someone else with the appropriate skills needs to'. Once done, the clinic can develop their service based on the review. We may still find that despite implementing best practice based on the evidence available, teenagers still miss appointments and our research question still needs answering.

Service development should not be dressed up as research or vice versa. However, service development and research can go hand in hand. It can be difficult to distinguish what is research and what is service development, but these issues are well described in research ethics guidance (see Resources).

Starting from best practice is important when evaluating a health intervention that aims to improve on current clinical practice. For example, in an evaluation of a new manual for patients living with type 2 diabetes which aimed to help them improve their blood glucose control (Sturt et al., 2008), the research team asked nurses already trained in best practice to participate in the study. This ensured that the results of the study showed the added value that the new manual could bring to best current practice. If the research team had asked any interested nurses to take part, the clinical practice of these nurses may have improved through their participation. However, some of this effect could have been achieved by training the nurses in best practice without the addition of the patient manual. We would therefore be unclear whether there was added benefit from providing the manual for patients, and how much.

Considering the ethical dimensions of doing research goes hand in hand with developing our research aims, questions and objectives carefully as described in Chapter 2. If we decide we need to do the research, we move on to consider whether we need to involve people.

Do we need to involve people in this research?

In general, it is rarely considered ethical to undertake research that collects data which is already available or where there is data available that would serve the same purpose. By 'available' I mean either available to anyone or available to *bone fide* researchers. Published research literature is just one of many sources of data we can draw on for our research. We will explore ways of undertaking research without involving people using the example in Box 3.2 of the physiotherapist wanting to evaluate a 'one stop shop' for assessing the elderly at risk of falling.

Getting started on research on elderly at risk of falls	**Box 3.2**

Health professional role: Physiotherapist specialising in care of the elderly.

Motivation: Improving the wellbeing of the elderly, reducing the number of people needing surgery for hip fracture.

Observation of difference or change: Increasing number of elderly having physiotherapy following hip fractures.

Overall aim: To reduce the incidence of falls among the elderly in the local population.

Research issue: Falls.

Research focus: The elderly people at risk of falling.

Research aim: To describe the number of elderly in the local population at risk of falling.

Research questions: How many elderly people are at risk of falling in the locality?

Our first thought may be to go out and collect new data about the elderly in the locality, but data that is already available may provide a good estimate that answers our question. For example, the **census** will give us an idea of the number of people living in the locality and their age. This information can be combined with published surveys of the age and risk factors for falling, undertaken in other parts of the country, to provide an estimate of the number of people we may expect to find in our own locality.

If an estimate as described above is not possible or perhaps does not take account of special circumstances in our locality, we could plan to collect new data. This does not necessarily need to come from the elderly themselves. Data already available within the health service may provide the answer. For example, we may have a list of criteria for deciding whether an elderly person is at risk of falling, such as use of antidepressants and treatments for hypertension, a history of previous falls and age. This data is available from general practice records in the UK and can be extracted without needing to involve the individual people. The researcher does not need access to the clinical records directly but can guide a search of the clinical records undertaken by someone who uses them in their clinical practice. The search results will be along the lines of Box 3.3. It is not possible to identify individuals from this report as it gives **aggregate data** (for example, total number of people of a certain age), not details of individual cases. We will return to consider the use of clinical data and when individual consent is needed in the following section.

Box 3.3	**Aggregate data about falls in the elderly from one general practice**

Number of people in the practice aged 80 years or over = 100
Of the 100 people aged 80 or over:
 	
   15 have a note in their records of a previous fall
   35 are on at least one of the medications considered to increase the risk of falls
 	
All 15 with a note of a previous fall are on one of the medications.	

The use of existing data for our research is considered further in Chapter 5. If we decide we do need to involve people in our research, our research aims, questions and objectives will suggest who they need to be. However, we must consider whether any of these people are more vulnerable than most and whether their inclusion is necessary.

Do we need to involve these people in this research?

Who to involve in our research will depend on our research question, but the inclusion of people from vulnerable groups within our society needs careful consideration. We must think through the ethical principles in relation to what makes the people vulnerable and whether they are vulnerable in relation to our research question.

People can be vulnerable for many different reasons. These include: being young or very old; having a sensory impairment such as blindness or hearing loss; having problems with understanding due to learning difficulties; not understanding the language; being very ill both mentally or physically; and being in a social situation where people are easily pressurised, persuaded or coerced, such as being in prison, being very poor or socially marginalised.

The balance between the risk of harm and the potential benefit depends on the research question. If the research question will only be answered properly by including vulnerable groups, then it is important to include them. For example, if people from a minority ethnic group are not included in research about a particular medical treatment because of language difficulties, it may be unclear whether the research results apply to this group. However, if we are researching the use of an immunisation for healthy young adults, we do not need to include those in prison, as there are enough healthy young adults within the non-prison population with sufficient diversity of characteristics for such research.

As researchers we should avoid making assumptions about how other people view the balance of risk of harm and potential benefit. For example, there has been debate about asking people who are terminally ill to participate in research, yet many of these people are glad to participate as far as they are able to as they feel they want to offer what they can to help others. We can avoid making erroneous assumptions by involving users in our research or undertaking an interview study to explore the issue.

As researchers we have an obligation to ensure that people involved in our research are fully informed, able to understand the information and able to consent on the basis of this information. We therefore need to ensure that our research information is in a form that can be understood by all participants. Examples include providing translations of information for those who speak other languages and audio tapes for those who are unable to read because of visual impairment or limited literacy. Where participants have learning difficulty or cognitive impairment, the information should be tailored to their needs. Resources are needed to provide information in these various forms. If it is important for the research to include people needing adapted forms of information, then the cost of doing this should be included as part of the cost of the whole research project. However, for each research project we need to consider why we are including people. We also need to avoid excluding from research those people needing information in an adapted form through omitting to consider their needs.

Some people are deemed unable to give informed consent for themselves. These include children and people with severe cognitive or learning problems. If your research needs to include anyone where there may be concerns about their ability to give informed consent, then it is important to seek advice. Sources of advice include other researchers working with similar groups, advocacy and support groups for the potential research participants, ethics committees and advisors, and other published research with similar groups. The obligation rests with the researcher to seek out this advice.

Many researchers shy away from undertaking research with vulnerable groups. However, if we avoid undertaking research with vulnerable groups which may lead to improvement in their health and wellbeing, we are in danger of discriminating against these groups, which is itself an ethical issue.

Gaining informed consent from research participants

As health professionals undertaking research in our own health care context we have ready access to patients, clinical notes and our colleagues. Researchers who are not health professionals are envious of this access as they have to work much harder than we do to persuade people to participate in their research. However, this ease of access brings with it the responsibility for ensuring clarity about when we are in our researcher role and when we are in our health professional role, and the ethical regulation of each of these roles. Our research also needs to be transparent, so everyone can be clear what the research is about, how it is done, how the results may be used and the possible implications of the research results for the locality and more generally. These issues are explored further in this section.

Clarity about our role and the use of data

It is very easy for us to ask colleagues and patients about our research topic, or to collect relevant clinical data within our normal working day as a health professional. There is no problem about this if it is data collected within our clinical role. We can analyse it and think about it with a view to developing research. This is not research data but clinical data. It needs to be treated according to the guidance on confidentiality for all clinical information.

Once we have designed a research project based in our own health care setting, we need to be clear about when we are doing research and when we are acting in our clinical role. We have to be clear about this to ourselves, and we have to explain our different roles clearly to others, including when our roles may change, when we are in both roles at the same time, and how we distinguish the roles. When I first started undertaking interviews with people as a researcher I was also working in the locality as a health professional. I found I had to write out and practice my explanation for people, as it was very easy, in the stress of the moment when starting an interview, to fudge the issue. I found a clear explanation was well received. If the research involves talking to other health professionals we should also take care to clarify our role, as we will be perceived as a colleague rather than researcher unless we explain. Issues of consent are explored further using the example in Box 3.4.

Getting started on research on older people and depression in primary care	Box 3.4

Health professional role: Psychiatric nurse managing the mental health team providing services for older people.

Motivation: Prevent older people developing severe depression wherever possible; reduce number of people needing mental health services so service can focus on those most in need.

Observation of difference or change: Older people report having symptoms of depression for longer than younger people before receiving medication.

Overall aim: To improve the mental health of older people.

Research issue: Depression, older people.

Research focus: Diagnosis and treatment decisions in primary care involving older people with symptoms of depression.

Research aim: To understand why treatment for depression is not started earlier in primary care for older people with symptoms of depression.

The nurse described in Box 3.4 may have decided that her research question is: Why do GPs delay diagnosing depression in the elderly? Let us consider her situation:

> The nurse has worked in the locality for over 20 years. She has known many of the doctors since they first came to work here. She contacts doctors about the study, and as they know her well, many agree to be interviewed. She undertakes five interviews which are very long as the doctors discuss not only their patients but also their own mental health and how this affects their clinical practice.
>
> When reviewing her research the nurse realises she did not make it clear enough that she was in the role of researcher. The interviews were really conversations between colleagues who had known and trusted each other for years. She feels she may be too close to her colleagues to be able to undertake this type of research in the locality.

In the UK, the nurse would have needed to apply for ethical approval for this study. The process of applying for ethical approval makes us think through all the implications of our study, so the nurse would have realised the problem before doing the interviews. She could have clarified the boundaries of the research interview and how she would keep within these boundaries (for example, interview content not relevant to the research question could be edited out of the interview recording with the agreement of the participant) or rethought her research question and approach.

If the nurse had not known her colleagues so well, perhaps having moved to the locality recently, she might more easily have undertaken research interviews maintaining clarity about her role as researcher. However, she may well have problems persuading GPs to participate when they hear her research question 'Why do GPs delay diagnosing depression in the elderly?' as the question implies that the GPs are at fault. Those that do agree to be interviewed may be very defensive about what they do when consulting with an older person who may be depressed. If we revise the research question and removing the assumption, it becomes: 'What happens in general practice consultations with older people who have symptoms of depression?' The research question has improved and the GPs are more likely to consent to the research.

As a first step in her research, the nurse may want to find out how many older patients are diagnosed with depression in general practice by searching the clinical records. In the previous section I mentioned the use of data from clinical records for research, where the data was extracted from the records in aggregate form without the consent of the individual patients. In the UK and elsewhere there is ongoing debate about whether data about an individual collected in the course of clinical practice can be used for research without seeking the consent of the individual (see Resources for up-to-date guidance). If the individual is not identifiable, such as in the example of aggregate data in Box 3.3, the consent of the individual patients may not be required, but the consent of the practice will be needed. If individuals are identifiable from clinical data used for research, then consent is usually required. At present there are exceptions, for example, if a study involves thousands of clinical records and gaining consent is impractical, then researchers may not be required to gain consent. However, the debate about consent is likely to continue, so if your research involves using data collected for clinical purposes it is important to check the latest guidance and seek advice.

Transparency about the research process

The whole research process, from the aims and research questions through to the potential use of the research results, needs to be clearly explained to people for gaining informed consent. The process of gaining ethical approval can help you think this through. The research process needs to be carefully explained in the information given to potential research **participants**. Here we explore particular issues for undertaking research in our local health care context.

The nurse described in Box 3.4 may decide she wants to record GP consultations with older people to see what actually happens in the consultations in relation to diagnosing and treating depression. She may be concerned that the

GPs will change what they do if they know the research is about depression, and so considers telling them the research is about doctors consulting with older people without mentioning her interest in depression. This does not allow the doctors or patients to give fully informed consent, as the purpose of the study has not been made clear. The nurse can either look for a different approach for her research or, through reading up about research involving recording of consultations, may decide she can take account of this effect within the research design.

All research should be undertaken as well as possible and be reported clearly so that others can judge the quality of the research and the reliability and usefulness of the results. Research undertaken in our own context should reach the standard of the best research. Within our local health care setting, if we undertake research we will become known as being enthusiastic about our research issue. We therefore need to take particular care to demonstrate that our conclusions are based on high-quality research and not a limited interpretation of the data that prove what we want it to.

Research may demonstrate that a particular aspect of health care provision is not effective. This can lead to changes in how health care is provided, so threatening our own job or those of our colleagues. This possibility needs to be considered before starting out on the research as it may be difficult to undertake this research when also working locally.

Participants are able to give fully informed consent to participate in our research if we distinguish clearly between our roles as a health care professional in clinical practice and as a researcher, and the whole research process from start to finish is clearly explained. Information for participants should also explain about confidentiality and **anonymity** of research data, the subject of the next section.

Confidentiality of research data and anonymity of published and stored data

One of the ethical principals for research is protecting confidentiality. We need to provide information for participants about the data we will collect and how we will keep it confidential. The resources listed at the end of this chapter provide detailed guidance on this. Questions include:

What data will be used in the research?

Who will have access to the research data?

Where will data be stored?

How long will it be stored?

How will data be transferred, for example between research sites?

How will data be disposed of?

What data will be used in the research will depend on the research question. It is usual to collect only data that is necessary for answering the research question, so this has to be thought through carefully. Some data is collected in order to carry out the research, such as names and addresses of participants. This is treated differently from data for the research question.

Data that identifies people including name, address, date of birth, used in the research process

Where data is collected from individual people, we may have details of their name and address for contacting them. This is usually stored separately from the research data, in a secure place (for example, a locked cabinet in a locked store room) and destroyed as soon as the research is complete. As soon as possible after data collection, anything that identifies the source of the data is removed. This applies to all kinds of data, including interviews and observational data. Where necessary, identifying codes are substituted (for example, a unique number for each research participant) and the list of codes and who they refer to is kept securely and separately from the data. If we take data away from a clinical setting where it was collected, names and addresses are first removed. Age may be substituted for date of birth as it is less identifiable, although some types of research will need the date of birth.

Any original sources of data which contain details of research participants, such as note books or audio recordings, are kept securely until the research is complete and then destroyed securely (for example, shredding paper copies). The normal post and e-mail are not considered secure ways of transferring such data between people or places.

Access to data that identifies people should be limited to only those who really need to see it. In many countries including the UK all health care, academic and research organisations have policies about personal data as they must comply with **data protection** legislation. All researchers should check these policies and comply with them.

Anonymised research data

When we have removed participants names, addresses and dates of birth from the data, we may consider that it is now not possible to identify any participant so it can be considered to be anonymised. We need to think about this carefully, especially when it comes to writing and publishing reports of our research, and storing data in an archive.

Consider research involving interviews, for example, with young people with diabetes (see Box 3.1). In the process of transcribing the interviews, the nurse would have removed anything that might identify a participant, such as the name of their school or the town they visit for shopping. Once the interviews have been typed up as transcripts, the nurse can destroy the recordings of the interviews. She then analyses the data, writes a report and gets it published in a journal. People reading the research report need to know who did the research and where, as this helps them assess the quality and relevance of the research. In any one locality there are only a certain number of young people living with diabetes. If the report included a quotation from a participant about what they eat before they play a particular sport, and included this participant's age and gender with the quotation, it may just be possible for someone to work out who the participant is. We have to ensure that participants are not identifiable by their characteristics through the piecing together of information in the research report. If it is not going to be possible to report the research without identifying the participants, we must ask for their consent at the very start of the project.

When our data is an aggregation of clinical data about individuals, the aggregation can make the data anonymous (see Box 3.3). However, undertaking research in health care practice often involves relatively small numbers of individuals, and this can reduce the anonymity of the data. For example, the physiotherapist (Box 3.2) undertaking research on the elderly at risk of falls, may identify a small group of elderly people at very high risk of falling; for example, people who are visually impaired, who have a mobility problem and live alone. Imagine that the physiotherapist writes a report on pilot work undertaken in one general practice, which identified three people in this high-risk group and named the practice in the acknowledgements. A local elected councillor may sit on the health board that reviews the report and realise that she knows at least two of those three people through her role as councillor. The small number of cases combined with the type of detail about each case has led to loss of anonymity of the individuals. Although this example may sound extreme, we need to think about how far we can anonymise our data when undertaking research in our local health care setting. If the only way to ensure that our participants remain anonymous is to disguise the setting of the research, then we need to consider drawing participants from a number of different places and ensuring nothing in the report indicates which participant was from which research site.

Research data with no personal identifiers is often stored for many years to allow researchers to return to the data and reanalyse it if necessary. The data should be stored securely as it may be possible to identify the individuals from piecing together their data. Many research organisations have secure archives for such data. The arrangements for storing data should be included in the information for research participants. As research data can sometimes be used to answer different research questions developed by other researchers, there are now national and local archives gathering data sets for future use. If data from a research project will be deposited in such an archive, this needs to be stated in the participant information. When using data from an archive, researchers abide by the same ethical principals as if they were collecting the data directly from research participants.

Conclusion

The ethical principals of balancing the risk of harm with potential benefit, ensuring consent and protecting confidentiality should be considered from the very start of developing our research, with particular attention to the local nature of our research and any vulnerable groups. Encountering ethical issues for our research challenges us to review what we are doing, to reflect on our motivations, aims, questions and objectives, and to explore ways of undertaking our research in a different and perhaps more robust way. As researchers we are responsible for keeping up to date with legislation, policy and guidance on research ethics and abiding by them.

References

Hearnshaw, H. (2004) 'Comparison of requirements of research ethics committees in 11 European countries for a non-invasive interventional study'. *BMJ*, **328**: 140–41.

Sturt, J., Whitlock, S., Fox, C., Hearnshaw, H., Farmer, A.J., Wakelin, M., Eldridge, S., Griffiths, F. and Dale, J. (2008) 'Effects of the Diabetes Manual 1:1 structured education in primary care'. *Diabetic Medicine*, **25**: 722–31.

Resources

National Research Ethics Service

The UK body overseeing research ethics and governance in the UK National Health Service. Its website includes valuable guidance and advice and details of the ethical approval process and forms for anyone undertaking research in the UK NHS. Available at www.nres.npsa.nhs.uk

National Institutes of Health Bioethics Resources on the Web

National Institutes of Health is a major funder of health-related research in the US and provides this wide-ranging web-based resource on research ethics. A useful resource for further reading and enquiry. Available at http://bioethics.od.nih.gov.

Further reading

Royal College of Nursing (2004) *Research Ethics: RCN guidance for nurses.* London: Royal College of Nursing.

This is a brief but clear introduction to ethical issues for health professional research.

4 Involving Users in Your Research

This chapter explores the role of users in our research. Research users can be anyone with a contribution to make about our research and with an interest in its results. User involvement can allow previously unheard voices to contribute to research for health care practice.

As health care professionals undertaking research, we move between health care practice and research. This can bring benefits to our research as we understand the health care context and have experience of working with patients and those providing services. In the same way other people, such as those using health care, can provide insight of benefit for research. Over the last two decades, in the UK and elsewhere, the benefits of involving users in research have been recognised. Many organisations that fund or oversee research, including ethics committees, now expect researchers to consider how they could involve users in their research.

Research for health care practice often involves patients or other health professionals as research participants. They provide us with data for our research. Although this is a form of involvement in research, as research participants they have little say in what research is carried out and how it is done. This chapter considers the involvement of users in planning and carrying our research. This type of user involvement in research is often usefully classified into three types: consultation, collaboration, and user-led or user-controlled research. Consultation may involve asking members of the public for advice about what research is needed, or forming an advisory group of interested people for a research project. Collaboration is where interested people work with the researcher on developing research and carrying it out. This may include assisting with data collection, **analysis** and **dissemination** of research results. User-led or user controlled research is where researchers take the role of adviser or assist and support the research, and is often led by community or voluntary groups (Tarpey and Royle, 2006). When undertaking research for health care practice in our own local context, the division between these three types of user involvement is not always clear, and sometimes the distinction between being a research participant and being involved as a research user is not clear. However, the categories help us reflect on how far we really have involved users in our research.

Ideally, users are involved from the very beginning of our research, even from before we have formed an idea for research, through every stage of the research process to publishing and promoting the results of the research and its implications. Our ideas for research often arise from our interaction with patients who are potential users of our research. This is a form of user involvement; however, patients within a health care setting are in the position of receiving care and often feel relatively powerless, unable to say what they really think about an issue. When we involve users in our research we need to set up a situation where they feel able to express their opinions and that their contribution is valued.

There are now excellent resources available to guide researchers on how to involve users, and to guide users in how to get involved in research (see Resources at end of this chapter). As you get started on your research, use these resources to help think through how to involve users in your research. The resources include guidance on practical issues for involving users, including how to find users, how to arrange for their involvement and ensure that people are not excluded through inattention to details such as access and whether and how to pay users for their time (INVOLVE, 2006 and 2008).

Involving users in our research is time-consuming for the users and for us, and may seem to delay the research. However, every time I have taken the time to consult with users about my research I have found their input of great value. They have prevented me wasting time going about research in an impractical way and have given me insights that have moved my thinking on, helped me see my research in a different way and be more critical of my analysis.

I have used the term 'research users' in this chapter but other terms are used, all with slightly different emphases, including 'consumers', 'lay people', 'the public'. What is important for undertaking research for health care practice is to think through who has something to say about what we want to research.

In this chapter we consider who are research users and how they can be involved in research through considering some examples of potential research. Who to involve and how depends on the research issue, focus and aim. The first example explores the involvement of representatives of the public and stakeholders and the second involves patients as research users. The final example includes the public, stakeholders and patients as research users in what is termed '**action research**'.

Public and stakeholder involvement in research

The public all use, or potentially use, health care and know people who use health care. They therefore bring a mixed experience of health and health care to their involvement in research. **Stakeholders** are those with an interest in the research issue because of their role or occupation. Where appropriate, stakeholders can include representatives of patient support groups or organisations that act as advocates for a particular patient group.

Getting started on research on emergency drugs for use by paramedics	Box 4.1

Health professional role: Paramedic working for emergency ambulance service.

Motivation: To ensure that paramedics have the best drugs available to them that will make a difference to the outcome of emergency situations so saving lives.

Observation of difference or change: Drugs traditionally carried by ambulances and used by paramedics may be less effective than drugs now available and safe for use with modern paramedic training and technology.

Overall aim: To improve the cost-effectiveness of the paramedic service.

Research issue: Drugs for emergency situations.

Research focus: The drugs.

Research aim: To draw up a list of the most **cost-effective** drugs to be carried by ambulances for paramedic use.

Consider the paramedic described in Box 4.1 who wants to ensure that the drugs available to paramedics are the best within a reasonable financial budget. For this research aim, he is likely to undertake an extensive literature review and so is not sure whether he needs to involve users. In Box 4.2 I have listed some of the potential users of his research.

Potential users of research on cost-effective drugs for use by paramedics	Box 4.2

- Emergency ambulance services can use the research in planning their service.
- Hospital emergency departments likely to receive patients from the ambulances can use the research to plan their response.
- Policy makers deciding on the funding for emergency services can use the research to decide on the budget for drugs.
- The public will be interested as they may be receiving the emergency treatments.
- Developers and manufacturers of new treatments and monitoring technology will want to know how and why their products are included and how they could improve their products.
- Educators of health care professionals can use the research in their teaching.

Each of these potential users will have a different perspective on cost-effectiveness and the drugs used by paramedics. For example, based on published research, there may be a drug that is cost-effective in the sense that the drug is itself not expensive and many patients seem to benefit. However, an ambulance service manager may ask about how long it lasts when stored in an ambulance and an educator may query the level of skill needed for its use. These are important considerations and so by including representatives of potential users as an advisory group, the paramedic ensures the research is relevant to all aspects of health care provision.

Patients carried by ambulance and receiving the drugs clearly have an interest in the results. However, this experience is hopefully brief and relatively rare for any individual. Patients as users may therefore be best represented by someone who has taken on the role of representing the public perspective in another setting, such as a lay member of a health board or a local elected representative.

Patient involvement in research

We are all potential patients, however, those who live with a health problem or receive health care have different perspectives because of this experience. Here I use the word 'patient' to mean anyone with experience of health care. To explore the involvement of patients as research users, we will consider the example in Box 4.3 of a midwife concerned about women living with diabetes.

Box 4.3	**Getting started on research about women living with diabetes and pregnancy**

Health professional role: Midwife working in hospital.

Motivation: Wanting to reduce the number of women living with diabetes who experience the distress of a serious problem with pregnancy such as still birth or congenital malformation.

Observation of difference or change: Published evidence that women with good control of their diabetes on entering pregnancy have fewer pregnancy problems than those with less good control.

Overall aim: To improve pregnancy outcome for women living with diabetes through improved blood glucose control at conception and in early pregnancy.

Research issue: Diabetes control, conception and early pregnancy.

Research focus: Women living with diabetes who may become pregnant.

Research aim: To understand the experience of women living with diabetes at the time of conception and early pregnancy.

Conception and early pregnancy are issues that may be considered very private or sensitive. Although the midwife is used to talking about sensitive issues in her clinical practice, few women would reveal details of their uncertainties and dilemmas when becoming or finding themselves pregnant. By asking users to be involved in the research the midwife can seek their advice on how to ask questions about these issues. Women living with diabetes and experiencing pregnancy may be the best people to involve. However, there are a number of reasons why it may not be possible to include these women as research users. They are often very busy with being pregnant, while managing their diabetes as well as life in general. They are very close to what could be a difficult issue for them and so may find it distressing to discuss the issue in a group with researchers and other users. There are few of them in any one locality, so the midwife may want to invite all these women for interview rather than to be research users. Other people could act as research users such as women with experience of pregnancy, particularly those with other chronic health problems.

To involve patients as research users the midwife could consider the different levels of involvement described in Box 4.4, where I also refer to examples of published projects involving patients as research users. Health professionals undertaking research in their local health setting need to consider whether they should involve their own patients as research users or not. There need be no problem in doing this if the patient is clear about their role as research user and the role of the health professional as researcher. Patients are likely to find it easier to undertake their role as research user as part of a group and where meetings and communication about the research are kept quite separate from any health care contacts.

To explore the involvement of users, the public, stakeholders and patients and their carers in research, we will consider research on health care for those living with chronic obstructive pulmonary disease (COPD) (see Box 4.5). As you read through the motivation, aims and research issue, you may notice a tension between them. As for many health professionals engaged in research, the motivation is about improving the quality of life for patients but the aim is about just one aspect of patients' lives: time spent in hospital. Those responsible for the financing and provision of services may hope to release health service resources for other patients if this can be done without making the situation worse for those with COPD. Clinicians treating patients in hospital may feel the treatment could be provided at home but community services may feel this is impractical. Patients may want to spend less time in hospital but when they feel they need hospital treatment they want to be able to access it easily. Tensions such as these are very common in research for health care practice. Early establishment of a user group representing the different perspectives provides a forum for these tensions to be discussed. Without this such tensions can make the research impossible.

Box 4.4	Involving patients as research users

Advisory group: This can be formed for the project or can be an ongoing group advising on research, such as a research user group for diabetes (Lindenmeyer et al., 2007). Groups formed for other purposes, such as general practice patient panels, local public participation groups, patient support or advocacy groups and other interest groups, may agree to act as an advisory group for research. The groups may meet in person or virtually, for example an e-mail group (Jesper et al., 2008).

Users involved as collaborators: This can include involving users in designing the study, recruiting participants, undertaking data collection, data analysis, writing up the research and disseminating the results. Involvement may be only advisory for parts of the study. Examples include advising on design, recruitment and data collection and participating in analysis, writing and dissemination (Griffiths et al., 2008) or full participation in design right through to dissemination (Belam et al., 2005).

Users having the idea for the research and taking the lead in developing it with help and support from researchers (Staniszewska et al., 2007): Health professionals working with particular groups of patients are well placed to hear their concerns, support them developing their research ideas and assist them in undertaking their research.

Box 4.5	Getting started on research about health care for those living with chronic obstructive pulmonary disease (COPD)

Health professional role: Specialist nurse working with individuals living with chronic obstructive pulmonary disease (COPD).

Motivation: To improve the life quality of those living with COPD.

Observation of difference or change: Wide **variation** in the number of times patients with apparently similar disease are admitted to hospital with exacerbation of their COPD.

Overall aim: To reduce the amount of time those living with COPD spend in hospital with exacerbation of their disease.

Research issue: COPD and health care services.

The next step in developing the research on COPD and health care services (Box 4.5) is for the nurse to clarify the focus and frame of the research (see Chapter 2). Box 4.6 is a list of those who may have an interest in, or something to say about, COPD and health care services (there may be others too).

Brainstorm on the many different perspectives on the research issue, COPD and health care services	**Box 4.6**

Who may have an interest in, or something to say about, COPD and health care services?

- Patients
- Those caring for patients (including family, neighbours, paid carers)
- Those living with patients but not the main carer
- Family of patients living elsewhere but concerned with patient
- Health care professionals providing day-to-day, week-to-week care (e.g., community nurses, physiotherapist, pharmacist, GP)
- Ambulance service called when patient needs hospital admission
- Hospital admissions unit staff
- Hospital staff working on wards where patient admitted (doctors, nurses, physiotherapist)
- Health service managers
- Health service policy makers (local and national)
- Self-help groups for those with COPD
- Advocacy groups working on behalf of those with COPD
- Providers of facilities that impact on health (exercise facilities, social care organisations, transport facilities, community organisations including social groups and voluntary organisations)
- Others, including politicians, ethicists, lawyers

The list in Box 4.6 is also a list of the roles of those who are research users. In relation to the research issue, different users have different roles and associated with this role, different levels of interest. For patients and carers, COPD is ever present in their lives. For health professionals, patients with COPD may be their main focus or only a small part of their role. Policy makers, politicians, ethicists and lawyers may only be interested in COPD and health care services as one of many examples when considering broader issues.

Associated with the different roles in relation to the research issue are different levels of power. The power associated with different roles is often the inverse of the level of interest in the issue. For example, policy makers have the task of making decisions that affect allocation of resources for health services. Health services managers make decisions about local health service configuration, including who is employed within the service. Health professionals work within current policy and resources for their organisation but have expertise and make day-to-day decisions about patients. Carers and patients may have considerable expertise but are vulnerable because of the disease. They have to engage with the current health care services for the professional help they need, so will avoid saying things they think may affect their care.

As the nurse develops her research focus, and clarifies what frames this research, it should become clear how to involve research users in a way that takes account of tensions within the research issue and the different levels of interest and power of users in relation to the research issue.

Box 4.7	**Developing research about health care for those living with chronic obstructive pulmonary disease (COPD): research focus on people living with COPD**

Health professional role: Specialist nurse working with individuals living with chronic obstructive pulmonary disease (COPD).

Motivation: To improve the life quality of those living with COPD.

Observation of difference or change: Wide variation in the number of times patients with apparently similar disease are admitted to hospital with exacerbation of their COPD.

Overall aim: To reduce the amount of time those living with COPD spend in hospital with exacerbation of their disease.

Research issue: COPD and health care services.

↓

Research focus: People living with COPD.

If the focus of research is people living with COPD (Box 4.7), the health care services form just one aspect of the frame of the research along with all the other aspects of the lives of patients, including their social networks, housing and community environment. People living with COPD are the experts on living with COPD and so are the key research users for this research focus. Their expertise is based on their own experience and they can draw on this in their role as research user. They can collaborate with developing a research aim and question, which they consider important and relevant to those living with COPD, and participate throughout the research as advisors or collaborators, or become research leaders. The way in which they are involved with the research should be empowering, giving them scope to really influence the research. People with a role within the frame of the research should also be considered as research users; for example, health care professionals, local government housing officers, providers of local facilities such as exercise facilities, and leaders of local social organisations. These people have a lower level of interest in the research, so their engagement with the research can be less. However, they are powerful, so the process of engagement needs to ensure a balance between the power of the users who live with COPD and these other users. The users who live with COPD could decide who to involve and how to involve them. For example, a user group formed of people living with COPD may decide to invite them to advise them on specific issues. With people living with COPD as the focus of the research and involved as research users, the research issue, COPD and health care services, will be approached from their perspective. The aim of the research and developments resulting from the research may not be focused only on health care as provided by health professionals, but include other related services such as social support through voluntary organisations, exercise facilities and access to transport. The research aim will guide decisions as to exactly who to involve as a research user.

Public, stakeholder and patient involvement in research

The nurse developing research on health care for those with COPD may decide to focus on the health care service and that her first step will be to describe the patterns of hospital admission (Box 4.8). This may be just one part of a larger project to develop and evaluate health care for those with COPD. Box 4.8 includes a list of likely research users and the type of expertise they bring to this research aim.

Health service managers, policy makers and those representing the public have expertise about the health care service as a whole and about the many people providing and using the service. The health care professionals have expertise about the care of many individual patients. Those with COPD and their carers have expertise about their own experience of health care. This experience is valuable but is only one experience, whereas the other users can claim to know about many individual experiences, although only from their own professional perspective. Those living with COPD and their carers can engage as research users on the same footing as the others if they can represent not only their own individual experience, but also the experience of others living with COPD. For example, they may have been chosen by a local self-help group to represent the group, or they may have undertaken their own research with people living with

COPD. People who themselves are not living with COPD may represent those that are, for example, people who work as patient advocates or for an advocacy organisation run by and for those with COPD.

Box 4.8	**Developing research about health care for those living with chronic obstructive pulmonary disease (COPD): research aim to describe the pattern of hospital admissions – the role of research users**

Health professional role: Specialist nurse working with individuals living with chronic obstructive pulmonary disease (COPD).

Motivation: To improve the life quality of those living with COPD.

Observation of difference or change: Wide variation in the number of times patients with apparently similar disease are admitted to hospital with exacerbation of their COPD.

Overall aim: To reduce the amount of time those living with COPD spend in hospital with exacerbation of their disease.

Research issue: COPD and health care services.

Research focus: Health care service for those with COPD.

Research aim: To describe the pattern of hospital admissions for people with COPD in the locality.

Research users:

- Health service managers, policy makers and those representing the public.
- Health care professionals involved in caring for people with COPD.
- People living with COPD and their carers.

Research user expertise of particular relevance for the research aim:

- Health service managers, policy makers and those representing the public; service resources and configuration, available data sources, and wider policy issues.
- Health care professionals involved in caring for people with COPD and people living with COPD and their carers; how the service functions day to day, reasons for admissions both those formally recorded and those not recorded, impact of policy and resource allocation on decision making (e.g., early or delayed discharges, readmissions soon after discharge).

When making decisions about engaging users in our research, we consider the focus and aim of our research and the interest and power of different users. Engaging as research users people whose voices have not previously been heard is of particular importance in action research and is discussed in the next section.

Action research is a term used to describe research closely linked to development, such as development of a health care service. Action research involves as many as possible of the people with an interest in the research and development, whether this be as members of the public, as stakeholders or as users of the services. This approach has been used within health care practice and is also known as **participatory research** or **emacipatory research**. A review of action research and its use in health care is included in the further reading for this chapter. I discuss action research here as user involvement is a key element of its approach. It aims to include users in every aspect of the research and values equally different perspectives and contributions. Action research brings into one research project the whole process of undertaking research for health care practice described as a research spiral in Chapter 1 – identifying the research issue, undertaking the research, using the results for change, identifying more research issues, undertaking more research and so on. Research for health care practice can become action research that goes beyond an individual project to become the normal process for research and development of health care.

Conclusion

As health professionals undertaking research for health care practice in our own clinical setting, we are, at least in part, a research user and can represent the health professional perspective within our research to some degree. We may also understand a great deal about living with health problems from our contact with patients. However, we need to involve users in our research to avoid making assumptions about other people's perspective on the research issue. As both health professional and researcher, we are in a powerful position with regard to the research as we have expertise in health care and in research (we may not feel we are experts in research, but we are likely to be perceived as such by others). How we involve users needs to take this into account so that users feel they can challenge us. Involving users in the research can also provide us with support if we encounter dilemmas in our research. For example, during our research we may uncover poor professional practice. Our research users can advise us on what to do, perhaps even before we find ourselves in such a situation. Involving users in our research takes time and requires careful planning (see Resources at end of the chapter). It needs to be considered early in the process of developing our research, at a time when we may not feel confident about undertaking our research. However, rather than avoiding engagement with users, we should seek advice and help from people who have more experience of this even if their research was on a different issue. We should aim to involve users at every stage of our research, and continually review who is involved and how. If for some reason we think user involvement would be inappropriate or difficult, we can use this as a prompt to stop and think, and perhaps ask some potential research users for their opinion.

References

Belam, J., Harris, G., Kernick, D., Kline, F., Lindley, K., McWatt, J., Mitchell, A. and Reinhold, D. (2005) 'A qualitative study of migraine involving patient researchers'. *British Journal of General Practice*, **55**: 87–93.

Griffiths, F., Lowe, P., Boardman, F., Ayre, C. and Gadsby, R. (2008) 'Becoming pregnant: exploring the perspectives of women living with diabetes'. *British Journal of General Practice*, **58**(548): 184–90.

Jesper, E., Griffiths, F. and Smith, L. (2008) 'A qualitative study of the health experience of gypsy travellers in the UK with a focus on terminal illness'. *Primary Health Care Research & Development*, **9**: 157–65.

Lindenmeyer, A., Hearnshaw, H., Sturt, J., Ormerod, R. and Aitchison, G. (2007) 'Assessment of the benefits of user involvement in health research from the Warwick Diabetes Care Research User Group: a qualitative case study'. *Health Expectations*, **10**: 268–77.

INVOLVE (2006) *Guide to Reimbursing and Paying Members of the Public Actively Involved in Research*. Eastleigh: INVOLVE.

INVOLVE (2008) *Good Practice in Active Public Involvement in Research*. Eastleigh: INVOLVE.

Staniszewska, S., Jones, N., Marshall, S. and Newburn, M. (2007) 'User involvement in the development of a research bid: barriers, enablers and impacts'. *Health Expectations*, **10**(2), 173–83.

Tarpey, M. and Royle, J. (2006) *Public Involvement in Research Grant Applications*. Eastleigh: INVOLVE.

Resources

INVOLVE promotes public involvement in the NHS, public health and social care research. Available at. www.invo.org.uk.

INVOLVE is a UK organisation funded by the government. It has an extensive website providing advice for members of the public wanting to be involved in research, for researchers and for research commissioners. It publishes a very helpful series of guides, available for free download and which include further reading. Guides for researchers include those listed in the References and:

Hanley, B., Bradburn, J., Barnes, M., Evans, C., Goodare, H., Kelson, M., Kent, A., Oliver, S. and Sted, R. (ed.) (2004) *Involving the Public in NHS, Public Health, and Social Care Research: Briefing notes for researchers.* Eastleigh: INVOLVE.

Further reading

There are many studies now published where users have been involved in different ways with the research. Lindenmeyer et al., 2007; Jesper et al., 2008; Griffiths et al., 2008; Belam et al., 2005; and Staniszewska et al., 2007 are just some examples (see References).

Waterman, H., Tillen, D., Dickson, R. and Koning, K. de (2001) *Action Research: A systematic review and guidance for assessment*, No. 23. London: Health Technology Assessment, NHS.

This review provides a definition of action research, reviews the use of this approach in health care settings and provides guidance on evaluating action research projects. The guidance is equally useful for planning action research. It is freely available on the Web.

5 Preparing to Design Research for Health Care Practice

This chapter takes you through preparations for designing your research, including defining what you want to research, finding out what is already known about it, and considering the different approaches you could use for the research. It considers models of the focus of our research, comparing models of individuals, health care use and populations and how they relate to each other.

This chapter considers the preparations needed for designing your research once you have decided on the focus of your research. Designing research is relatively straightforward if the research focus and research question are clear. However, once we start the process of designing our research we often realise that these are not as clear as we thought and we have to go back and review them. This chapter describes the process of review at this stage of designing our research and points towards future data analysis. This iterative process of going back over what we have already done while also moving forward is a normal part of research.

The thinking, reading, discussing, writing and reviewing that we need to do to get our research focus, question and method right takes time but it is all part of our research. We tend to feel that we haven't started our research until we start our data collection. This is not so; our research starts when we conceive of the initial idea.

The first section of this chapter discusses our own preferences for research methods and how this may shape our research. The chapter then considers how we define the focus of our research, including its time dimension. We then consider how we can use literature to understand more about the focus and frame of our research, how our research fits with what is already known and how we can carry out our research. Finally, the chapter considers modelling the focus of our research to help us in prioritising our research questions and designing our research, and how these models can also assist in data analysis.

Examining our preferences for our research approach

Before getting started on our research we may have a preference for a particular research method. We may enjoy reading certain types of research more than others as we find them interesting, easy to understand or particularly relevant to our clinical practice. Influential colleagues may also have preferences. Just as our motivations for research influence what we do (see Chapter 2), so can our preferences for research methods. We should write down our preferences in our research diary to help us reflect on our research and what influenced it.

Our preferences may be very appropriate as we understand our research context and we know about research methods from our professional education. However, we need to pause to consider other possible research approaches. This is not easy as, if we undertake this process rigorously, we may find our research question would be best answered using a research approach that we do not know much about, that we think will not be supported by our colleagues or managers, or that seems impractical in our setting. We will explore this using the example in Box 5.1.

Getting started on research on access to podiatry services	**Box 5.1**

Health professional role: Podiatrist.

Motivation: Concern that the people in most need of podiatry are not getting to podiatry clinics.

Observation of difference or change: Case mix in local podiatry clinic is different, with fewer serious foot problems than the case mix reported in a similar clinic elsewhere.

Overall aim: To understand how people gain access or do not gain access to podiatry.

Research issue: Access and podiatry services.

Research focus: Patients in need of podiatry.

The podiatrist described in Box 5.1 may phrase his research question as: What are the experiences of people in gaining access to the health care service?

This research question indicates that he wants to hear accounts of people's experiences and so requires research methods for listening to people such as interviews or focus groups. The podiatrist may be keen on doing interviews as he is new to research and has little available time. A small interview study appears easy to do and will give him results fairly quickly. However, he could ask the research question:

What is the incidence of foot problems in the community?

This question requires gathering data from a large number of people, so he would be thinking of undertaking a **survey**. If the podiatrist knows how to do a survey but not an interview study, he may favour the second question. He may also feel a survey will be more acceptable to the clinic manager, who has agreed to reduce his workload to allow him time for research. His colleagues may suggest that it will be easier to find a journal to publish his research if it is a survey. The clinic manager may be keen on the survey as she urgently needs to review the clinic service and the survey could feed into this review.

Both research questions can contribute to the overall research aim, but provide very different types of results.

We should note our final decision about the research question and research methods, and the reasons for the decision, to refer back to during analysis and writing up the research. Developing our research question and deciding on our research approach often go hand in hand, but we need to think critically about what we want to do, why we want to do it, what and who is influencing us.

Defining the focus of our research

Researchers have learnt to isolate particular aspects of the world in order to study it in the process known as abstraction. Researchers have found this useful in order to move forward with research and not become overwhelmed by the complex interactions of the world. Part of this process involves placing boundaries around parts of the world where in reality there is no boundary. Understanding how and why we isolate and define the aspects of the world we want to study is important when designing our research and understanding its limitations. Chapter 2 considered how to clarify the focus and frame of our research. In this section we take this a step further, exploring how to define the focus of our research. Defining the focus is essential for data collection.

To define our research focus we need to make decisions about how we carve it out from the rest of the world, where we place a boundary to separate it out. To explore this we will take as an example a doctor working in a clinic with elderly patients who wants to improve understanding about medication (see Box 5.2). She makes a list of possible research foci and research aims (Table 5.1). We will discuss the issues to be considered when defining each of the research foci.

It may seem straightforward to define a patient. If we perceive the boundary to be the patient's skin, we could stand a patient up against a white wall and draw around them with a pen to provide an image of the boundary of the patient. However, think of any patient you have encountered and consider who they are as people and how they have become who they are. I suspect you will start thinking

Getting started on research on elderly patients and understanding medication	Box 5.2

Health professional role: Doctor in clinic seeing mostly elderly patients.

Motivation: To improve health care for the elderly patients.

Observation of difference or change: Increasing number of telephone calls from relatives about problems or uncertainties about medication.

Overall aim: To improve understanding about medication between doctors and patients.

Research issue: Medication communication and information.

Table 5.1   Research foci and research aims for research on elderly patients and understanding medication

Research focus	Research aim
Patients	To understand why patients take or do not take medication recommended by a health professional
The clinic	To explore what aspects of the clinic enables/inhibits patients from bringing relatives/carers/friends with them to the clinic
The interaction between patients and clinic staff (and communication systems used by staff such as posters, leaflets)	To understand how information about medication is communicated in the clinic
Information sources that could potentially be accessed by patients or on behalf of patients	To explore the information sources available for patients to access about their medication (e.g. books, Internet)
The family of the patient	To understand how patients' families talk about medication

in terms of where they are from and how they relate to other people. So, is the boundary of a patient at their skin or does it include their relationships to others and their environment? Similar problems occur when we consider the clinic (see Box 5.3).

For understanding the interactions between patients and clinic staff, we would need to decide whether to include all face-to-face interactions a patient may have at a clinic (including conversations with receptionists, nurses, doctors, pharmacists and so on) or whether we focus on interaction between patients and health professionals within specific consultations. Do we include interaction via posters and leaflets? Do we include communication by telephone or e-mail, or indirect communication via other people such as relatives?

Box 5.3	**Problems of defining the boundary of a clinic at the focus of research on elderly patients and understanding medication**

Place

It may be straightforward to identify the boundaries of the clinic as a place, including how long it has been there and who works there. However, there may be outreach services elsewhere and staff may work partly at the clinic and partly elsewhere.

People

Are the patients who attend the clinic part of the clinic? For the time the patients are in the clinic or communicating within the clinic they will be affecting how it runs, so could be considered part of the clinic.

Organisational boundaries

If the clinic is mostly funded by the health service but community groups, patient advocate organisations and charities also work within the clinic, are they part of the clinic or not?

For exploring information sources, the focus of the study is the information, although the clinic frames the research as we are interested in information that could potentially be accessed by patients who attend the clinic. Where would we stop looking for information? We can specify boundaries such as including only information in certain languages or in particular formats such as written, audio, printed or websites. We need to be clear about why we are placing these boundaries and how they may limit our research. If the clinic serves a multi-ethnic community, people may access information about medication from websites written in their language of origin, which would be missed by limiting the research focus by language. If the aim was to understand what information patients access about their medication, we remain focused on the information, but the patients' recall of the information they access and their willingness to tell us about it provides the boundary of what is included. If the research aim was to explore how or why patients access information about their medication, then the patients become the focus of the study rather than the information.

The doctor (Box 5.2 and Table 5.1) may be interested in how families talk about medication as this may influence the patient's understanding of medication. However, how do we define family? We could include only those in the patient's household or all first-degree relatives wherever they live. We could decide to include only relatives living close to the patient, but a daughter living on another continent may be frequently in touch and very influential. Someone who is not a relative but who has been considered part of the family for decades may be a key person who would be missed if we only include relatives. The definition of who to include as family could be decided by the doctor doing the research, or she could ask each patient to define it for themselves. Whatever she decides to do, she is placing a boundary where there is no clear boundary.

There is growing interest in the role of social networks on health, for example, how social interaction that is not family interaction influences obesity (Christakis and Fowler, 2007). If the doctor in the example in Box 5.2 was to focus on social networks with the research aim 'To understand how medication is talked about in social networks', how would she define the social network? Networks can have almost no limit. For example, talk about medication between a patient and their daughter may be taken up in conversations between the patient and their neighbour, and then the neighbour may discuss it with the local pharmacist and a group of friends over coffee. Meanwhile the daughter, who lives on another continent, may talk to her work colleagues, some of whom mention it to friends and so on.

We are accustomed to placing boundaries around people and organisations, so much so that these boundaries often seem well defined, although when we look closely they are not. We are less accustomed to thinking in terms of networks in health care research, and so it is perhaps easier to see that a network such as a social network has no boundary that we can easily define. All people and organisations are within networks as they communicate and relate to many other people and organisations, and so in this sense their boundaries are not easy to define. However, to move forward with our research we need to define what we focus on.

We define the focus of our research in the process of designing our research. Table 5.2 gives examples of how **research design** has the effect of placing a boundary around the research focus and so defining it.

When we define the focus of our study, it is important to keep in mind that as researchers *we* are deciding on the definition of our research focus, it is not a given. It is not easy to go through this process of clarifying, reflecting and refining the focus of our research and we may feel uncertain and insecure about what we are doing. It may seem easier to use boundaries and definitions developed by other researchers. This has its advantages as it enables comparison of results across studies. However, if the boundaries and definitions developed by others do not fit with our research focus and aim, then we need to use different ones. Sometimes we may work with two different definitions, our own and another that enables us to compare our research with that of others. Whether we plan to work with boundaries and definitions used by other researchers or our own, we need to remain open to changing this decision as we develop our research.

Our decisions about how to define the focus of our research are not claims about how the world actually is, but enable us to move forward with research in our complex world. We can change our decisions if we realise we are missing something during the

Table 5.2   Research design and definition of the focus for research on elderly patients and understanding medication

Research focus	Defining the research focus: examples of how research design places a boundary around the research focus
Patients	Boundary is often the skin surface of the patient. Relationships with other people and the environment are placed on to the patient as if they were within the patient (e.g. marital status, occupation, level of social support).
The clinic	Boundary is usually based on common understanding of what is the clinic. Details of the boundary are often pragmatic (e.g. ignore outreach clinics; include people present in clinic at time of data collection). Relationships with other organisations and the environment are placed on to the clinic as if they were within the clinic (e.g. level of deprivation in the local community, sources of funding).
The interaction between patients and clinic staff	Boundary defined by data collection method. For example, video recording captures data about interactions between people easily, but where the video recorder is set up defines what interactions are recorded.
Information sources that could potentially be accessed by patients or on behalf of patients	Boundary defined by placing filters at the point of data collection. Filters may be linked to the aim of the research (e.g. patients recall of information used) or due to limitations in the research process (e.g. the researcher's ability to access data in other languages).
The family of the patient	Boundary defined by placing filters at the point of data collection. Filters may be linked to the aim of the research (e.g. the patient's view of what is family) or due to limitations in the research process (e.g. a family member providing data may not know about a relative who has not been in contact for years).

early stages of our research. We can also explore those aspects of the world that we have not included when we undertake further research.

Defining the time focus of our research

Time and the nature of everything in the world are so interrelated that when we define the focus of our research we may also define the time focus. For example, the focus on information sources available to patients (see Tables 5.1 and 5.2) includes a definition of the time focus of the research although it is not made explicit. The information has to exist in such a form that it is available to patients at the time of the study. Information from 30 years ago is less likely to be available than information produced and published recently. As discussed above, in the process of designing our research we also define its focus. In this section we discuss defining the time focus of our research.

Defining the time focus of research on information and renal failure	Box 5.4

Health care professional role: Nurse working with people living with renal failure.

Motivation: Improving experience of health care for patients; increasing patient self-reliance; reducing patient reliance on health care professionals.

Observation of difference or change: Many patients and their families understand very little about renal failure, but when he takes time to give them information and explain about it they are more able to manage their treatments.

Overall aim: To improve the provision of information for people living with renal failure.

Research issue: Information and renal failure.

Research focus: Patients living with renal failure.

Research time focus: From confirmation of diagnosis to end of life.

We will explore this using the example from Chapter 2 of research on information and renal failure. The nurse developing this research may decide that he wants to consider patients at all stages of living with renal failure from confirmation of diagnosis to end of life (see Box 5.4). This definition places what happens before confirmation of diagnosis in the frame of the research rather than within its focus. Characteristics of the patient from before the start of the research time focus could be placed onto the patient as if they were within it, such as previous illnesses. Experiences of previous illnesses may well influence the patient's experience of renal failure, so in this sense these earlier experiences are expressed within the time focus of the research. How we decide to deal with this indistinct boundary in time will depend on what we are trying to find out and on our research methods (as discussed above). For example, a survey of patients may collect data about past illnesses from clinical records and use this data as if it was a characteristic of the patient at the time of the survey. An interview study may use the patient as a filter, relying on the patient to mention any past illness experiences that have made a difference to their current experience of renal failure.

The boundary of the research time focus needs careful consideration and definition when designing the research. For example, when do we consider the diagnosis of renal failure to be confirmed? Is it when the specialist is as sure as she can be that this is the diagnosis? Is it when the patient realises this is the diagnosis? As the focus of the research (Box 5.4) is patients living with renal failure, the end of their life provides a clear time point. However, if the research focus included their families, this end point would be less clear as the impact of the patient's illness can go well beyond the patient's death.

Through the process of clarifying and defining the time focus of our research, we clarify what forms the frame of the research (see Chapter 2). Although the focus and frame of our research will be constantly changing over time, there may be particular changes in the research frame that we need to take into account. For example, the launch of a new health care policy related to renal failure or the introduction of a new treatment may rapidly change the research frame and is likely to affect the patients at the focus of the research. Changes in the frame of the research are sometimes known as **secular trends**. Such change may not have an even effect on the research focus. For example, the availability of information from the Internet has increased rapidly over the past decade but has not had the same impact on everyone, as younger people have more rapidly taken up use of the Internet than older people (a **generation effect**).

The definition of the time focus of our research includes its duration: from the boundary at the start of the time focus to the boundary at the end of the time focus. For people living with renal failure this may be many years. For other research foci the time duration may be relatively short, for example, if we focus on an event such as admission to hospital or a health care consultation. Whatever the duration of the time focus, it is possible to divide it up through how we design our research.

When we collect data at one point in time, for example an interview, a survey or a period of observation, our data is about that point in time. It is known as **cross-sectional** data as it is about one section or period of time. The data collected at one point in time is likely to include data about both the past and the future, but this is filtered through the present. For example, how a person perceives the future may depend on how he or she feels at the present time, how a receptionist describes a clinic in the past may depend on how he or she perceives the clinic now. All this data can be used to understand the present time. However, we may also use this data to understand the past, and perhaps the future. There are data collection techniques to assist in collecting data to understand the past and future through the present time, as discussed in Chapters 7 and 8. The other research design option is to collect data at a number of different time points. This is known as **longitudinal** data as data is collected as time goes along. Data collected at each time point is about the present at that time plus the past and future as perceived through the filter of the present time. This data can be used to understand the present time at each of the data collection time points, and each present time can be compared to other time points, both those before and after it in time sequence.

For both cross-sectional and longitudinal data collection, we need to consider the duration of present time. The world is constantly changing so present time could be considered infinitesimally small as, almost before we have realised it, the world has changed. However, for the purpose of our research we usually consider the present to be longer that this. The focus of our research and how we design our research influences the definition and so the duration of present time. Examples of ways of defining present time are given in Table 5.3.

Table 5.3   Defining the boundary of present time

Definition of present time	Examples of how the boundary of present time may be defined
Phase or stage of illness	Disease stage defined by assessment, e.g. physiological measures of renal function. Phase of illness as described by individual in interview.
Duration of event or occurrence	People's perceptions of when event or occurrence started, e.g. acute illness. The place of an event, e.g. cubicle in emergency department or consulting room.
Actions or utterances	End of previous action or utterance and start of next action or utterance, e.g. in a health care consultation the actions or utterances could be the type of talk or action such as greeting, asking a question, expressing empathy, giving information, prescribing.
Position in pathway	End of previous position in pathway and beginning of next, e.g. in a clinic the position in pathway may include diagnostic tests, confirmation of diagnosis, treatment decisions.
Duration of measurement process	How long it takes to complete a measurement, e.g. a second or two for a blood glucose monitor, half a minute for a blood pressure monitor.
A specified duration of clock or calendar time	The specified duration should be tailored to the aim and focus of the research and the research design. For example, some questionnaires about symptoms, e.g. back pain, may ask about symptoms in the last four weeks as research has shown this provides a useful assessment of symptoms. Other questionnaires ask about symptoms at the time the person fills in the questionnaire and can be used more frequently with the same person in a longitudinal study.

The definition of the boundary of present time may be developed from the research data, such as defining the present time based on interview data or making the boundary the previous and subsequent utterances in a conversation. There may be a standard definition of the boundary of present time such as 'the last four weeks' or the duration of a measurement process. We may decide to use two definitions, one based on our research data and another that is standardised, so we can make comparisons with other research.

When collecting data over time, we need to decide when to collect the data. The timing may be determined by the nature of the data. For example, if we record a health care consultation, each utterance of doctor or patient is data collected at a time point. The timing of these time points is determined by the consultation. However, if we undertake data collection from a group of patients to explore how their symptoms change over time, we need to decide whether we ask the patients to record change if and when it occurs or whether we collect data at pre-planned time points, for example, four times a day or once a month.

Time is an important dimension to consider in the process of designing our research for health care practice. As we design our research we need to think about what we are considering to be the present time and how this is defined by the nature of our data and how we design data collection. We also need to consider whether we collect data at one point in time or over a period of time and the timing of data collection. These decisions will influence how we analyse our data and are discussed in Chapters 9 and 10. We may want to review and revise our design a number of times to ensure that the time focus, definition of the present time and timing of data collection are the best possible for our research.

Reviewing literature in preparation for designing research

This section considers how to use existing literature to assist in research design. Literature of particular importance in the design of research for health care practice includes reports of research, descriptions of current health care activity and health policy documents. Other literature may also be needed depending on the research issue. As health professionals, we are likely to have read about our research issue as part of our continuing professional development and this forms a good basis for developing our research. Researchers who are not health professionals often spend a great deal of time reading up about an issue before developing their research. However, even if we consider ourselves experts on our research issue, when we reach the stage of designing our research, if we have not already done so, we need to pause and take time to look carefully at the literature as discussed in this section. This process will help with research design and may also prompt us to review our research aims, focus and questions. We may even need to abandon our original ideas and start again.

We will consider the example in Box 5.5 of a doctor interested in the quality of care for people living with diabetes in residential care homes:

> The doctor is only just starting on his research, so wants to examine what the care homes say they are doing. Later on he hopes to look in detail at what they are doing and the impact of this on indicators of health, such as the level of diabetes control measured by HbA1c. With advice from an **information scientist** or librarian with experience in the health field, the doctor searches for literature that will help him design his research

Information and library sciences are rapidly developing, and systems for finding relevant literature are continually changing. Researchers seek advice on finding relevant literature however experienced they are in research. The literature can help the doctor answer a number of questions about his research. First, he should consider whether to proceed with the research at all, then he decides whether the

Getting started on research on the provision of diabetes care in residential care homes	Box 5.5

Health professional role: Doctor overseeing diabetes services in a small city.

Motivation: To ensure equality of care for people living with diabetes.

Observation of difference or change: People with diabetes who are living in residential care homes do not seem to receive the same quality of care for their diabetes as those living in their own homes.

Overall aim: To improve the quality of care for diabetes for those living in residential care homes.

Research issue: Diabetes care and residential care homes.

Research focus: Residential care homes.

Research aim: To describe the policy and practice for diabetes care as reported by residential care homes in the city.

Research question: What current provision of diabetes care is reported by residential care homes in the city?

research can use the literature as its data. If new data collection is needed, he then considers how to use the literature in the design of the research.

Can the literature answer the research question?

Occasionally someone has answered the exact research question. The doctor may feel disappointed, but this gives him the opportunity to tackle his next research question, building on the research already undertaken. It is more likely that there is research that answers a similar question but not exactly the same one. If one or a number of these studies are similar to what he is planning to do, this may provide a sufficiently good answer to the research question to enable him to move on to the next research question. For example, research undertaken two years earlier in a similar locality may give him a sufficiently good answer. However, if the research is five years old and there has been a major change in the recommendations for diabetes care in that time, then it may no longer be relevant. Research undertaken in a very different setting may also not be directly relevant.

Can the literature be used as research data?

There may be a number of research reports that give partial answers to the research question and when combined give a sufficient answer. There is now so much research literature available that the doctor should start the process of doing a systematic review of the literature (as discussed in Chapter 6) before he can be sure whether there is sufficient research literature to answer his research question. This will take time, but will be time well spent because if we need to design new research his knowledge of the relevant research literature will inform this.

Other literature may also provide research data (see Chapter 6) such as policy documents, minutes of meetings and information on the Internet. This may be used to understand the frame of the research or as data for analysis. Finding this data would follow the same principles as collecting qualitative data (Chapter 7), and the approach to analysis would be similar to analysis of new data such as interviews (Chapters 9 and 10).

How does the literature inform the design of research involving new data collection?

The literature can inform every stage of developing and designing research. It can be helpful to write down the questions about the research design that the literature may be able to answer. The following are examples, of questions the doctor (Box 5.5) may ask, but there may be many more.

- *What questions have already been answered about the research issue and focus?*

   Mapping out the questions that have already been answered helps the doctor clarify how his research fits with and adds to existing research. For example, there may be research that answers questions about the educational needs of residential care workers, communication issues between health and social care or the health care of those with other chronic disease in residential care.

- *How does the literature define the focus of the research?*

   The research is focused on residential care homes. The doctor will need to consider what organisations to include as residential care homes in his locality. There may be policy documents from governmental and non-governmental organisations that suggest what is commonly understood to be a residential care home. He could also read about how other researchers have decided what to include in similar research. How to decide on who or what to include in research is discussed further in Chapter 7.

- *Is there research from a different time or place which provides useful comparison for the research focus?*

   One of the ways in which local research for health care practice can contribute to the wider body of knowledge is through comparison with other places, or the same place at other times. Early on in designing his research the doctor needs to identify other research for use in comparison, as he may need to adapt his data collection for making the comparisons. This is discussed further in Chapter 8.

- *How has data been collected about the focus of the research in similar studies?*

  Literature assists with the design of data collection. The doctor should read the detail of how and why data is collected in other studies. For example, if data was collected using a **questionnaire,** he needs to read about its development and use. He can then decide if it is useful for his research.

- *What are the important issues for the frame of the research?*

  The frame of the research – what is happening around the research focus – is important for understanding research undertaken in one locality. The doctor may be aware of local, regional or national policy about the provision of diabetes care and any guidelines on care for diabetes but he may need to update his knowledge. However, the doctor also needs to read more widely, beyond the immediate research issue of diabetes care and residential care homes, to explore what other issues may be important in the frame of the research. These may include changes in the number of frail elderly, trends in migration in and out of the city, changes in the training requirements of care staff, or changes in the allocation of resources for residential care.

- *Is there local data about the important issues in the frame of the research?*

  If the doctor wants his local research to be useful for other people, he needs to describe his own locality so other people can consider how similar or different it is from their locality. The data needed will be guided by reading about the issues that are important in the frame of the research (see above). This information may be available in published literature, local reports and surveys such as the census.

- *How have other researchers tackled similar research questions?*

  We can learn about research design, what has worked well and where there have been problems through reading other people's studies. These studies may have nothing to do with the research issue but tackle a similar type of research question. For example, a study on the reported provision of care for people with chronic illness in prisons may provide insights about research methods. There are also many books and articles about research methods that are relevant to research for health care practice.

Some of the literature that can help us design our research is written in styles unfamiliar to health professionals and published in journals which we would not read for our clinical work. It can be very difficult to know where to start with this unfamiliar literature, and it is tempting to stay with the familiar. However, this wider literature can improve our research and may save us time and resources in the long run. There are a number of strategies to use for finding your way into and around unfamiliar literature:

- Ask people you know for advice; they may know people who can help even if they can't themselves.

- Look for books on unfamiliar topics that are designed for undergraduate university students as these often provide a general overview of a topic.

- Look at the references of papers in your research field and from this identify literature that may be helpful but is unfamiliar, as the authors of the paper found it helpful.

- Find people who are experts on the unfamiliar literature and ask them for help. For example, check the websites of academics at your local universities, look at the references of literature you have read to see who writes about the topic, ask a librarian to help you find experts.

'Start reading' is perhaps the most important strategy. You will soon discover what is helpful and what is not. Remember that books may provide the easiest way in, as these will introduce topics in some detail whereas papers tend to summarise the background issues. You may not read right through a book as you may discover after a few chapters that its focus is not relevant, but in finding that out you will have learnt about the topic in general. This reading takes time and can feel frustrating as it seems to delay starting on your research. However, reading the literature is part of doing the research.

Matching the research approach to the research aim

At this stage of designing our research, we should consider the whole range of research approaches before committing ourselves to a particular one. This includes the many different types of data collection and analysis. By going through this process we clarify why we are choosing a particular approach and how this will give us data that most closely resembles the real world (**validity**), and what we may miss through making this choice. Our notes on this process are valuable when we analyse our results and write about our research.

The range of research approaches appropriate for our research will depend on its aim. Once we have decided on our research approach we can then adapt it to the focus of our research. We will consider the example in Box 5.6 of a religious leader or chaplain wanting to investigate mental health at the end of life. We consider a number of potential aims for his research.

Research aim: To explore the meaning of mental health near the end of life

In his initial discussions about the research issue, a colleague asks the chaplain what he means by mental health when a person is near the end of their life. This prompts him to develop this research aim. He realises he could focus this in a number of different ways, including a focus on people at the end of life or those

Getting started on research on mental health care for people near the end of life	**Box 5.6**

Health professional role: Local religious leader or chaplain working mostly with people near the end of their life.

Motivation: To ensure that people can enjoy life up to its end.

Observation of difference or change: Change in outlook by people near the end of life when their mental health needs have been addressed.

Overall aim: To provide the best possible mental health care for those near the end of life.

Research issue: Mental health near the end of life.

caring for people at the end of life, or people in general – the public. There are a number of possible research approaches for exploring meaning, some involving direct data collection from people and others using data provided for other reasons but available to the researcher. Possible approaches for understanding meaning are listed in Box 5.7. The list of ways of collecting data directly from people is actually a list of research methods – interviews, questionnaires, **write and draw**. The list of indirect sources of data depends on what is available. These indirect sources of data could be used in **secondary analysis** which is the term used for when data collected for another purpose is used in research. Where the data is in the form of stories an approach called **narrative analysis** may be used that seeks to understand both the meaning and the purpose of the story.

Research approaches for exploring the meaning of mental health near the end of life	**Box 5.7**

Ways of asking people directly

- Individual interview (e.g. face to face, telephone, e-mail exchange).
- Group interview or focus group (usually face to face but could be on-line/video conference).
- Questionnaire involving a series of questions requiring short answers (delivered face to face, by telephone or in writing).

(Continued)

(Continued)

- Requesting people to write or draw in response to the research question (Oakley et al., 1995) (this is similar to a questionnaire but with one or two very open questions, or similar to an interview but the responses are on paper).

Sources of indirect data for analysis

- Published research.
- Notes made by health professionals about patients' understanding of mental health.
- Case studies or projects undertaken by professionals in training.
- Reflective writing of people at the end of life.
- Writing about mental health and end of life in general literature, such as books written about the experience of terminal illness, weblogs, novels, poetry, films and plays.
- Media (TV, radio, web, newspapers, magazines and so on) coverage including reports, opinion writing and discussions.

Research aim: To describe the provision of mental health care for those near the end of life

The chaplain may decide he wants to find out what actually happens, or not, in terms of providing mental health care at the end of life. For this aim he needs to observe what happens or have access to other people's observations. Possible approaches for this research aim are listed in Box 5.8.

Box 5.8	Research approaches for describing the provision of mental health care near the end of life

Direct observation of what happens

- Observation in health care settings as **non-participant observer** present in the setting.
- Observation of health care as **participant observer** (e.g. while working in the setting as chaplain).
- Observation without being present, using audio-visual recording technology.

Sources of indirect observation data

- All data sources listed in Box 5.7.
- Clinical and administrative records.

As in Box 5.7, the list of ways of collecting new data is actually a list of research methods. For this aim this includes different observation methods. Indirect observation depends on what is available. Clinical and administrative data records of health care processes may include data about what happens to people nearing the end of life. In addition, all the data sources in Box 5.7, both data collected directly from people and indirect data sources, could provide data about health care as well as meaning.

Research aim: To describe the diversity of meaning of mental health and experience of mental health care near the end of life

From his reading about mental health near the end of life, the chaplain may observe differences in peoples' understandings and experiences. To explore this further, the chaplain will need data collected from lots of people to be sure he has, as far as possible, included the whole range of meaning and experience. As this involves observing or talking to lots of people, we use the term survey for this type of research approach. The chaplain needs to compare data from each person with data from all the other people in the survey. Due to the inevitably large volume of data, it will need to be in a form that makes comparisons relatively easy. This research aim therefore needs data that has been **coded,** processed, analysed or structured in some way (Box 5.9).

Research approaches for surveying the meaning of mental health and experience of mental health care near the end of life	**Box 5.9**

Methods of collecting structured data from people

- Structured interviews.
- Questionnaire involving a series of questions requiring short answers (delivered face to face, by telephone or in writing).

Indirect sources of structured data for analysis

- All data sources listed in Box 5.7 and 5.8 once analysed.
- Clinical and administrative records, particularly coded data and measurements.
- Existing relevant survey data sets.

When developing a structured interview or questionnaire, the researcher imposes a structure on the data that is to be collected. The person answering the questionnaire also processes the data they provide. This processing of data by researcher and research participant also occurs during observation and exploratory interviews, but there is flexibility to ask further questions during data collection.

For the chaplain's research aim it is unlikely that there is existing relevant survey data; however, there are many large survey data sets, so this possibility should always be considered (see Chapter 6).

Research aim: To describe the impact of mental health care on the mental health of those near the end of life

During his discussions with colleagues about his research, the chaplain may encounter some scepticism about whether health care can improve the mental health of people nearing death. In response he formulates this research aim that requires data from before and after mental health care. The chaplain will need to decide whether collecting data at one point in time will tell him what he wants to know about past, present and future, or whether he needs to collect data at different time points. None of the research aims so far have required time ordered data. All the research approaches described in Boxes 5.7, 5.8 and 5.9 can be used to collect time-ordered data.

Research aim: To evaluate the effectiveness of mental health care near the end of life

This aim is a further refinement of the research aim that considered the impact of mental health care, and implies measurement of the change in health status of the people receiving the care. This research would require an experimental approach, such as a randomised controlled trial, and is beyond the scope of this book (see Further Reading).

This section has explored the range of research approaches that we can use depending on the aim of our research. For any one aim, we can use more than one approach. The process of deciding which to use involves going back and forth between considering our aim, appropriate methods and any existing data. Each decision shapes the research so needs care and should be noted in our research diary. We then design our research, as discussed in the remainder of the book.

Modelling the research focus

Before moving on to design our research in detail, we can use the understanding we have gained so far to **model** the focus of our research. The model summarises what we know. It helps us prioritise our research questions (see Chapter 2) and work out what data we need. The model is also a first step in our analysis. In the very early stages of developing research, the model may be very simple, based on our initial ideas about what is happening. We develop it based on our reading and preliminary investigations. In the later stages of research, when we are analysing data, the model can be reviewed and revised and perhaps completely redrawn based on our research findings. In this section we use the example in Box 5.10 to consider how to develop models of individual people, people using a health care service and people in a population.

Getting started on research on the variation in blood pressure control in one locality	**Box 5.10**

Health professional role: Doctor with a special interest in cardiovascular disease prevention.

Motivation: To reduce the number of people having strokes and other disease related to high blood pressure.

Observation of difference or change: Variation in the control of blood pressure among people identified as having high blood pressure despite the widespread provision of health care and health information on the issue in the locality.

Overall aim: To improve the control of blood pressure in the local population.

Research issue: Control of blood pressure.

Research focus: People identified as having high blood pressure.

Modelling individual people

We can develop a simple model of individual people to assist in deciding which research questions to give priority. The model would consider individuals going from being unaware of their blood pressure, realising they should have it checked, finding that it is raised and going on to take treatment for it. One such model is represented in Figure 5.1 along with what may influence them as they move through the pathway. This model could be thought of as a 'patient pathway'. Early in our research the model will be based on our experience and knowledge of the literature. As we continue to read about our research issue, we can add more stages and influences to the pathway. The model clarifies what we already know about the research focus.

The simple model in Figure 5.1 seems to represent an individual person, although it is really a caricature; it does not represent an actual person. The model includes stages many patients go through, but it is unlikely that any one patient would go through them in the standardised way represented in the model.

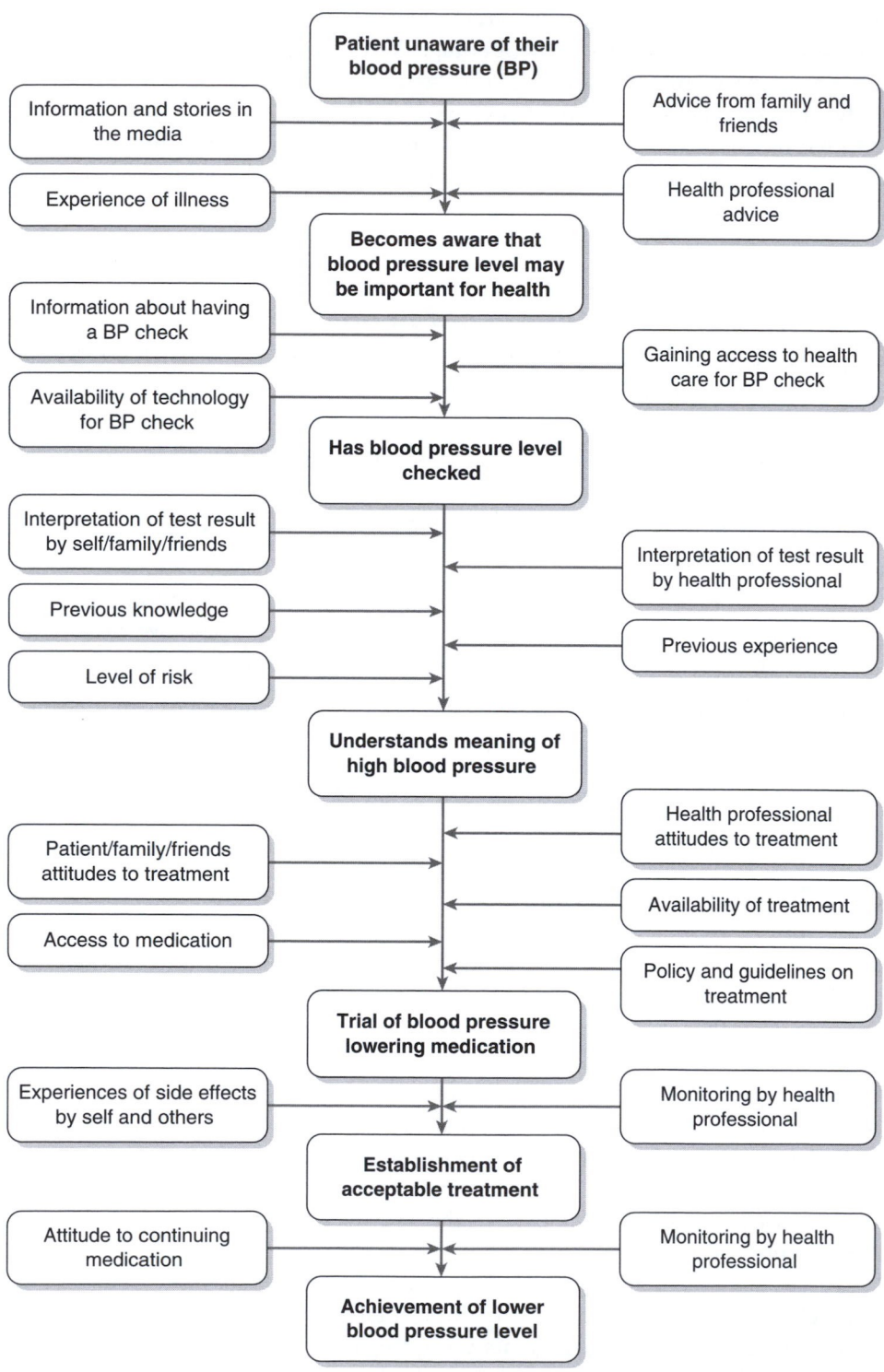

Figure 5.1   Model of a caricature patient pathway to good blood pressure control

For example, moving between having blood pressure checked, understanding the meaning of a high result and trying medication may happen within a day for one person, whereas another person may have their blood pressure checked many times and gradually come to understand the meaning of the high result. The influences on the pathway as indicated by arrows may happen in a different order and some may have no impact on some people. Influences may interact with each other. The patient may also change the influencing factors so the arrows should perhaps be in both directions. Despite all these caveats, drawing out such a model can be helpful in developing our research, but we need to take care how we use it. This type of modelling is similar to mapping out the different perspectives on an issue, as discussed in Chapter 2.

The simple model can help the doctor decide on his priority for research questions (see Chapter 2). For example, he may decide that he needs to understand the meaning of high blood pressure for patients before investigating the use of treatment guidelines by health professionals, or that more research is needed on the experience of side effects of medication before investigating why patients do not take their medication.

Later in our research, when analysing data we may develop models of individual people that represent their particular pathways. Each model would summarise what happened to a particular individual. The model for each individual would be slightly different from the model for every other individual. Analysis of the data would include comparison of each model with every other model to identify similarities and differences as these provide clues as to why there is variation in blood pressure control.

Modelling the use of health care services

We can develop models of the flows of patients through a health care service. Early in his research the doctor in Box 5.10 could collect data from his own clinic, such as how many patients attend, what investigations and treatments they have, whether they are asked to come back for follow-up and whether they do come back. This data can be used to develop a simple model such as Figure 5.2. The doctor would put in the model the actual numbers of patients seen in his own clinic during a specified period. This type of model can help with deciding on the priority of research questions. For example, the priority may be to find out why 45 out of 70 people given treatment and appointments for follow-up do not attend. The model can also help with the detailed design of research, particularly whether the doctor is likely to recruit enough people for his research within the time he has to do it. For example, if the doctor wanted to survey patients about taking long-term medication for blood pressure, he may consider sending a questionnaire to patients who have not had a recent change in their medication. Five patients did not have their medication changed during the period covered by the model. The doctor can calculate how long it would take to complete his survey and decide whether this is the best approach to use.

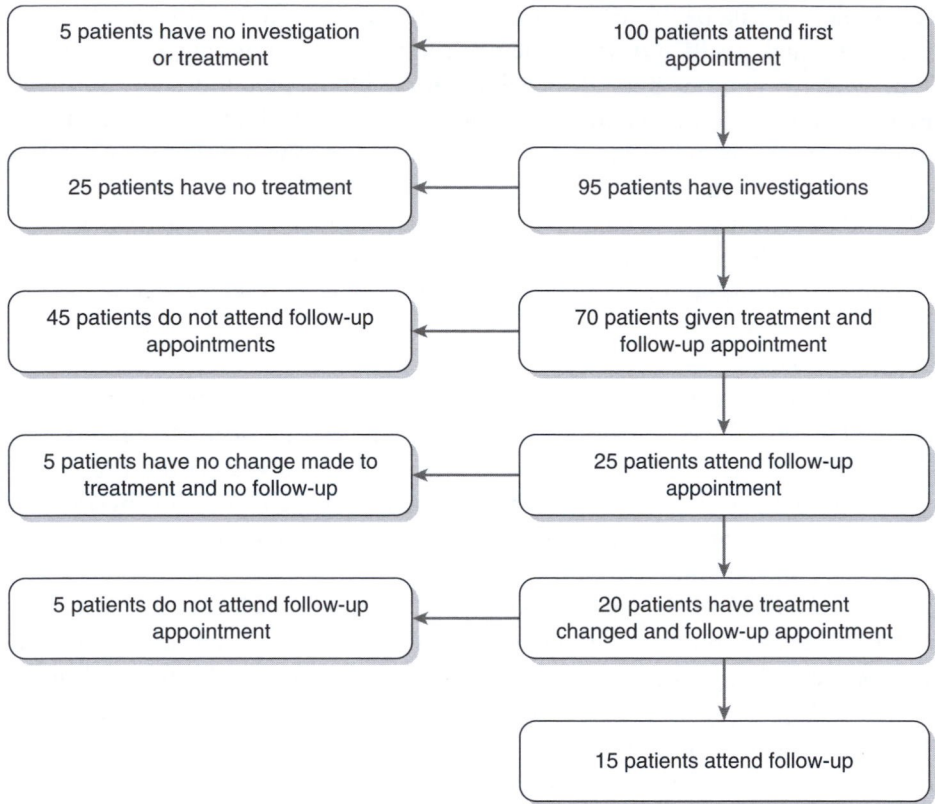

Figure 5.2   Model of patient flow through a local clinical service in a specified time period

After the preliminary data collection from his own clinic, the doctor may decide to undertake a larger study about what happens to people known to have high blood pressure when they attend all the relevant clinics in his region. Although the focus of the research remains on people identified as having high blood pressure, it is only concerned with when they are in contact with the clinics. Data collection would record what happens to each individual patient, as discussed in the previous section, but only about their contact with the clinics. The way clinics are organised provides the structure through which the patients flow and so provides the structure to the data. The structure will be similar to the model in Figure 5.2 although perhaps more complicated, for example, certain groups of patient may follow a different pathway of investigation and treatment. Analysis would include counting how many patients have a particular type of contact with the clinic. Understanding who comes into and leaves the clinic system and at what point may give us clues as to how the health system contributes to the variation in blood pressure control in the population.

An example of research on flows of patients through an emergency department was discussed in Chapter 1 (Box 1.1), but the focus of the research was the emergency department as a system rather than the patients. If we drew a model of the flow of patients through the emergency department it would look very similar to Figure 5.2 but with stages in the model such as 'reception', 'waiting area', 'triage nurse', 'x-ray department'. The number of patients at each stage of the emergency department at any one time is important for understanding how it works as a system and how it could be improved. In the example discussed above where the focus is on patients this data is not needed as the doctor is interested in who reached each stage rather than whether there was delay or congestion in the clinic system. Delays and congestion may of course be a reason for patients not attending follow-up appointments, so the doctor may want to focus on both individual patients and the clinic system.

Modelling populations of individuals

We will now consider modelling what is happening in the population of people studied by the doctor (Box 5.10). The doctor has noticed variation in the control of blood pressure in the local population. As a first step to understanding why this variation exists he could draw a model of all the possible reasons for the variation he can think of, based on his own ideas and his reading of the literature. This may include biological mechanisms, psychological factors, the meaning of blood pressure for people, and the way health care is provided. Figure 5.3 is an example of such a model. Such a model, even though only capturing some of the issues, can be quite complex. Figure 5.3 does not include wider social issues such as employment opportunities, health policy and migration, nor issues such as genetics. The arrows in the model suggest direction of influence. For example, access to medication influences regularity of taking medication. Although this may be the main direction of influence, there can be influence in the opposite direction at the same time. For example, if medication is taken regularly by a number of people, the supply chain becomes more consistent. The model does not include interaction between factors, such as the interaction of health care services and community understanding. The model in Figure 5.3 captures our ideas about the issue and can be developed and refined, and perhaps redrawn, as research proceeds. The model can help the doctor to decide which research questions he will give priority, and clarifies others which he is not including in his current research but which form the frame of the research.

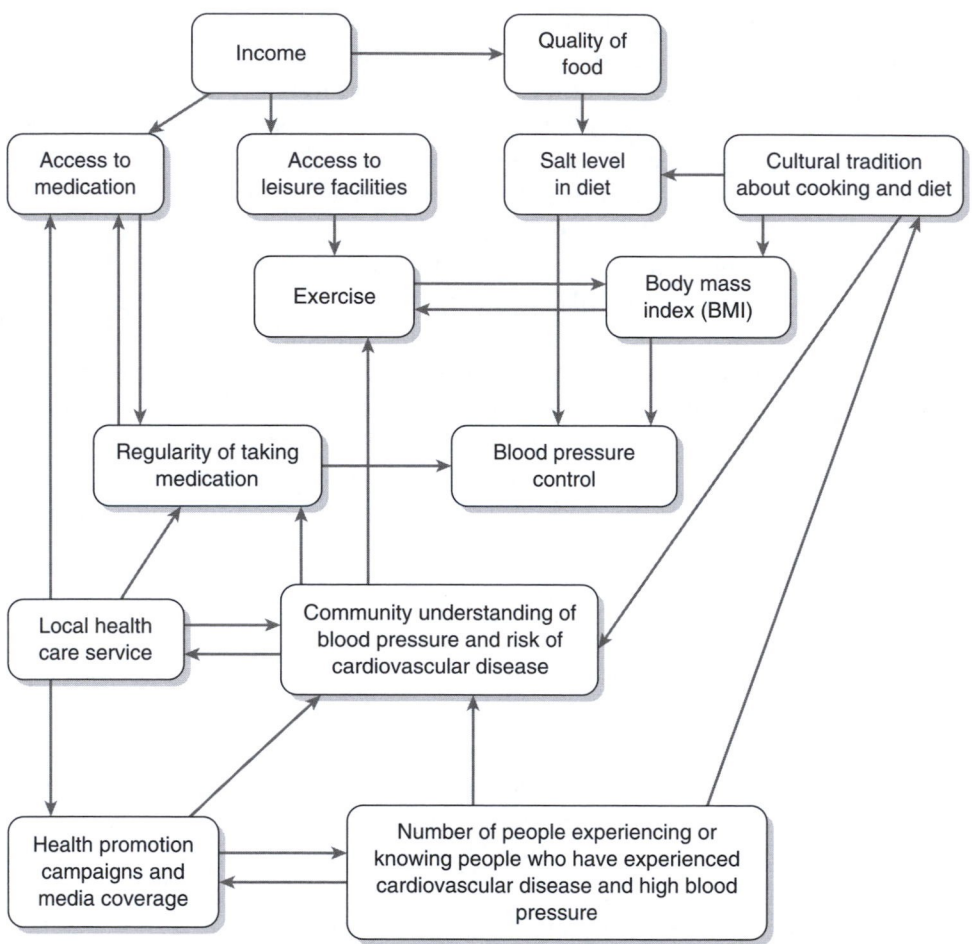

Figure 5.3   Model of reasons for variation in blood pressure control in the population

Epidemiology has refined methods for developing models of population health and testing them against research data. The remainder of this section introduces this research approach to clarify how it fits with the modelling of individuals discussed above. The approach will not be considered further in this book except as an important source of comparison for our research focused on health care practice. See Further Reading for more about the approach.

Developing models of what is happening in populations can prompt questions that need further investigation using other research methods. For example, an epidemiological study may examine data about one part of the model in Figure 5.3 and may demonstrate that income and community understanding of blood pressure seem to interact and influence the regularity of taking medication.

To understand the mechanism for this, the doctor (Box 5.10) could undertake an interview study. This may reveal that for people who have to pay for their medication, those with low incomes often take it only during certain weeks of the month. However, people of low income who live in a community where people are aware of the importance of blood pressure are encouraged by family, friends and colleagues to take their medication regularly, and so tend to give it priority when making decisions about their spending. Family members also help them to budget for it. Thus, models about what seems to be happening for populations can suggest where we should investigate further to understand more about what is happening.

The element of time is included in the models discussed above. Individuals change over time, from being unaware of their blood pressure to being on treatment for high blood pressure (Figure 5.1). Individuals using the health care service move through different stages of assessment and treatment (Figure 5.2). In the model of the community (Figure 5.3) time is present, but it is less clear how the passing of time and the different influences identified in the model are linked as there are no people in the model. To consider how such a model links to models of individuals, we will consider just one section of Figure 5.3. The model suggests that if the number of people in the population taking their medication regularly changes, then the number of people in the population with well-controlled blood pressure would change. For our discussion here we will assume that taking medication, or not, occurs before blood pressure control is assessed. This is a simplification of what is happening in the world as there is likely to be feedback both positive (good blood pressure control encourages regular medication) and negative (good blood pressure control prompts less regular medication), and the person and their context is constantly changing.

If we looked in detail at how individuals come to take medication for high blood pressure each individual will have a slightly different pathway although different pathways may lead to a similar outcome in terms of blood pressure control. For the doctor wanting to understand the variation in blood pressure control across the local population, the difference between two individuals with the same outcome are not important. However, if two people have similar pathways in all but one aspect and one has good blood pressure control and the other does not, then this suggests the one difference is important for blood pressure control. For example, one of the two individuals may take his medication every day and the other takes it three weeks out of four. Of course it is difficult to find people who are similar in everything except one aspect. However, if we include a large number of people, all different from each other, and find out if they have good blood pressure control or poor blood pressure control, we can then compare the two groups. If there is a feature common to a substantial number of people with poor blood pressure control and this feature is rarely found among the good blood pressure control group, then this feature is likely to be important for the pattern of blood pressure control in the population. For example, if one-third of the poor blood pressure control group only take their medication for three out of every four weeks and only 1 in 10 people in the good blood pressure control group do this, then we know that taking medication three out of every four weeks contributes to the pattern of variation in blood pressure control for the community. This is illustrated in Box 5.11.

Box 5.11	The different combinations of regular medication or not and blood pressure (BP) control for individual people in a population of 60
Regular medication → Good BP control (27 people) Not regular medication → Good BP control (3 people) Regular medication → Poor BP control (20 people) Not regular medication → Poor BP control (10 people)	

We will now consider just the people who have good blood pressure control. There are different ways of achieving good blood pressure control for different people; some take regular medication and some do not. If we had more information about these people, for example, whether they have a salty diet and whether they take exercise, we may find more variety in the pathways to good blood pressure control.

All the possible combinations of salt in diet, exercise and regularity of medication are listed in Box 5.12. Each of the combinations could apply to an individual. If we had more data about the individuals we could add more about them on the left of the arrows. If we do this we increase the number of potential pathways. Some pathways may be followed by many people and some by very few or none. For example, from what we know about blood pressure, for people who have established high blood pressure the combination at the bottom of the list is unlikely. If we continue to add more information to the left of the arrows, we will eventually be able to distinguish each person from all the others. We may also have potential pathways that do not apply to any individual in our study. We noted above that if the doctor focuses on variation in the population, the different pathways to the same outcome are not important. However in clinical practice we may tailor our health care differently for different pathways. Chapter 9 discusses analysis of data to identify and understand these different pathways.

<table>
<tr><td>Possible combinations of salt in diet, exercise and regularity of taking medication leading to good BP control</td><td>Box 5.12</td></tr>
</table>

Possible combinations of salt in diet, exercise and regularity of taking medication leading to good BP control	**Box 5.12**

Low salt diet + exercise + regular medication → Good BP control
Low salt diet + no exercise + regular medication → Good BP control
High salt diet + exercise + regular medication → Good BP control
High salt diet + no exercise + regular medication → Good BP control
Low salt diet + exercise + not regular medication → Good BP control
Low salt diet + no exercise + not regular medication → Good BP control
High salt diet + exercise + not regular medication → Good BP control
High salt diet + no exercise + not regular medication → Good BP control

Finally, we briefly consider how individuals changing may or may not impact on how we describe the community as a whole. Imagine the doctor in Box 5.10 was to assess the variation in blood pressure control in the population over several years. Individuals within the population may have changed even if overall the variation in blood pressure control remains the same. For example, at one point in time, an individual with poorly controlled blood pressure who does not take medication regularly contributes to the description of the community at that point in time. If data is collected at a later time, this individual may have started taking his medication regularly and have well controlled blood pressure but other people in the population may have changed, for example taking their medication less regularly, so overall the variation across the population remains the same. Over a number of years, although the variation across the population remains the same, the average level of blood pressure may change. This could result from lots of individuals improving their blood pressure control or from factors affecting everyone in the population.

In research for health care practice, we often focus on individual people or organisations. Understanding the health of populations is important for suggesting where to focus our research and for understanding the frame of our research. I have clarified the link between models of individuals, individuals using health care, and models of populations because a great deal of health-related research is based on populations. This includes research evaluating the effect of health interventions and identifying causes of ill health in populations. Epidemiologists and statisticians are the experts for these research approaches (see Further Reading). This book does not cover these approaches but it does discuss how to describe a population, such as a local community (see Chapter 9), as it is often important to describe the health of the local population when researching health care practice.

Conclusion

This chapter has discussed the preparation for designing research. The next step is to design the research in detail, working out exactly how to do it, as discussed in the remainder of the book. This may include testing out in a small way how we will collect data and analyse it before we commit ourselves. Such small studies are often called **feasibility studies** as they check whether it is possible to do the research in a particular way. They may also be called **pilot studies,** particularly if they provide data that guides the design of our main study. In research for health care practice undertaken in our own health care setting, the early stages of our research can act as our feasibility or pilot study. We start the research but, early in the process, pause and review whether it is feasible to do it this way and whether the data we have collected suggest we need to alter the design of the study.

References

Christakis, N. and Fowler, J. (2007) 'The spread of obesity in a large social network over 32 years'. *New England Journal of Medicine,* **357**: 370–79.
Oakley A., Bendelow G., Barnes J., Buchanan M., Nasseem Husain OA.
Health and cancer prevention: knowledge and beliefs of children and young
people, *BMJ,* 1995 **310**: 1029–33.

Further reading

Adam, B. (2004) *Time*. Cambridge: Polity Press.

This book discusses the standardisation of time and explores the different ways time is experienced in various life situations. It is an excellent introduction to the issue of time, prompting us to take a critical view of what we mean by time and how we work with it in our research.

Ragin, C.C. *Fuzzy-set Social Science* (2000) Chicago: University of Chicago Press.

Part I of this book entitled 'Diversity orientated research' is an excellent exploration of the link between individual cases and populations.

Dawes, M. (2005) *Evidence-based Practice: A primer for health care professionals,* 2nd Edition. Oxford: Churchill Livingstone.

This book is written by a team with extensive experience in teaching health professionals how to find and evaluate evidence for clinical practice. It includes a chapter on 'Finding the evidence: an information skills approach'.

Jadad, A.R. (1998) *Randomised Controlled Trials: A user's guide.* London: BMJ Books.

A highly recommended book for those wanting to understand randomised controlled trials.

The following are recommended introductions to epidemiology:

Bhopal, R. (2002) *Concepts of Epidemiology.* Oxford: Oxford University Press.

Swinscow, T.D.V. (1997) *Statistics at Square One*, 9th Edition, revised by M.J. Campbell. London: BMJ Publishing.

Coggon, D., Rose, G. and Barker, D.J.P. (1997) *Epidemiology for the Uninitiated*, 4th Edition. London: BMJ Publishing.

Using Existing Data in Research for Health Care Practice

Research can be undertaken without collecting data. This chapter discusses using existing data to assist with designing research and as the data for analysis in research, particularly large longitudinal data sets. The chapter also considers the systematic review of research literature to generate new knowledge.

In the last decade, the amount and availability of data for health-related research, without needing to approach individual people, has increased dramatically. Using existing data reduces the time and cost of research both for us as researchers and for research participants. If data is already available for our research we may be able to go further in exploring our research issue than if we had to collect new data. Sometimes existing data only partially answers our research question, so we still need some new data. This chapter first considers sources of existing data for research then considers the use of such data for designing our research and as data for analysis. The remainder of the chapter describes how to use published research literature as the data for our research.

Sources of existing data for research

Published research reports are important sources of data for further research but there are many other sources of data that may be relevant, depending on the research focus and question. With the computerisation of data recording, many data sets are now relatively easy to access. Examples of data available for research are listed in Box 6.1.

The Resources at the end of this chapter include websites with information about data available for research. Publicly available data can be used by anyone, but access to other types of data will be limited to those using it for bona fide research (for example, achieved research data) and with the approval of those responsible for the data (for example, clinicians or managers of health service data). Using data about identifiable individual people usually requires their individual consent (see Chapter 3).

Examples of sources of existing data for research	**Box 6.1**

Published literature (publicly available)

- Research reports
- Policy documents
- Guidelines
- Opinion and discussion writing
- Newspaper reports
- Other forms of literature such as novels and biography
- Blogs, Internet forums

Health service data

- Data recorded as part of normal daily clinical practice:

  - administrative data, e.g. clinic attendance
  - clinical data, e.g. diagnoses, medication, clinical tests such as blood pressure

- Data collected for a specific purpose, e.g. patient satisfaction survey, audit data
- Documents about policy and guidelines
- Minutes of meetings
- Letters and e-mails

National or regional data sets (summaries of this data are publically available but access to the data set itself is limited to bone fide researchers)

- National census
- Health surveys
- Social surveys

Data from completed research

- **Clinical trial**, survey and interview data held in national archives
- Research data in local archives

There are problems with using existing data. Data is collected at a particular time and place, by particular people, in a particular way and with a particular purpose in mind, all of which affect what is collected. We need to understand the data in terms of what it is, where, when, how, why and by whom and from whom it was collected. Understanding this enables us to decide if the data is useful to us in our research, and what we need to take into account when analysing it.

These considerations also apply to data we collect ourselves and are discussed in the remainder of this book.

Using existing data for research

Existing data can assist us with designing our research or may be used as research data. We will consider these different uses in this section.

Box 6.2	**Using existing data to understand the research frame for research on access to podiatry services**

Health professional role: Podiatrist.

Motivation: Concern that the people in most need of podiatry are not getting to podiatry clinics.

Observation of difference or change: Case mix in local podiatry clinic is different, with fewer serious foot problems, than the case mix reported in a similar clinic elsewhere.

Overall aim: To understand how people gain access or do not gain access to podiatry.

Research issue: Access and podiatry services.

Research focus: Patients in need of podiatry.

Existing data about the research focus: Census data, for example, age structure of local population; clinical data, for example, general practice registers of people living with diabetes and the clinical notes of these people.

Research frame: This includes the current configuration of the podiatry service and related health care services.

Existing data about the research frame: National and local policy documents, annual reports of local health care services, health care service meeting minutes.

Using existing data for designing research

Take the example of the podiatrist discussed in Chapter 5, who wants to understand how people gain access, or not, to the podiatry service. Examples of existing data about the focus and frame of his research are given in Box 6.2. The podiarist knows that older people need his services more than younger people and people living with diabetes need to attend regularly. From existing data he can get some idea of the number of these people in his locality. Understanding how and why the podiatry service functions the way it does is important background for his research. For example, one local area may have been served by a different podiatry service in the past and not all the people from that area may have transferred to the current service.

Existing sources of data may also help the podiatrist to decide what new data he needs and how he will collect it. For example, general practice clinical records will include some data of relevance to foot health, such as chronic illness and prescribed medication, but the podiatrist may need to collect other data directly from individuals. Documents may provide background necessary for understanding the local podiatry service, but interviews with long-standing staff members may add useful data.

The results of other people's research can help the podiatrist refine his use of existing data. For example, if research in a similar locality describes the incidence of foot problems, the podiatrist can estimate the likely incidence of foot problems in his own locality using what he knows about the local population.

The use of existing data as our research data

Depending on our research issue, qualitative and quantitative data may be available for analysis (see Box 6.1). It is analysed in the same way as new data. Each type of existing data has its own particular strengths and weaknesses, so it is important to read about the data and check that you understand how and why it was collected. For large data sets, getting to understand them can take considerable time. When undertaking analysis of data collected by other people or for another purpose (secondary analysis), we have to keep in mind that there may be problems about the data that are not obvious.

There are large data sets collected in the course of clinical practice available for use in research. These data sets are checked for quality and consistency of recording. For example, in the UK there is a large data set of general practice records, called the General Practice Research Database. This database has been collected for over a decade from several hundred general practices. Data is also collected through surveys, including the census that is undertaken every ten years in the UK and longitudinal social surveys undertaken annually. In addition there are studies of individuals born in a particular year and followed up over time, known as **cohort** studies (see Resources). These data sets are of particular value because they have been collected over time and are used by epidemiologists to study the health of populations. However, they also have a local role in research for health care practice. The existing longitudinal data sets can be used to understand the frame or focus of our research. The data can tell us about the local community, and we can compare the people we are studying with the population as a whole. The data can also be used to explore what is happening to individuals or communities over time. Cohort studies collect data from the individuals at set time points, for example, every year or every five years. The timing of the data collection is determined by the design of the study. This is a limitation of the study; however, these data sets still provide rich data for understanding what is happening to individuals over time (Elliott, 2005). The way the health service functions influences the data collected during routine clinical practice. However, unlike cohort studies where data collection is initiated by the researcher, data collected in clinical practice is to some degree initiated by the individual making contact with the health care service. In the UK, the patient initiates most health care by going to see their general practitioner, and so general practice data can indicate change in the community in relation to health. For example, the start of an influenza epidemic (Fleming, 1999). Data collected over time about the number of people attending a health care service, can assist in planning the service. For example, if there has been a steady rise in the number of people attending, the service may need to expand. The data can be explored for recurring patterns, such as peaks and troughs in the numbers attending at certain times of year. This can be useful for planning services, and the timing of these patterns may give clues as to why these peaks and troughs are happening, such as seasonal variation for asthma. Clinical data about an individual can also be studied as a sequence of health care events. The analysis of existing data is considered further alongside the analysis of new data in later chapters of this book.

Using published research as the data for our own research – a systematic review

Reading published research related to our research issue is an important step in the preparations for our research, as already discussed in Chapter 5. There is now so much research literature that we need a system for reading and reviewing this literature, otherwise we can end up either totally overwhelmed or restricting ourselves to one corner of the literature and so potentially missing important research. The system we use needs to include finding the relevant research literature, assessing its quality, extracting the relevant data and then analysing or **synthesising** the data to develop new knowledge. The way we do this needs to be clear, so that it may be repeated by someone else to reach a similar conclusion. These literature reviews are known as **systematic reviews**.

Within health care the term 'systematic review' is often used as shorthand for a Cochrane systematic review, which was the first type of systematic review to be widely established and is the appropriate approach for reviewing research about whether a health care intervention is effective or not. This includes interventions such as drugs, surgery, psychological interventions and health service design.

Cochrane reviews are mostly based on experimental research, although they may include other types of research where this is not available or to increase understanding of the research issue. This section does not consider Cochrane style reviews further, as experimental research is beyond the scope of this book. However, for anyone embarking on a systematic review of research literature, I recommend reading publications about how to do a Cochrane review as their guidance provides valuable advice, some of which can be adapted for other types of review (see Resources).

This chapter describes the process of undertaking a systematic review of a health issue. Using comparative analysis such a review can include studies that have used very different methods of data collection such as surveys (quantitative data), interviews (qualitative data) or several types of data collection in one study (**mixed methods** studies). Such reviews can be termed 'systematic mixed studies reviews' (Pluye et al., 2009). There are many excellent sources of advice about undertaking systematic literature reviews, some of which are listed at the end of the chapter.

The first steps for undertaking a systematic review are the same as for any research, as described in the earlier chapters of this book. Using published research as our data does not lessen the importance of getting our research question clear and ensuring that it is the one we really want to tackle. The remaining sections of this chapter take you through preparation for and undertaking a systematic literature review.

Preparations for a systematic literature review

The process of clarifying our research issue, defining it and developing our research question includes looking at the literature – often called '**scoping' the literature,** as it gives us an idea of the range of literature there is related to our research issue. For example, if our research issue is hypertension, a quick search of the medical literature will reveal thousands of research papers examining it from many perspectives, including the physiology, pharmacology, epidemiology, clinical outcomes, patient experience and health service configuration. Searching the social science literature will reveal much less, but we will find some papers on the social understanding and social implications of hypertension and its treatment. If our research issue is the admission of terminally ill patients to hospital, we will find almost no papers that specifically examine this wherever we search, as this has not been the focus of much research. Knowing the extent of the research literature available helps us refine our research question and plan our review of the literature. During this scoping exercise we can also look out for relevant literature reviews. If someone has already done a review similar to ours, this is a bonus as we can build on it, for example, bringing the review up to date or taking a different perspective.

The scoping exercise familiarises us with the process of searching for literature, including how to gain access to libraries and **search engines,** which search engines are good for different types of literature, and how to construct a search. Information scientists and librarians are experts at finding information and research literature, and keep up to date with the rapid developments in search engines, journal formats, accessing issues and software, so do seek their advice and guidance at an early stage.

Early in our planning we need to decide how to keep a record of the literature we find. There are a number of software packages now available for managing databases of literature. These allow us to sort and categorise the literature and, when we come to write up our research as a report or paper, enable us to reference the literature very easily. Librarians, colleagues, academic teachers and supervisors are usually the best source of advice about the latest software and access to this software. Our decision needs to take account of how we will sort the research literature we find and how we will analyse it.

To consider the process of undertaking a systematic literature review in more detail we will use the example of the mental health nurse concerned for the health and wellbeing of people caring for those with dementia (Box 6.3).

Box 6.3	**Getting started on research on the health and wellbeing of those caring for people living with dementia**

Health professional role: Mental health nurse working with people living with dementia.

Motivation: To improve the wellbeing of those caring for people with dementia.

Observation of difference or change: The health and wellbeing of those caring for people with dementia often deteriorates.

Overall aim: To find ways of supporting those caring for people with dementia to reduce the deterioration in their health and wellbeing.

Research issue: The health and wellbeing of those caring for people with dementia.

In her scoping exercise the nurse has found literature about a number of aspects of caring for people with conditions such as dementia, including the description and evaluation of support systems, assessments of psychological distress, descriptions of the socio-economic situation of carers and accounts of the experience of caring. Some research focuses on early dementia, excluding the elderly with dementia. The literature also comes from all over the world, with a great deal from North America. She also notices that there is research on care homes of various types, on professional carers of people living with dementia at home and research that particularly interests her about carers who live with the people with dementia.

The mental health nurse decides that she is really interested in the experience of caring for someone with dementia at home when the carer lives with the person with dementia as, in her professional role, she provides support to these people.

By looking at the many different experiences of carers, the nurse may begin to understand what can make a difference to their health and wellbeing (see Box 6.4).

Scoping the literature clarifies the research question on the health and wellbeing of those caring for people living with dementia	Box 6.4

Health professional role: Mental health nurse working with people living with dementia.

Motivation: To improve the wellbeing of those caring for people with dementia.

Observation of difference or change: The health and wellbeing of those caring for people with dementia often deteriorates.

Overall aim: To find ways of supporting those caring for people with dementia to reduce the deterioration in their health and wellbeing.

Research issue: The health and wellbeing of those caring for people with dementia.

Research focus: Those living with and caring for people living with dementia in their own home.

Research aim: To understand the experience of living with and caring for people living with dementia in their own home.

Research question: What is the diversity of experience of living with and caring for a person with dementia at home?

The nurse now needs to define her research focus further. This process clarifies what literature to include or exclude from the literature review. These decisions should be made before undertaking the full literature search. So far her research focus suggests she should include literature that:

- is about carers living at home with the person with dementia
- describes some aspect of the experience of caring

and exclude literature about:

- care homes and similar institutions
- non-resident carers (such as professional home care staff).

The nurse has not specified that the carer is a relative, so professional carers who live in the home of the person with dementia are included. If her research focus was the experience of caring for a family member with dementia, this would need to be clear in the research focus and question.

Dementia has a number of different forms and can affect people at different ages. It is also a progressive disease with different impacts on carers at different stages. The nurse needs to decide if she will include all types of dementia at any age and stage or whether she wants to restrict the focus to a particular sub-group, such as carers for people developing dementia before the age of 60. The scoping exercise will have given her some indication of the available research literature. There is no point deciding to define the research focus as a specific sub-group if there is no research on this sub-group. The lack of research may suggest the need for new research on this sub-group, although we need to consider why we think the experience of this sub-group would be different from other groups for which there is existing research.

The nurse is interested in the diversity of experience of carers, so she may want to include research from very different places. The other option is to restrict her research focus to the diversity of experience in places similar to her own. For example, carers living in countries with different health and social care services may have different experiences. A nurse in the UK may decide that the health and social care service in the US is so different that she will exclude research from the US, but as some European countries have similar health and social care she will include research from those countries. However, although a great deal of research literature from all over the world is published in English, some research is published in other languages. The decision about what languages to include is unfortunately often a pragmatic decision based on language ability. The nurse will need to consider what she will be missing if she excludes research on the basis of language.

The nurse will also need to define her research focus in terms of time. She needs to consider what may have impacted on the experience of caring. For example, a major political upheaval may have precipitated a change in social support for carers. Literature from before this event, although interesting as background to the current situation, is unlikely to reflect the experience of carers now. Decisions on the time focus of the research will suggest how far back in time to go with her search.

Scoping the literature may reveal there were very few studies published on a particular issue before a certain year. Caution is needed, as the topic we are interested in may have been described differently and so is not appearing in our searches (McPherson and Armstrong, 2006). Where this may impact on our literature review, it is important to seek advice of a librarian or information scientist and read about the history of the research issue.

The types of research study that provide data about the experience of living with and caring for a person with dementia at home include:

- Interview studies with carers

- Surveys of carers

- Assessments undertaken within a study evaluating some type of intervention for carers

- Studies of people with dementia where their carers are included within some part of the study

- Research on population health where people with dementia and their carers are identified and described as a sub-group

- Research describing services for carers, such as self-help groups or online peer support groups.

If there is very little research literature on a chosen topic, then all these sources may need to be included and the data relevant to the research question teased out of these very different sources. If, however, the mental health nurse finds a substantial number of papers that are specifically on the research focus as she has defined it, she may limit her review to these papers. For example, ten papers reporting interviews with carers living with people with dementia in a context similar to that of the nurse and seven surveys focussing on these people would probably provide enough data for the literature review. Other research papers, not specifically on the research focus, may provide background information for the review and so should not be discarded.

Through the process of defining the focus of her research and scoping the literature, the nurse has identified the **inclusion** and **exclusion criteria** for her literature review. Inclusion criteria should be written tightly tied to the definition of the research focus and its frame. Exclusion criteria deal with unusual cases. An example is given in Box 6.5.

The quality of the reported research is an important criteria for whether or not to include research in the review. Different types of research require different quality criteria (see Resources). The criteria for judging the quality of other people's research is the same as those we use when designing our own research so the guidance throughout this book can be applied to other people's research as well as to our own. When undertaking a systematic review we should, as far as possible, decide in advance the criteria we will use for judging whether a research report is of good enough quality to include in our review. Where there is plenty of research available about our research focus, we can have fairly tight criteria for quality using an existing quality framework (see Resources). However, when undertaking research for health care practice based in a particular locality, there may be research that might not be of high quality or is not published but tells us about our research issue for our context. We may want to include this because of its specific relevance for our research, but we must take care in how we use the results of the research because of our concerns about quality. Describing our decisions about this allows someone reading our literature review to make their own judgement.

Box 6.5	**Inclusion and exclusion criteria for a systematic literature review on the experience of those living with and caring for people living with dementia**

Inclusion criteria

Focus of research: Those living with and caring for people living with dementia in their own home.

Frame of research: England since the introduction of social care policy in [date].

Exclusion criteria:

Focus of research:

- Research that is exclusively on those caring for people with early onset dementia (under 60 years of age).
- Research that is exclusively on carers who live in and care for people with dementia in an institutional setting.

Table 6.1 provides a summary of the preparations for undertaking a systematic literature review and how to do them.

Finding and sorting literature for a systematic literature review

Searching for literature should use a number of different searching methods, whether for scoping the literature or for undertaking the systematic review. Take advice from a librarian or information scientist or other sources of guidance on what searches to undertake. For a systematic review we aim to include all research relevant to our defined research focus, and so when searching we need to include everything that may be relevant and then sort out whether or not it really is relevant.

Table 6.1   Preparations for a systematic literature review

Preparations for a systematic literature review	How to undertake preparations
Defining the research focus and developing the research question	Developed iteratively while scoping the literature and planning inclusion and exclusion criteria.
Scoping the literature: • using literature search engines • searching databases such as archives of research reports • using web search engines • hand-searching specific relevant journals • finding and searching personal collections of literature (e.g. a health care team's resources)	Seek advice from an information scientist/librarian. Talk to colleagues. Ask advice from academics and professionals known for their expertise on the topic.
Refining the process of searching the literature	Build on your literature scoping. Seek further advice. Try out search terms and review the results. Build on the experience of published literature reviews on a similar topic. Consider how each decision impacts on the review.
Database/software for handling literature	Seek advice and try out software before starting the full search. Consider whether it will support your process of sorting and final analysis.
Inclusion and exclusion criteria	Decide what to include and exclude whilst also refining the research focus. Too much literature: consider narrowing focus or narrowing the type of research (e.g. only surveys). Too little literature: consider widening focus or teasing out data from a range of published research.
Assessment of quality of research	Consider the use of published guidance. Consider including research of particular relevance to the research and its context even if quality is not high.

Sorting the literature requires a staged process, as mapped out in Figure 6.1, and each stage needs some quality checks. The most rigorous quality checks are when two or three researchers undertake each stage independently and then compare results. Any literature on which the researchers do not agree is then reviewed and discussed by the team before a final decision is made. This is time-consuming, so if the number of titles/abstracts/papers for review is large, the second and third researchers may only check a sample at each stage. The mental health nurse (Box 6.4) may, however, be working alone and so needs strategies for reviewing her own sorting decisions. These include noting when she is unsure and reflecting on how her decisions are changing as she goes through the sorting process by comparing later decisions with early ones.

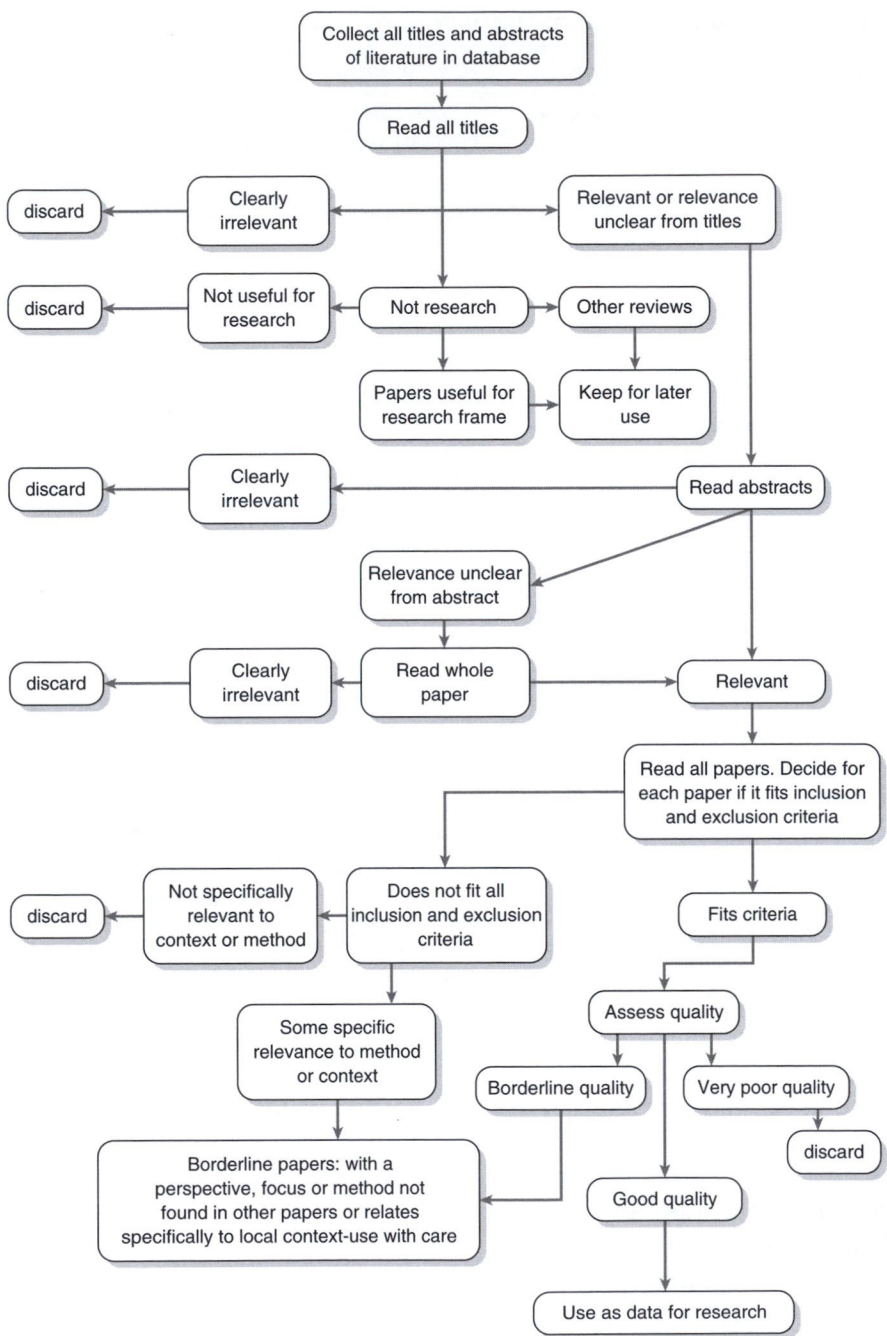

Figure 6.1   A process for sorting research literature

Extracting data from published research for comparative analysis

We need to be able to compare the different research papers for analysis. If we have only a few research papers to read and compare, this is relatively easy. However, with more than a few papers we need a system for comparing so that we do not miss important similarities or differences. This section describes how to develop a system for extracting data from published research for comparison. Reading how other researchers have undertaken this process can inform our plans, even if the topic of their research was very different (see Resources). However carefully we plan the **data extraction**, it is best to try out the system on a small number of papers to ensure that all the relevant data is extracted (and not irrelevant data) before working through lots of papers. Most researchers use an electronic spreadsheet for recording the relevant data from the literature.

When analysing the data we will compare the results of the research from the different papers. However, to understand whether our comparisons are appropriate, we also need to know about where and when the research was undertaken, how and why it was done, and on and by whom. We will consider the example of the mental health nurse (Box 6.4). If in her scoping exercise the nurse found many surveys of carers regarding their health or wellbeing, she may decide to review these surveys. The data she will need to extract from each paper and put into her spreadsheet is summarised in Box 6.6. We will explore why these different aspects of the papers are needed for comparison.

Details of the paper (title, authors, year, journal reference) acts as the data identifier. However, keeping the details in the data extraction sheet, rather than using an identifying code, allows the nurse to spot where several papers have been written about the same survey. Where this has occurred, the papers are often best considered as one source of data as it is all from one study.

The results of the survey need to be carefully summarised into the data extraction sheet as the results of all the papers will be compared. To know whether results can be compared, the nurse needs to know how research participants were selected and what survey instruments were used. For example, a survey of carers recruited through a carers' support group may be very different from carers identified through the general practitioners of the people with dementia. If the survey assessed the mental health of the carers, a number of different **standardised questionnaires** could have been used. The nurse may need to look for other research about these to understand the results. If surveys are undertaken at times and in places that are very different in ways relevant to the research, such as the availability of health and social care services, results may not be comparable. The way data is collected may also make a difference to whether we can compare results; for example, Internet surveys only include those with Internet access.

Box 6.6	**Data extraction for a systematic review of surveys**

Data extraction will include:

- Details of the paper (title, authors, year, journal reference)
- The results of the survey
- How research participants were selected
- What survey instruments were used (e.g. standard questionnaires, questionnaires developed by the research team)
- How the analysis was done, including how they controlled for confounding variables
- Where the survey was undertaken
- When the survey was undertaken
- How data was collected
- Why the survey was undertaken
- Who funded and carried out the survey.

How research participants were selected, what survey instruments were used and how the analysis was done, in particular how they controlled for **confounding variables,** are all essential for assessing the quality of a survey. This may have already been assessed before data extraction, or the two processes may be undertaken simultaneously.

Motivations and preferences can shape how research is undertaken, so it is useful to note why the survey was undertaken and who funded it and carried it out.

The process of extracting data from the literature makes it much easier to then compare research results. The process involves very careful reading of each paper and so is also a final check on whether the paper should be included in the review. Data extraction for other types of research will be similar to that described above. The details of the paper and the results will always be needed. The other data needed will vary a little depending on the research method used. However, by asking the questions what, where, when, how, why and who, and considering each stage of the research process, all the necessary data extraction will be covered. In the next section we consider how to analyse the data. The Resources and further reading at the end of this chapter provides further guidance.

Qualitative analysis of data for a systematic review

This section discusses analysis of data for a systematic review using a qualitative approach. This includes comparing numerical data from the research literature included in the review. Additional statistical analysis such as meta analysis is used in systematic reviews of health interventions and is not covered here; details can be found on the Cochrane Collaboration website (see Resources).

The analysis of data for a systematic review is very similar to the approach used for the analysis of text data discussed in Chapter 9, such as field notes from observation or transcripts of interviews. The first step is to decide what data can reasonably be compared to what other data (see above).

Let us consider further the example of the nurse described in Box 6.3. The nurse may find five interview studies and four surveys that have explored and assessed the health and wellbeing of people living with and caring for those with dementia. The studies may have selected participants in a similar way, used similar interview questions or survey questions and have been undertaken in similar health and social care settings. The results of these studies can be considered together and their results synthesised. This involves asking: What do we learn that is new from looking at all these results together? The process involves very careful reading of the data, identifying similarities and differences and developing ideas about what may account for these similarities and differences. Techniques used in the analysis of qualitative data can assist this process (see Chapters 7 and 9), including thematic coding, comparison of themes, analysis discussions with other researchers and advisors, along with drawing models of what we think might be happening (see Chapter 5).

Although the studies included in the review are similar, no two studies will be exactly the same. These differences may lead to different results or to similar results. This is helpful in teasing out what the literature suggests is happening in the world and why. For example, the variation in wellbeing, as measured by a standard questionnaire, may be less in one research report compared to another. Clues as to the reasons for this may come from comparing every other aspect of these two research reports, including, for example, the age and socioeconomic status of the participants and their access to support services. In interview studies, social isolation may be a dominant theme in one study and not in another. Understanding why this might be involves asking questions of the rest of the data in the two studies, where they were undertaken and how. For example, does the data suggest that the social isolation has come about because of the caring role, or was there social isolation before taking on this role? Were the studies undertaken in similar areas in terms of geographical isolation or not? How were participants recruited? Those recruited via support groups may not feel socially isolated, whereas participants recruited via their health care service may be more likely to be isolated.

The nurse may find that although there are a number of relevant research papers for her review, there are very few that are similar to each other. It is then difficult to undertake the type of analysis described above. The nurse can describe the different studies and their results. This should include a detailed account of why she thinks the studies cannot be compared with each other. Writing down these reasons can lead us to revise our initial impressions that studies are too different to be compared. For example, consider two studies that have interviewed people about the experience of living with and caring for those with dementia, one in the US and one in the UK. The health and social care systems are very different, so the experience of these people may be very different. However, the interviews may suggest that health and social care services have very little impact on the experience of the carers and so the studies may be comparable.

The analysis of data extracted from research literature requires similar methods to that of textual data and requires the same close reading of the data, attention to details, noting of similarities and differences and discerning clues as to why things happen the way they do. Undertaking a systematic review of research literature with a qualitative analysis provides research results just as the collection and analysis of new data would do. It is a piece of research in itself that contributes to the overall research effort and provides a good starting point for research involving new data collection, which will be discussed in the next two chapters.

References

Elliott, J. (2005) *Using Narrative in Social Research*. London: Sage.

Fleming, D.M. (1999) 'Weekly returns service of the Royal College of General Practitioners. Communicable disease and public health'. *Communicable Disease and Public Health*, 2: 96–100.

McPherson, S. and Armstrong, D. (2006) 'Social determinants of diagnostic labels in depression'. *Social Science and Medicine*, **62** (1): 50–8.

Pluye, P., Gagnon, M.P., Griffiths, F. and Johnson-Lafleur, J. (2009) 'A scoring system for appraising mixed methods research, and concomitantly appraising qualitative, quantitative and mixed methods studies: Critical literature review of systematic mixed studies reviews in the health sciences'. *International Journal of Nursing Studies*, doi:10.1016/j.inurstu.2009.01.009.

Resources and further reading

Information about data sets available for analysis

The following websites provide information about UK-based data sets:

UK Data Archive: www.data-archive.ac.uk/introduction.asp
The General Practice Research Database: www.gprd.com
UK Centre for the History of Nursing and Midwifery: www.nursing.manchester.ac.uk/ukchnm
The National Archives: www.ndad.nationalarchives.gov.uk

Department of Health Publications and Statistics: www.dh.gov.uk/en/publications
andstatistics/statistics
UK Statistics Authority: www.statistics.gov.uk

Undertaking secondary analysis

Elliott, J. (2005) *Using Narrative in Social Research*. London: Sage.

This book considers the analysis of cohort study data as narrative of an individual.

Heaton, J. (2004) *Reworking Qualitative Data*. London: Sage.

This book provides guidance on the analysis of data such as interviews that other people have collected.

Guidance on undertaking systematic reviews

Aveyard, H. (2007) *Doing a Literature Review in Health and Social Care: A practical guide*. Maidenhead: Open University Press.

Dixon-Woods, M., Agarwal, S., Young, B., Jones, D. and Sutton, A. (2004) *Integrative Approaches to Qualitative and Quantitative Evidence*. London: Health Development Agency.

Higgins, J.P.T. and Green, S. (Editors) (2008) *Cochrane Handbook for Systematic Reviews of Interventions*, Version 5.0.1 (updated September 2008). Oxford: The Cochrane Collaboration. Available from www.cochrane-handbook.org

Popay, J., Roberts, H., Sowden, A., Petticrew, M., Arai, L. and Rodgers, M. (2006) *Guidance on the Conduct of Narrative Synthesis in Systematic Reviews*. London: ESRC.

Pope, C., Mays, N. and Popay, J. (2007) *Synthesizing Qualitative and Quantitative Health Evidence: A guide to methods*. Maidenhead: Open University Press.

Spencer, L., Ritchie, J., Lewis, J. and Dillon, L. (2003) *Quality in Qualitative Evaluations: A framework for assessing research evidence*. London: Cabinet Office.

Databases of systematic reviews

The Cochrane Collaboration – reviews of evidence for health care interventions: www.cochrane.org

The Campbell Collaboration – reviews of social science evidence on education, crime and justice, and social welfare: www.campbellcollaboration.org

Examples of systematic reviews

These three literature reviews on e-health illustrate different types of systematic review:

Eysenbach, G., Powell, J., Engelsakis, M., Rigo, C. and Stern, A. (2004) 'Health related virtual communities and electronic support groups: a systematic review of the effects of online peer-to-peer interactions.' *BMJ*, **328**: 116–1170.

Eysenbach, G., Powell, J., Kuss, O. and Sol, E-R. (2002) 'Empirical studies assessing the quality of health information for consumers on the world wide web: a systematic review.' *Journal of the American Medical Association*, **287**: 2691–700.

Griffiths, F.E., Lindenmeyer, A., Powell, J., Lowe, P. and Thorogood, M. (2006) 'Why are health care interventions delivered over the Internet? A review of the published literature'. *Journal of Medical Internet Research*, 8 (2): e10. Available at www.jmir.org/2006/2/e10/.

For a literature review combining qualitative studies to understand patient experience, see: Campbell, R., Pound, P., Pope, C., Britton, N., Pill, R., Morgan, M. and Donovan, J. (2003) 'Evaluating meta-ethnography: a synthesis of qualitative research on lay experiences of diabetes and diabetes care.' *Social Science & Medicine*, **56**: 671–84.

7 Collecting and Exploring New Data Using Qualitative Methods

This chapter discusses the importance of reflection in research, describes how to tailor data collection to the research focus and how to access research participants. These issues are important for collecting qualitative and quantitative data. The chapter then considers in detail the design of data collection using observation and communication, including interviews and research with groups and the initial exploratory analysis of this data.

The term 'qualitative methods' is used in health and social sciences to refer to the use of observation and communication for collecting data. These are often used together, although with varying emphasis. For example, we may decide to interview people about our research issue but in the process of arranging and undertaking the interviews, our observations provide background data for our interviews: if we mainly observe, for example, a clinic, we will also talk to people in the clinic. These methods of data collection have been developed and refined within sociology, anthropology and organisation science, and by researchers working in the commercial world. In this chapter we consider their use for research in health care practice. The term 'qualitative methods' is used to distinguish these data collection methods from those involving counting and measurement (quantitative methods), which are considered in Chapter 8. However, many of the issues considered in this chapter are relevant to the collection of quantitative data.

Collecting data through observation and communication can give us a lot of detail about what people do and what they think and feel about a research issue, including what influences them and why. Observing and asking questions is the way we find out what is happening in real situations. The data we collect is what we observe or what other people tell us about. The data is filtered by our own ability to observe or by other people (see Chapter 5). If we ask other people how a clinic works, they tell us their perception of how it works, which may be different from our own. If we are interested in what is happening within individual people, such as how they perceive their illness, we can ask in different ways and so hear different accounts from the same person. We can also ask many different people about how they perceive their illness. We aim to collect many different accounts of the focus of our research so that in the analysis process we can compare these different accounts for clues about what is happening that we are unable to see directly.

The way we observe or communicate with people influences what we observe and what people tell us. This chapter discusses how to collect data by observation or communication so that we notice and hear as much as possible about our research issue. This involves taking care over how we design our research and taking time to reflect on how our data collection process may influence the data.

We need a well-defined research focus and a clear research question (see Chapters 2 and 5) for successful design of data collection, and must keep them in mind as we think through every step of our data collection. When I am planning data collection, I imagine myself going through each step in the process to work out whether what I hope to do is possible and what problems I may encounter. If you are new to doing research you may find this difficult, so rather than imagining yourself doing the research, imagine yourself being researched whether as a health professional or patient. This will also help you to be sensitive to the needs of those you are researching. This chapter will guide you through the many issues you need to consider in designing your research and planning the data collection process. Once you have a good idea of how you want to collect your data, I suggest you also read other books on your chosen data collection methods for further detail (see Further Reading at the end of this chapter).

Although I have separated data collection and analysis to make the text easier to follow, data collection and analysis should be undertaken alongside each other, as we use early data analysis to develop and refine our data collection.

Reflection in research and clinical practice

When collecting data through observation or communication we need to reflect constantly on the data, including how we may have influenced the data by the way we have collected it and what needs further exploration. Our experience of clinical practice can sensitise us to the need for this reflection.

As health professionals we have experience of how a person or situation influences what we do or say. For example, when a student accompanies us on our work for a day, we behave slightly differently and so do our patients. Although we may perform the same task with the same skill, there will be subtle differences in what we do and say. If the student is around for a long time, becoming part of the team, our behaviour changes again. When we talk about our patients we do it in different ways depending on the situation. In a multi-disciplinary team meeting we may present a patient and their problems in a formal way, following a set structure for case presentations. When chatting over coffee with colleagues, through the conversation we may work out the next steps in caring for a patient. When we go home in the evening we may talk to someone close to us about how a patient made us feel. Reflecting on what we ourselves do and say in different situations in our own professional practice sensitises us to how our data collection activity may influence the data we collect. Here are some examples of questions we can ask ourselves about collecting data, which we will consider in the remainder of this chapter:

- *Where*: Will it make a difference if I interview people in their homes, at a community centre, in a café or at my clinic?

- *When*: Will the timing of my observation or interview make a difference?

- *How*: Will the phrasing of a question (how it is asked) influence the response?

- *Why*: Will the purpose of my research (why I am doing it) influence what people say?

- *Who*: How will the data be affected by who I am in my professional role and as a person?

When we are assessing a patient or health care situation in our health professional role we often collect information from a number of sources. For example, if a patient tells us about an operation they had a few years earlier, we may also look at their medical notes to check the details. If we are concerned about a patients' mental health, we may talk with their family. If we are developing the services provided at a clinic, we would talk to various members of staff to hear their perspective on how the clinic runs and how it could develop. In the same way, when we collect data for research we use many sources of data. By increasing the data we have about the focus of our research we are less likely to miss out important data. It also enables us to look for differences in the data which give us clues about what is happening that is difficult to see directly. We use this approach in our professional practice too. For example, if we are assessing a patient who seems depressed, we would take careful note of differences between how the patient describes their daily life and how their family describes it. If we were to hear very different stories about how a clinic functions from different members of staff, this would alert us to look into why the accounts are so different.

Throughout our research we need to keep reflecting on what we are doing. However, this can lead to a feeling of not being able to get on with the research because we are so busy thinking about the inadequacies of what we are doing. Nevertheless, we need to get on with collecting data to see what we find. We can then review what we find and reflect on the data we have before undertaking more data collection and improving how we do this. Our data collection plans need to include opportunities to review and reflect.

Tailoring data collection to the research focus

Data collection should be tailored to our defined research focus. However, as with all other stages of research, we often need to go through an iterative process, going forward and back, between different stages of the research. In the process of designing our data collection we may find we have to change our research design to fit with the definition of our research focus or we may find we have to review how we define the focus of our research. The definition of the research focus and the research design are interlinked as discussed in Chapter 5. To explore this further we will consider the example in Box 7.1 of a health psychologist newly appointed to a substance misuse service for one region of the country.

Box 7.1	**Getting started on research on health care for those seeking help for substance misuse**

Health professional role: Health psychologist newly appointed to work with people seeking help for substance misuse, including alcohol and drugs.

Motivation: Deaths from substance misuse in the region reported in the media. Regional managers suggest undertaking research that will indicate how the health service could improve its care for people seeking help for substance misuse, including alcohol and drugs.

Observation of difference or change: Higher number of deaths from substance misuse in the region compared to other similar regions.

Overall aim: To reduce the number of deaths from substance misuse through improving how the health service responds to these people.

Research issue: Health care for those seeking help for substance misuse.
Research focus: The health service response to people seeking help for substance misuse.

Research aim: To describe how the health service responds to people seeking help for substance misuse.

Research questions: How does the health service in the region respond to people seeking help for substance misuse?

The research focus is the response of the health service, but this needs further definition to work out how best to collect data. The psychologist may be thinking of how the health care service as a whole responds to everyone in the region who seeks help from the service or who may potentially seek help. Data about the activity of the health service can be found in policy documents, financial information and activity reports. Data about how many people are potentially in need of help may be available in health and social surveys; the use of such existing data for our research is discussed in Chapter 6.

The regional managers of the health service may have already reviewed the overall activity of the service and over the last few years allocated additional resources specifically for services to meet the needs of those seeking help with substance misuse. However, they remain concerned at the number of deaths from substance misuse. The psychologist may therefore decide to look at what happens when people ask the health service for help with substance misuse, not the overall response of the service. She therefore defines her research focus as the response of individual people working in the health service to individual patients seeking help. The frame of her research focus is the health service and the population of the region, particularly those with substance misuse problems.

The definition of the research focus guides what data will be needed and from where. The psychologist needs to identify where it is in the health care service that people seek help for substance misuse. The psychologist will know about the specialist services in the region, but she needs to consider where else people may seek help for this problem. For example they may contact community nurses, general practitioners, community advisory services, police and probation services, friends, neighbours, family and support groups, including Internet-based groups. Some of these are outside of the research focus as they are not part of the health service, but may be important to consider in the frame of the research. Limiting her research to people who have made contact with the health service may mean the psychologist misses important data about the research issue. She may review her research focus to include all people seeking help. If not she needs to be clear as to why and write this down. People reading her research will want to know why she focused on people making contact with the health service, to help them understand the research and decide whether the results are useful for their situation.

Such decisions about the definition of the research focus are sometimes driven by practical considerations, such as lack of time and resources and the difficulty of contacting people who have not been in contact with the health service. However, the psychologist needs to consider carefully whether she is likely to uncover any new knowledge with her research focus. How is the research going to add to what is already known about the response of health services? This is not easy to do as it takes time to read the relevant literature and reconsider the research issue. It can also be very difficult to let go of a well-defined research focus and clear research question and rethink them, but it is often worthwhile.

The psychologist faces more decisions about the focus of her research and data collection. She could decide to collect data from clinics specialising in substance misuse, or look at health services more widely, or both. Those working in specialist clinics for substance misuse will be responding frequently to people seeking help, within the clinic work pattern (appointments, home visits, group therapy sessions and so on). Those working in other parts of the health service, such as general practice, will respond infrequently and at times and in places that may not be predictable. These different health care settings need different data collection methods. As responses in specialist clinics happen frequently in a predictable time frame and place, it would be possible to observe these responses.

Where responses are relatively infrequent and unpredictable in time and place, it is not possible to observe the responses and so data about the responses will have to be collected from other sources, for example, asking people about these events in an interview. When the psychologist observes the responses, the way she observes acts as a filter on the data. When the psychologist interviews other people about what happens, the other people act as a filter. However, when asking people about what happens, the psychologist can also hear their attitudes and opinions about what happens and the meaning it holds for them.

Access to people and places for data collection

How we approach research participants and those with responsibility for the places where we want to research will make a difference to how far they co-operate and what they tell us.

Gaining the co-operation of the people at the focus of our research

People are more likely to co-operate with research if it is clear that the researcher is genuine about wanting to discover new knowledge, if the motivation for the research is clear and if they know what use will be made of the data. We will explore this further with the example of the psychologist described in Box 7.1.

Each research participant and research setting must be approached with an open mind, setting aside any assumptions or judgements, and with an expectation of finding out new and interesting data. Participants soon pick up whether a researcher is genuinely interested in them and what they do, and this will make a difference to how much they co-operate. For example, if the psychologist is perceived as someone coming to find out what the health professionals are doing wrong, then she is likely to find they are unwilling to co-operate.

The psychologist's research is motivated by deaths reported in the media, so people working in the health service may have heard about them. The psychologist may be tempted to conceal her motivation due to concern that it could influence what people tell her but this could have unintended consequences. If a research participant has not heard about the deaths and later they hear that this prompted the research, they may feel deceived. If a research participant has heard about the deaths they may assume this is the motivation for the research and adapt their responses accordingly, but the psychologist will be unaware of this. In general it is best to be open about our motivations so we are sure that the participants know why we are doing the research. We can then take this into account when collecting and analysing our data.

The psychologist wanting to observe a clinic would approach those supervising the clinic to discuss the research, and perhaps ask them to tell the clinic staff about the research. This helps the staff to feel able to spend work time talking to the psychologist. However, if the use of the data is not explained the staff may suspect the data is to be used to justify closing the clinic and become un co-operative.

Establishing the trust of those at the focus of our research

When collecting data through observation and communication, we want the research participants to behave as normally as possible and to be open to talking about the research issue. Gaining their co-operation is an essential first step to establishing the necessary trust. We also need to clarify our role as health professional and researcher and clarify who will see or hear the data as discussed below.

In interviews people may talk about an issue in a certain way because they think that is what the interviewer wants to hear, or because they think it is the generally accepted way of talking about the issue, rather than saying what they really think. For example, a patient may be reluctant to mention that they do not take medication prescribed by a doctor because they assume the person interviewing them will disapprove. When people are observed they may change the way they behave to what they think is the accepted behaviour. To some degree, this effect can be reduced by making it clear that we are genuinely interested in and value what the individual says or does and that we are not there to judge them. It may be tempting not to mention that we are a health professional as well as a researcher to reduce the tendency of people to tell us only what they think a health professional wants to hear. However, if they find out later about our role as health professional, they could feel deceived. When I introduce myself at the start of a research interview, I emphasise that I am here as a researcher, that I do also work as a health professional, but the role I am in currently is as researcher. I sometimes remind people during an interview that I am here as researcher, particularly if they seek advice about a health issue.

People are usually more willing to talk openly about an issue if they know that what they say will not be passed on to other people. When telling people about our research we should explain that the data will be kept confidential but clarify what this actually means. We are likely to share the data with others working on the same research, including a secretary transcribing interviews from audio to text and other researchers or academics. These members of the research team should understand about keeping the data confidential. The psychologist described in Box 7.1 may observe or interview people who work in the same clinic. To encourage them to be open about what happens in the clinic, the psychologist will need to ensure that data from each individual is kept confidential and not disclosed in any form to others in the same clinic, even as a passing comment over coffee. Confidentiality and making data anonymous is discussed further in Chapter 3.

People have the experience of being asked for data in many different situations, such as health care, for financial issues including tax, banking and claiming benefits, housing, legal and police issues. Those working in health care will have the experience of assessment in education and appraisal in their jobs. These experiences are far more common than being involved in research. People are used to saying what they want each particular audience to hear. Some are very suspicious of people asking questions about themselves as they have had difficult experiences in the past. If we are open about our research, why we are doing it and what will happen to the data, those we observe and interview are more likely to trust us and let us see and hear as much as they can show or tell us about our research issue.

Gathering data about the frame of the research to understand the focus

Our research needs data about our defined research focus, but we also need data about the frame of the research. We need to keep this in mind when planning data collection. It is often best to collect data about the frame of the research before we collect data about the focus. The psychologist described in Box 7.1 may decide to observe a specialist clinic (see below). Before going to observe a clinic, she should read about the clinic, the wider health service and the local area so when she is observing she has some idea of why things happen, for example, knowing what administrative data is recorded for financial reasons.

When observing it is important the psychologist looks not only at the particular behaviour of interest but also observes the wider context as this may increase understanding of why things happen the way they do. For those being observed it also helps to reduce their awareness of being observed. If the psychologist asks a patient attending the specialist clinic for an interview, the patient may start by describing their recent experience attending the clinic. This may be what the psychologist wants to know about, but to understand it within the context of the patient's life she needs to know more about the patient. If the psychologist introduces the interview as being about the person themselves and their experience of substance misuse, including their experiences of seeking help, this allows the psychologist to find out more about the patient so their experience of seeking help can be understood in context. An interview undertaken in the clinic setting will tend to focus the interview on the experience at that clinic. If undertaken at the patient's home, the interview may range more widely.

Although we talk to people about our research, we also need to provide the information in writing and in other forms, such as audio recording where participants are unable to read our text. Guidance about the provision of information to research participants is available in the resources listed at the end of Chapter 3. In the next two sections we will discuss how to plan and undertake data collection.

Planning and undertaking data collection using observation

Observation as a method of data collection is particularly suitable where the behaviour to be observed happens fairly frequently and in a reasonably predictable timeframe and place. The psychologist in Box 7.1 could observe the response of individual people working in a specialist clinic to those seeking help for substance misuse.

For planning data collection using observation the psychologist needs to consider what, where, when, how and who she wants to observe (see Table 7.1).

Table 7.1 Planning data collection through observation of a specialist clinic for those seeking help with substance misuse

Consider	Question	Observation
What	What do we want to observe?	How the health service responds to those seeking help with substance misuse. This may include arranging appointments, reception and waiting areas, and consultations with health professionals.
Where	Where can we observe this?	Where this activity happens frequently, such as in clinics specialising in helping people with substance misuse.
When	When can we observe this?	When people who are seeking help (not those already receiving help) attend the clinic.
How	How can we observe this?	Being present and observing the clinic in all its areas from reception through to encounters with health professionals. Consider the use of audio or video recording, particularly for consultations with health professionals. Consider the use of photographs.
Who	Who should we observe?	To observe a 'response', the observation needs to be of both those seeking help and those working in the health service.

The psychologist will need to ask advice of the people working in the clinic about when and where to observe. This is part of the research, and the information and advice given by those working in the clinic forms part of the research data. This will include information that is important for interpreting observed behaviour, such as clinic routines. The working practices of the clinic place a structure on the observation that the psychologist works within but should also question. For example, why is there so much similarity between how people respond or why is there nothing happening at certain times? A request not to observe at a particular time must be respected. The psychologist should ask about the reason, but needs to respect a refusal to give a reason.

Observation periods should, as far as possible, vary in terms of time of day, day of week and place of observation in the clinic. The psychologist would draw up a timetable for observation in consultation with clinic staff. This would include where to position herself so that she can observe what she needs to see without hindering the clinic's normal activity.

During periods of observation everyone in the clinic needs to know this is happening. Methods for informing everyone include displaying a notice in the waiting room, wearing a T-shirt with appropriate printed text, introducing herself to people as they arrive and formal consent forms, particularly for video recording.

The psychologist takes notes as she observes, initially noting as much as possible about what she sees and hears, even though it may not be apparent how relevant it is to the research question. This includes places and things such as the layout of the waiting room and posters on the walls, as well as who does what, when and why. All notes must be labelled with date and time and include details of the observed behaviour and background data, such as what was going on generally in the clinic and who was present. It is also important to note when nothing happens or when things which usually happen do not happen.

After each observation session the psychologist reviews her observation notes and reflects on:

- what she has observed and its relevance to her research question

- patterns of activity and behaviour that are emerging, in relation to her research question.

From these reflections she then plans further observation including:

- questions she needs to ask to clarify what she has observed and why

- who to ask follow-up questions, and when

- who, what and where she has not observed, and her plans to observe them.

During further observation she would also actively look for examples of activities that do not fit the patterns she initially observed, as a way of testing her perception of what is happening. It is very easy to assume that what we are observing is the same as, for example, what we observed the previous day. Observation is an active process, with each session of observation building on earlier observation, so planning in sufficient time for reflection in between observation sessions is important. When the psychologist is sure she is observing nothing new in that setting, she then knows she can stop observing.

If there is more than one specialist clinic in her region, the psychologist needs to decide how many to observe. Ideally she should observe as many as possible, until she is finding no new data or until she has observed them all. After the first clinic, the psychologist will be observing and at the same time comparing what she observes with other clinics. This alerts her to what is different about the clinic she is observing and what she may have missed noticing or understanding in other clinics. If she has enough time she may be able to return to a clinic and observe again.

Table 7.2 provides examples of what the psychologist should include in her **field notes** made before, during and after observation. The notes will be made in date order, so the categories of data in the Table will be mixed in together. They can be teased out during analysis. Notes should include when photographs or audio/visual recordings are made or other materials collected. The photographs, recordings and any other material must be labelled with date, time, place and people present. It is important not to throw anything away, even a leaflet picked up during observation, until the research is complete and written up. For ease of storage, analysis and archiving, notes made during observation are often typed up. Other materials can also be stored digitally. All notes, photographs and audio/video recordings must be kept secure and remain confidential.

Table 7.2   Examples of the type of field notes made during observation and reflection on these observations

Observation subject	Content of field notes
Research process	
Access and recruitment process	Details of all contacts made in process of arranging observation, both successful and unsuccessful.
Researcher impact	Peoples' responses to researcher and researcher's reflections.
Research frame	
The context of the observed behaviour	Includes: policy, plans and resources, clinic structure and processes, activities and people present during observation.
Research focus	
Detail	What is observed, what people say about the observed activity.
Diversity	Variety in time, place and people engaging in observed activity.
Similarity	Observed patterns of activity that are similar; why they are similar?
Difference	Unusual occurrences and what people say about them.
	Differences noticed through comparison with other places/times/people.
	What is expected but is not happening.
	What people say about the differences.

It is sometimes possible to undertake observation while also taking part in the activity being observed. For example, the psychologist could work as a clinic receptionist. This can provide rich observational data but is not easy. Observing and taking notes is hard work in itself. For health professionals undertaking research, this option is usually impractical. Anthropologists may undertake observation in this way, but often with much more time and exploring much broader research questions than we usually undertake for health care practice.

Observational data is often complimented with interview data, where the people observed are asked their perception of what happens. These may be informal conversations during a period of observation, or more formal interviews.

Planning and undertaking data collection through interviews

In this section we will consider planning and undertaking a study which seeks to find out how the health service responds to people seeking help for substance misuse from non-specialist services such as general practice, telephone advice centres and community clinics, such as women's health clinics (see Box 7.1). The psychologist could interview those working in the health service and those seeking help from it. There are different issues to be considered for these two groups. We start by considering how the psychologist will plan and undertake interviews with people seeking help and return later to discuss interviewing those working in the health service. The interviews will be **'semi-structured' interviews** as they have a structure in order to focus on the research issue but will allow exploration of the issue within or beyond this structure.

To plan her data collection the psychologist needs some idea of how many people seek help through non-specialist services, and where and when they seek help. She can ask advice of people who work in these services and look at activity data from the various services.

Recruiting people for interview

The psychologist wants to find out about the response of non-specialist health services when someone seeks help for substance misuse. Those interviewed therefore need to have had this experience (**purposive sampling**). If their request for help was recorded in clinical or administrative records, these people can be identified through these records. The psychologist could search clinic or general practice records for patients who have sought help for substance misuse in the last few months, and ask the clinic or general practice to write to them inviting them to be interviewed. The event of interest – seeking help – needs to have happened relatively recently so that it is reasonably fresh in the mind of the person being interviewed.

There are other ways of **recruiting** people for interview, such as advertising through relevant community groups or support groups or visiting places where people with substance misuse problems congregate. The psychologist could ask people she interviews to invite for interview other people who they know and who have substance misuse problems (**snowball recruitment/sampling**). Not all these people would have had the experience of seeking help for substance misuse from non-specialist services. However, these methods of **recruitment** have an advantage. The invitation to participate in the research comes direct from the researcher (or via a person known to the participant) and not from the health care service from which the participant was seeking help. The participants may therefore feel able to talk more openly about their experience.

Deciding who to interview

The psychologist wants to understand what is happening in the health service in the region but cannot interview everyone who has sought help in the region. Her plan of recruitment should be refined so that it leads her to the people she wants to interview. For example, if the psychologist knows that most people with substance misuse seek help from their general practitioner, then she can recruit most of the people from there. However, this will exclude certain groups of people, such as the homeless who seek help through a clinic for the homeless. The psychologist could recruit some people from this clinic to capture their different experience (**sampling for diversity**).

If the psychologist finds that there are plenty of potential interviewees, her next decision is how to choose between possible participants and, hand in hand with this, how many to recruit for interview. All participants seeking help are likely to have had different experiences, but there are some characteristics of individuals that mean they are likely to have more or less in common. For example, the experiences of someone aged 50 years may be different from the experiences of someone aged 20 years. Someone who grew up in one country may have different experiences from someone who grew up in another.

If she decides to limit her research to a particular age group, she needs to decide on its boundaries. This type of decision should be based on published research or information about her region. For example, in the UK where schooling is compulsory until age 16 years, the psychologist may exclude everyone under 16 years as their experience is likely to be different from that of people no longer at school.

We can only choose people using the data we have available. By recruiting through the health service the psychologist will know the age, gender and the area where a potential participant lives. However, she is unlikely to know about other aspects of their life, such as income and educational attainment. If it is important to recruit people according to characteristics we don't know about, then we have to recruit them first and then ask them to complete a brief questionnaire or to answer some questions in a brief interview, perhaps by telephone. Then we can decide whether to proceed to a full interview. It is important to keep a record of who was considered eligible for the study, who was invited to participate, whether they agreed and whether a full interview went ahead.

Interviewing people at the same stage of seeking help with substance misuse provides a basis for comparison of the accounts of different people. However, the psychologist needs to consider whether the stage in seeking help through the health service is a good basis for comparison, as it is just one small aspect of people's life experience. As health professionals we can easily over-estimate the importance of the health care system within the lives of those seeking help.

The recruitment process should prioritise finding people with the characteristics the psychologist thinks, from her preparatory work, are particularly important.

For example, the psychologist may decide that understanding experiences of people from across the age range is important. There may be many more people eligible for the study from one age group than from another; she should therefore start recruitment with the group where there are fewer people, so that there is plenty of time for contacting them and waiting for their responses and that no potential interview candidate is missed through lack of time. Priority should also be given to the recruitment of people who are difficult to contact, such as people who change their residence frequently and those who may be suspicious of the research, such as those living on the margins of mainstream society. If the psychologist invests time in gaining the trust of people who feel marginalised, they may be very willing to tell their story.

The psychologist will know that she has interviewed enough people when she is no longer hearing anything that gives new insights. For an interview study with a tight focus, such as 'the response of the health service to seeking help for substance misuse', undertaken within a region (not across the whole nation or internationally), it is likely that no new insights will be found after 15–20 interviews if the people interviewed are varied, for example, all ages, women and men and living across the whole region. If the people interviewed are similar in a number of ways, for example, young men living in a certain area, then it may take less than ten interviews to reach this point.

Planning the interview

Before undertaking an interview, the psychologist should write down what she wants to ask about. As a first step there is no need to worry about how to ask or in what order to ask, just getting the ideas down about what to ask is important. These ideas then need to be reviewed to check that they are consistent with the research focus and question. In our enthusiasm it is very easy to add more and more into interviews. The danger is that by asking about lots of things we fail to delve deeply into the focus of our research.

The list of questions then needs to be refined so that the wording enables the interviewee to answer how they want to, that they are in an appropriate order and that sufficient background information is collected. Start with more general questions and move onto more specific ones. Consider whether asking one question may influence how others are answered (**framing**) and order them to reduce this effect. Questions that are difficult to ask as they are about sensitive topics should be left for later in the interview, when some rapport has developed between interviewer and interviewee. Work out the wording of questions and check they will not lead the interviewee to a particular answer. For example, 'How did you find out about the service?' is an **open question** whereas 'Was it difficult to find out about the service?' is a **leading question**. Consider how you would answer each question if you were the interviewee. If data such as age, income, self-declared ethnicity and educational attainment is needed, ask for this at the end of the interview. This is often easiest using a short written questionnaire that the interviewee fills in.

Undertaking an interview

As health professionals we are used to asking questions of our patients, and we can bring these skills to conducting interviews. However, in our clinical work our aim is to make a clinical decision, and our questions to patients are driven by this aim. In an interview we want to hear from the interviewee what they want to tell us about the research issue, so we need to be less directive than in our clinical work. As health professionals we may ask questions in a way that allows the patient to answer as they want to, for example, 'How do you feel?' (an open question), but we often move in quickly with questions which limit responses, such as 'Are you feeling better?' (a **closed question**). Our time is constrained in clinical settings by appointment times and other people waiting. Research interviews are different. They should be arranged so that the researcher has no immediate time constraint and, if possible, the interviewee has plenty of time. Writing out and practising the wording of questions helps to avoid slipping into clinical questioning habits. As health professionals we find it quite hard to say to an interviewee 'Tell me about your experience of seeking help for your alcohol problem' and then sit back prepared to listen with encouraging and open body language for however long the interviewee wants to talk. We need to watch ourselves very carefully during the interview and be prepared to listen to everything the interviewee wants to say, even if it doesn't seem immediately relevant. They may be getting slowly around to telling us very interesting things, but perhaps checking first that we really want to hear. Of course there may be times when we need gently to bring the interviewee back to the topic of the interview. There will also be times when the interviewee says 'What do you want to know?'. Our response needs to give them a pointer, such as 'Why not start with when you first considered seeking help'. During the interview we want to hear about what happened, the story of the experiences of the interviewee, and with this their thoughts, attitudes and feelings about the experience and what it meant to them.

When we ask people about what happened in the past, what they tell us is filtered by their memory and all that has happened to them since. This is not a problem if we are interested in their perceptions of what happened in the past and how they think this influences what they do now. If we are interested in understanding in more detail what happened to people in the past, we may need to help them remember. For example, several interviews over a number of months allows memories to surface. Key events in their lives such as getting married or the closure of a local factory can be used as markers, so that when the interviewee talks about an event they place it in relation to these time markers. Events related to the focus of the interview can be written out as a 'time line', for example, what has happened since first seeking help with substance misuse. The timeline acts as a reminder and helps them reflect on what has changed.

If our research seeks to understand how people change with time, we can ask them to keep a diary about the research issue. This can be a traditional paper diary, an audio, video or photo diary. Electronic diaries can include reminders to complete them. Mobile phones can be used to send text reminders to those participating. Regular e-mail exchange or brief telephone conversations with the researcher are also ways of asking about what is changing, and we can arrange a follow-up interview to find out what has changed in more depth.

Before an interview or set of interviews is complete, it is important to check that all the data needed for analysis has been collected (unless the interviewee does not wish to give certain data). Take time at the end of an interview to ensure that all questions have been covered, explaining to the interviewee what you are doing.

Almost all researchers undertaking interviews these days make an audio recording, as this captures everything that was said, and the technology for recording is usually easily available. It is, however, important to make notes about the interview immediately afterwards, including reflections on the process, notes about interruptions, thoughts and feelings about what was said, any new insights gained and issues to consider for future data collection.

Careful preparation for interviews is important, but so is learning from the first interviews. Take time to listen to the first few interviews, noticing the phrasing of questions and the responses given. The list of questions and prompts can be revised in the light of this. As interviewees raise new issues, these should be added to the list of questions for exploration in subsequent interviews with other people.

Interviewing people who work in health care services

For interviewing people who work in the health service, the preparation and conduct of the interviews follows the same principals discussed above. Different interviews may have different aims. Key people in an organisation can be interviewed about how an organisation works in general (**key informant interview**) but to find out about what actually happens and why for example in response to people seeking help with substance misuse, interviews need to be undertaken with those who respond to the requests for help.

A health professional may respond to many people seeking help with substance misuse. Therefore, if the psychologist (Box 7.1) asks a health professional 'What do you do when a patient asks for help with substance misuse?' the response is likely to be something like 'I always tell them to …'. This response is based on what they think they do in a general way and is rarely very informative. If, however, the psychologist asks the health professional to recall the last patient they saw with substance misuse, they may give some details about the patient including what they said and did and why. This answer is likely to be much closer to reality than the previous answer. It may be possible to interview health professionals after they have watched a video recording of their own consultation or of a simulated consultation to explore their responses to particular patients. Another way of bringing the health professional to focus on specific examples is to write a brief story or vignette about a patient and ask how they would respond to the patient. It takes some skill to develop simulated consultations and vignettes and so if you want to do this, seek the help of someone with expertise in this field.

As health professionals we are familiar with health care services and the activities of health professionals. This can make it more difficult to undertake an in-depth interview with other health professionals than if we were not familiar with what they do. It is very easy to make assumptions about details, but these assumptions may be wrong. When listening to our interviews with health professionals we need to check that we are not falling into this trap, and where we have failed to clarify issues we need to improve our interviewing skill for the next interview.

So far I have discussed interviewing individuals, seeking their stories about their experiences. Interviews can be undertaken with groups of people, which provides the added dimension of hearing how people react to each other. Undertaking **group interviews** and other data collection methods from groups is considered in the next section.

Collecting data through group communication

If we are interested in how our research issue is talked about between people, then we could consider collecting data from a group of people. Through this process we will also collect data from individuals as they speak about the research issue, but this data has to be interpreted in the context of the group discussion. Individuals may say something very different in a group than when alone. What they say in the group will be influenced by who else is there and what has already been said (**group dynamics**).

If the health professionals working in a specialist clinic were interviewed together about how they respond to people seeking help with substance misuse, the interview may reveal how they interact as a team, including who tends to lead, who dominates decision making and who says very little. However, the data can be difficult to understand as it will be influenced by how they relate outside the group interview as well as within the interview.

Group interviews can be useful for testing ideas with people, listening to how they develop their responses to a new idea in dialogue with others. For example, if the psychologist (Box 7.1) developed ideas for changes to the health service, she could put these to a group of health professionals or patients and encourage them to discuss them. This form of interview is usually called a focus group. It asks the participants to focus on a particular issue and discuss it. As a research technique, focus groups were developed by market researchers to find out what people thought about ideas for marketing products. The group members usually do not know each other, and so their interaction will not be affected by how they relate outside of the group. This could be the situation for patients invited to a focus group. However, if we draw a group of health professionals together for a focus group they are likely to know each other, or know of each other's role in the local health service. As this can affect the interactions within the group, the psychologist needs to take it into account when deciding who to invite. For example, district nurses may discuss the issue differently in a group with nurse managers, nurse assistants and doctors than in a group where they all have a similar role and status. As the aim of a focus group is to hear how people respond to an issue and develop their ideas in a group, it is best to plan the groups so that everyone is likely to feel able to contribute.

There are structured ways of undertaking group interviews to develop consensus on an issue, and some of these methods can be used without the group actually meeting (for example, using e-mail or web forum). An example is the **Nominal Group Technique**, where participants are asked for their responses to two or three carefully developed questions. One such question might be 'How should General Practice respond to people seeking help for substance misuse?'. Responses to this open question are categorised and a list drawn up of the categories of responses. The list is then circulated to all participants. The group may then discuss the list, and vote on and rank the responses to reach a consensus. One of the advantages of this method is that it allows those who are anxious about voicing their ideas to do so. A variation of this method is the **Delphi method**, where the participants are chosen as they bring a particular expertise to the issue. In the Delphi method the participants may be unaware of precisely who else is involved and there is no discussion stage (see Further Reading).

Collecting data from groups of people allows us to understand how they talk about the issue and perhaps reach a consensus. This is very different data from observation and individual interviews.

When have we collected enough data?

Knowing when we have collected enough data through observation and interviews depends on the research focus and research question. We will consider this further using the example discussed earlier in the chapter (Box 7.1).

To understand how the health service responds to people seeking help for substance misuse, the psychologist may interview people who have experienced this. The interviews will ask about the person and their context as well as the experience of seeking help and the response they received. However, the decision about whether the psychologist has enough data is based on the focus of the research, the response of the health service. Each person will have had a different experience, so the detail of each person's story will be unique. The psychologist has to consider whether, despite the differences in detail, there is sufficient in common between experiences to say they are similar or not in relation to the research focus as she has defined it. For example, interviewees may have contacted different health professionals seeking help, so their experiences are different in this detail. However, if the psychologist is interested in the responses in terms of what was said and done the difference in who responded may not be important. When the psychologist is not hearing anything new about what was said and done, then she has interviewed enough people about this particular research focus. This is known as **data saturation**.

When collecting data through observation and communication, we will at first be unsure about what is important and what is not. During her interviews the psychologist may find that there are other issues at least as important as her initial research focus, and so she may change her focus. The psychologist then needs to interview until she is hearing nothing new about this focus. The structure of the overall interview may change very little despite the change in focus. It is important to make a note of any change in focus and why it was made.

If the psychologist aims to collect accounts of help-seeking from a diversity of people, she needs to consider whether she has interviewed enough people from the range of potential interviewees. Take, for example, interviewing people from across the age range 18–65 years. The psychologist may decide to divide the age range into 18–24 years, young adults; 25–44 years, the age range when many adults have dependent children; and 45–65 years, when adults are still of working age but are less likely to have dependent children. The psychologist expects the experience of people in these different age groups to be different. Ideally, she needs to continue interviewing people until she is sure she is finding no new insights in each age group. This means undertaking a large number of interviews, which may be impractical. A useful rule of thumb is to include at least five interviewees from each group. With five interviews it is possible to identify some commonality and difference of experience. The psychologist also needs to keep an open mind as to whether age is as important as she first thought.

If the psychologist undertakes interviews with health professionals, it may be tempting to interview, for example, one health professional from a number of different health care settings to hear about the different settings. The one account from each setting is likely to be given by the health professional with the most interest in substance misuse and so the accounts are likely to be very similar with nothing new being learned after only a few interviews. The psychologist will obtain more diverse accounts if she interviews as many people as possible from one health care setting. Health professionals who work together in a clinic or general practice change and adapt to each other's strengths, weaknesses and interests and so within one setting, health professionals tend to be more different from each other than if they are compared between settings. The psychologist will have collected enough data when she has observed and/or interviewed everyone who works in one health care setting, as far as possible. The people working there who are least interested in the research issue will be the most difficult to observe or interview. However, their lack of interest in itself is useful data for the research, and they may be happy to explain why they are not interested. We also should not consider a lack of interest in our research as an indication of someone's ability or interest in the issue when in their clinical role.

The psychologist set out to understand how the health services in the region respond to people seeking help with substance misuse (Box 7.1). When has she collected enough data to have a full picture of what happens? She needs to reconsider the background data from the start of the project, including how many people there are in the region with substance misuse problems, where they are, and which services are approached by people seeking help. Are there groups of help seekers or of those responding who have been missed out? Are there localities where people seeking help have not been included? How different are these groups or localities likely to be from those where data has been collected? Is there data available to enable the psychologist to make this comparison? How does the data collected compare with other studies undertaken on a similar issue? Considering all these questions enables the psychologist to make a judgement about whether there is a need to collect more data or not. It may be that she does not have the time to collect more data, in which case she needs to be clear about the limitations of what she has; for example, explaining that a locality was missed out which, based on available background data, may be different from the localities included in the data collection. The psychologist may decide that she needs data from other people or places but, through the in-depth understanding gained through observation and interviews, she is clearer about the key issues and so can ask about these through a survey.

Managing data and preparing data for analysis

As we go through the process of developing our research and collecting the data it is important that we keep everything relating to the research, including notes made during meetings, reflections, diaries of meetings and interviews, as well as all the data we collect in the form it was collected (diaries, audio recordings, field notes and so on). During analysis it is not unusual to need to check something in original notes or recordings. As we prepare our data for analysis, and during analysis, we should keep detailed notes of what we do and why, plus our reflections on the process including ideas about the data and how different sections of data relate to each other.

As the data is collected it is important to check that we have recorded the date and place it was collected, who collected it and who participated in the research and note when it goes through each stage of processing in preparation for analysis. All consent forms should be kept secure.

Most people type up their main data, for example, recordings of focus groups or interview and field notes. Styles of transcribing vary according to the method of analysis used, so this needs to be considered before transcribing starts. Some data may be left in handwritten form. Pictures and diagrams may be scanned into a computer data set or kept in their original form. During the process of transcribing and collating data into a form for the computer, data should be made anonymous by removing all names of people and places. Names of research participants can be replaced with an identification number, and the list of participants' names and identification numbers kept separately and secure. In transcriptions where someone has referred to, for example, their husband by name, the transcript can have (husband) in place of the name. Similarly for names of places, for example (town where participant lives), (area where sister works) and organisations, for example (hospital ward), (employing organisation). Where we have photographs we need to ensure there is nothing to identify the person or location. For example, a photograph of a bed may not reveal anything about whose bed or where it is. If there are clues about people or places in the photograph, then the use of the photograph must be discussed with the relevant research participants and consent obtained. Any data that has any identification on it must be kept secure.

We also need to check the data for errors and omissions. Transcripts of audio recordings should be checked for accuracy while listening to the recording. This also allows the researcher to re-familiarise themselves with the data and become immersed in it. Throughout analysis the data needs to be assessed for quality, particularly looking for where the manner in which the data was collected may have had a strong influence on the data. Examples include leading questions or closed questions used in interviews. Sometimes we have to abandon the use of data where this has occurred.

In the next section we consider how we explore our data, getting to know all the data and coding it so we can locate it easily as our analysis proceeds.

Initial exploratory analysis of our qualitative data

The first stages of analysis should start early in the process of collecting data. Initially this will involve reading the data through and thinking about it, and discussing it with other researchers. Through repeated reading and reviewing our data we become familiar with it and start to make comparisons between data, looking for similarities and differences and how these give us clues about what is happening. This exploration continues throughout analysis. However, we use analysis processes to guide us so that we do not get lost in our data. In this section we discuss coding the data. This coding is undertaken so that portions of data about similar topics, ideas, actions or communications can be easily identified and compared. Coding involves reading, thinking about and labelling every piece of data so we can find it easily later in analysis. In Chapter 9 we consider further analysis of data for research for health care practice.

A code summarises the content of a portion of data, for example, a section of text, a short section of a video recording or a section of field notes. Codes are defined so that each one is only used to code portions of data that are comparable. Sometimes a section of data is given more than one code. What codes to use depends on the research focus, question and analysis approach. With small amounts of data, coding can be done using coloured pens. With larger sets of data, most people use computer software designed for this task. With small amounts of data in text form on paper, the coded data can be cut up with scissors and sorted into piles that have the same code. All the pieces of paper in one pile can then be compared. When first starting on qualitative analysis, you may want to do some coding and comparison in this way so you become accustomed to the process. Computer programmes designed for qualitative data analysis do the same thing but can easily handle large amounts of data. The computer programme does not do the analysis, it is only a tool to help handle the data.

Let us consider how to code data from individuals interviewed about seeking help for substance abuse (Box 7.1). We want to identify what people say about the response of health services to their request for help. The interview was designed to gather this data, so we can develop an initial list of codes based on the questions we asked. For example, if we asked the interviewee to 'Tell me about the first time you considered seeking help', the text of this question and its response can be coded 'First time considered seeking help'. If we then asked 'What was it like when you got to the clinic?', the question and response can be coded 'First experience of clinic'. I find it best to code the data initially using fairly broad codes such as these. It is then relatively easy to go back to coded data of particular interest and add more detailed coding. For example, the data coded 'First experience of clinic' could be further coded for the timing of this experience in relation to changes for the person, clinic or community or it could be further coded to indicate the sequence of events. As we go through the data to code it we also look for themes in the data that are new to us and code them. During our study we may read other research that suggests what to look for and code in our data. Our coding can also include issues that are in the frame of the research, such as the personal background of the interviewee. We should keep notes on why we have included a code and the date we added the code so that we can return to data we coded early in the process to add the new coding.

It is not unusual to find that we have more data from some sources than others. For example, in interview studies it is not unusual for a few participants to talk a lot more than others, and perhaps tell vivid and memorable stories. In an observation study we may have limited access to certain places compared to others. In our data analysis process we need to check that we are using the data from all sources and not just the sources providing the most data, nor the data that is most memorable. Where there is a lack of data this needs to be noted, and we should reflect on why this is. It is very easy to forget where there is a lack of data as we tend to consider what is there rather than what is not there but the lack of data is itself data and needs to be brought into the analysis.

When we are coding we make comparisons between portions of data to decide whether one portion of data is about the same thing as another portion of data and so should be coded the same way. These portions of data may be from the same source, such as observation field notes of one clinic or from different sources, such as different interviews. As we code we should note down what strikes us as we make these comparisons, what is similar and what is different, as this provides clues about what is happening and what may be important for the next stage of our analysis.

This chapter has considered the collection of new data using qualitative methods involving observation and communication including the preparation of the data for analysis. The next chapter considers collecting new data using quantitative methods, counting and measurement. In Chapter 9 we consider the use of both types of data in analysis that can directly inform health care practice.

Resources

NVivo and ATLAS.ti are the names of software designed for handling qualitative data. The software designers bring out frequent updates. Their websites provide an introduction to the software.

NVivo: www.qsrinternational.com

ATLAS.ti:www.atlasti.com

Further reading

Crabtree, B. and Miller, W.L. (1999) *Doing Qualitative Research*. London: Sage.

Written by health professionals, this continues to be one of the best introductions to qualitative research for health professionals.

Pope, C. and Mays, N. (Editors) (2006) *Qualitative Research in Health Care*. Oxford: Blackwell.

This book provides concise introductions to undertaking interviews, focus groups, observation, Delphi and Nominal Group Techniques and the contribution of qualitative method to case study, action research and data analysis. The editors and contributors have been leaders in establishing qualitative methods within health care research over the last decade.

Green, J. and Thorogood, N. (2004) *Qualitative Methods for Health Research*. London: Sage.

This excellent book includes very clear and helpful advice on approaches to analysis widely used for qualitative health research.

Flick, U. (Editor) (2007) *The Sage Qualitative Research Kit*. Thousand Oaks, CA: Sage.

An excellent recent addition for those using qualitative research methods.

Hine, C. (Editor) (2005) *Virtual Methods: Issues in Social Research on the Internet*. Oxford: Berg.

The Internet provides access to people and data for research, an approach discussed in this book, including how the way it is collected influences the data.

8 Collecting and Exploring New Data Using Quantitative Methods

This chapter considers how to define what we count or measure to fit with our research focus. It explores how to design data collection to minimise the effect of the process on the data we collect, an issue also important in qualitative data collection. The chapter then considers how to identify people for a quantitative study, including those in a local population and people using health care. The use of time-ordered data, particularly data collected at frequent intervals, is discussed and the chapter ends by considering preparation of data for analysis and how to explore and summarise data.

This chapter considers collecting data using quantitative methods involving measurement and counting. In health sciences these are distinguished from qualitative methods where data is often in text form, such as interview transcripts. However, qualitative and quantitative data collection methods are often used together, supporting and complimenting each other. There are many considerations common to collecting qualitative and quantitative data. In Chapter 7 we discussed issues of relevance for collecting quantitative data including reflection in research, tailoring the data collection to the research focus and accessing research participants. In this chapter, the section on designing quantitative data collection considers how to minimise the effect of data collection on the data, an issue of importance for qualitative data collection.

In clinical practice we are accustomed to measuring and counting. For example, if we want to know how many people in our community have diabetes, we would measure their blood glucose level and if it is over a certain level we count them as having diabetes. If we were planning to provide dietary advice for obese children, we would measure the weight and height (body mass index or BMI) of the children in our community and then count the number of children with a high body mass index. Questionnaires are also used to measure certain aspects of people, for example, symptoms of depression or satisfaction with health care. People completing a questionnaire about depression are given a score based on their answers that indicates whether they are considered to be depressed. We also count people, events or other things where measurement has not been used. For example, if we are reviewing the provision of health care services for pregnant women, we may count the number of women having a baby in our community in the previous five years. If we want to redesign an appointment system, we may count the number of people requesting appointments in one month.

If we have a measurement such as BMI or the score from a questionnaire about depression from many people in a community, we can use these measurements to describe the variation of these aspects of people in the community (see Chapter 2). If we classify people as 'obese' and 'not obese' or 'depressed' or 'not depressed' we can also look at the variation in the community, but without the fine detail that the measurement gives us. However, we need to be sure that the measurement is assessing something that relates closely to people's real experiences and are relevant to the aim of our research.

The design of our data collection using measurement and counting will be closely linked to the definition of our research focus and our research questions. However, data may be collected in the same way for research with a different focus and different research questions. For example, blood glucose measurements from people in our community may be used in research where the focus is the individual people or where the focus is the community. Maintaining clarity about our research focus and questions is important to reduce confusion about how we analyse our data.

We need to think through every step of our data collection in detail and consider carefully why we are collecting each item of data and whether the data we collect is really telling us what we want to know. We also need to consider whether it is possible to collect the data we want and the problems we may encounter in doing this. Collecting data through counting and measurement involves very careful planning because once we start collecting the data we need to continue in the same way. For example, if we are counting obese children in our community, we need to ensure that measurements are undertaken in a standard way so that they can be accurately compared. Sticking to a data collection plan may seem at odds with the need to be constantly reviewing our research, questioning our ideas, data and analysis; however, when collecting data using measurement and counting, we need to question our research as we plan it, stick to our plan during data collection and then question our research again as we undertake analysis. This chapter will guide you through the many issues you need to consider in planning and undertaking data collection using quantitative methods. There are specialist books listed at the end of this chapter that provide greater detail on these issues. The methods of data collection described in this chapter have been developed and refined within various disciplines including clinical sciences, epidemiology, psychology, sociology and statistics and by researchers working in the commercial world. In this chapter we consider the use of these methods for research in health care practice.

Defining the relevant characteristics of our research focus

Researchers isolate particular aspects of the world so that they can study them (see Chapter 1) and through this process define the boundary of what they are studying (see Chapter 5). However, relationships with what is beyond this boundary may be important. One approach is to include these relationships as if they are within the boundary; for example, a person's marital relationship is summarised as whether they are married or not, or the influence of the environment on a clinic is summarised as the clinic being 'rural' or 'urban' (see Table 5. 2). When we have decided where to place the boundary around the focus of our research, we need to decide how to bring within this boundary aspects of the world that are beyond the boundary. This first involves deciding what is important and needs bringing within the boundary; for example, what aspects of how individuals relate to their context are important for understanding their level of blood pressure control? These decisions will be guided by our research questions, our literature review and modelling our research focus (see Chapter 5). We then have to decide how to define these aspects of the focus of our research; for example, how we define marital status as a characteristic of an individual, or how we define a clinic as 'rural' or 'urban'? When we define these aspects of people, organisations or other things we lose fine detail about them; for example, there may be a great deal of variation in the nature of relationships between people who are married, but this variation is obscured within the summary of 'married'. However, by losing this detail we gain in our ability to compare lots of people. These comparisons can help us understand what is happening in the world across a whole community or population.

Decisions about how to define the relevant characteristics of our research focus need to be taken hand in hand with further refinement of the focus of our research. We will explore this with examples from Tables 5.1 and 5.2, first considering research where patients are the focus, then where the clinic is the focus.

With a research focus on the patients, we may consider the boundary to be the patient's skin; anything beyond this is external to the patient. Many aspects of the patient are influenced by how they function within their environment, including their appearance and biochemical measures such as glucose and cholesterol. However, these characteristics of the patient are definitely within our boundary. For the research question about why patients do or do not take medication (Table 5.1), we may suspect that their experience of side-effects is important and likely to vary between patients. To understand these differences, we could look at what influences patients' experience of side-effects. Existing research may suggest that important influences include aspects of their genetics, physiology, concurrent health problems, and how patients relate within their social and physical environment. Some of these factors are within our boundary or, in the case of medication, cross into our boundary. However, how patients relate to their social and physical environment is beyond our boundary. How do we define these aspects of the patient to bring them within our boundary?

Let us explore the idea that the amount of support patients have from their family is an important influence on the experience of side-effects. We need some way of describing what we mean by family support and defining it as a characteristic of the patient. Some of the options are listed in Table 8.1.

Table 8.1 Different ways of summarising family support

Method of defining family support	Characteristic given to patient
Develop a definition of what we mean by having family support or not (e.g. patient says they feel supported by family or not).	Family support = yes/no
Ask the patient to rate their family on a scale between supportive and not supportive.	Family support: scale 1–5 1 = no support 5 = very supportive
Count the family relationships (we could give more weight to some relationships than others, e.g. a daughter could count as 2 and a brother as 1).	Family support = count of family relationships
Describe the relationship between the patient and each family member in terms of frequency of contact.	Family support = number of contacts/week
Describe the characteristic of the family as a group and develop categories (these categories could include: family in household; close-knit but living elsewhere, dispersed with little contact).	Family support = a category describing the family

How we decide to describe family support will depend on how we refine the focus of our research. If we are particularly interested in how genetics and concurrent medication influence the experience of side-effects but want to take account of the effect of family support, we may decide to use a fairly crude method such as 'family support: yes/no' (**categorical data**). However, if we decide to steer our research towards understanding the influence of the patient's physical and social environment, we may want to describe family support in a more fine-textured way, such as a scale assessing family support (**ordinal data**) (see Table 8.1). We could also use more than one way of describing family support. It is important that we note down our decisions and our reasons, as we may need to review them later in the research.

For research where the clinic is the focus, we may need to consider how it is perceived by the community and aspects of the clinic's environment that influences how it functions. These could include its geographical position, transport links, stories about the clinic circulating in the community, media coverage and national health care policy. Although these are all external to the clinic they can also be considered as characteristics of the clinic, included within the boundary of what we mean by the clinic. They can be summarised as characteristics such as 'rural', 'high quality' or 'under resourced'. Each of these characteristics would need to be defined. We could also use counts or measurements, such as number of people in the community served by the clinic or the geographical size of clinic catchment area. Decisions about what to include and how to define it depends on our research focus. For example, for the question about what inhibits relatives attending with patients (Table 5.1), we may want to include clinic accessibility and describe it in several different ways, including the number of bus routes passing the clinic, distances travelled by patients to the clinic and perception of the safety of the local area.

In our research for health care practice, we are likely to use definitions of characteristics of people, organisations or other things that have been developed by other researchers. This saves us working out these definitions ourselves, which can be time consuming, and enables us to compare our results with other research that has used the same definition. This is an important consideration as the value of research in our own local context is greater if it can be compared with research undertaken elsewhere (see Chapter 1). However, we need to take care that definitions used by others makes sense for our own research focus, question and context. For example, the collection of data about the death of children under the age of one year is well established in many countries as research has demonstrated that it provides a very useful indicator of health status for a population in a region or country. A nurse working in a local community may be undertaking research prior to setting up health care services to support the families of infants who have died. By counting the number of children dying under one year of age and calculating the **rate**, the nurse can compare her community with others. However, she may also want to count the number of deaths beyond the boundary of the definition, such as the death of a child aged 14 months. As a health professional working in the community, the nurse will have experience of the tragedy for a mother of the death of an infant under one year; however, the death of a child aged 14 months is no less a tragedy. When establishing her new service, the nurse may be faced with difficult decisions about who receives help because of limited resources. If she has counted the number of deaths in all young children she can use this data to make these decisions. She can still compare her community with others as the data includes deaths of children under 1 year.

Definitions of characteristics of people, organisations and other things are not fixed but change with the development of scientific understanding, new technology and changing social norms. For example, diabetes is diagnosed when someone's blood glucose is above a certain level; however, the level recommended is now lower than it was 10 years ago as we understand more about diabetes and its long-term effects on health. New medical imaging technology gives images of the body that have not been available before, leading to changing definitions of diseases. Definitions of ethnicity and how to characterise a person by ethnicity have changed over the last few decades.

As health professionals, we have access to data collected during the day-to-day business of providing health care. This includes administrative data such as lists of patients, appointment schedules, clinical records of individual patients, communications between health professionals or between health professionals and patients. If we use this type of data we need to take care to understand its meaning and how this fits with our research focus and questions.

For example, if a GP records a diagnosis of 'urinary tract infection' and prescribes an antibiotic for a woman, this may indicate that the GP had established beyond reasonable doubt that there was a bacterial infection of the urinary tract. However, the story may be more complex. For example, the GP may not be absolutely sure about the diagnosis or the woman may have been concerned that based on previous experience she was developing an infection and wanted antibiotics with her as she went off on holiday. The usefulness of the clinical note 'urinary tract infection' depends on our research focus and question. When using existing data we also need to consider what is not recorded that may be important for our research. For example, if we are interested in the use of aspirin in cardiovascular disease prevention, as aspirin is cheap to buy many people taking it may not have this recorded in their clinical notes.

The most important consideration when defining the relevant characteristics of our research focus is our research questions. However, we also need to consider whether our definition allows us to compare our results with those of others and whether we can make use of existing data recorded during the provision of health care. There may also be practical considerations, such as the availability of a method of measuring such as equipment or a questionnaire. There is unlikely to be a perfect way to define the relevant characteristics of our research focus, it can only be the best possible at the time. Defining the relevant characteristics of our research focus and designing how to collect the data are often integrated in the process of planning our research. This is explored in the next section.

Designing quantitative data collection

The way in which we collect data influences the data, although there are ways of minimising this effect so the data resembles as closely as possible what is happening in the world. Many people work on this problem, including academics, researchers in disciplines such as psychology, sociology and clinical sciences and those developing technologies such as microscopes, imaging technology, detectors of sound, light and radioactivity and measuring instruments. We can draw on this expertise most effectively if we understand the nature of this problem for our research. Most research for clinical practice collects data from people, but the same issue of how to collect data that resembles what is happening in the world applies to all science disciplines. This section will consider the example of a physiotherapist interested in back pain (Box 8.1) so that we can explore how to define the relevant characteristics of our research focus and design our data collection to minimise the influence of the data collection process.

Getting started on research on chronic low back pain and behavioural therapy	Box 8.1

Health professional role: Physiotherapist with an interest in back pain.

Motivation: To improve the treatment of people with chronic low back pain.

Observation of difference or change: A clinical trial has demonstrated that people with chronic low back pain can benefit from a behavioural therapy.

Overall aim: To provide the behavioural therapy for local patients with low back pain who are most likely to benefit, and to evaluate the impact of this treatment.

Research issue: Behavioural therapy and low back pain.

Research focus: People with chronic low back pain.

Research aim: To describe how many people in the local population have chronic low back pain.

Research question: How many people in the local population have chronic low back pain?

The physiotherapist has read that behavioural therapy can help adults who have had pain for at least six weeks. The physiotherapist wants to survey his local population, find the people who fit this description and count them. For each person he needs to know the answers to the questions:

Are you an adult?
Do you have back pain?
Have you had back pain for more than six weeks?

The physiotherapist's questions may seem relatively simple, yet they can illustrate what we need to consider when collecting data to ensure that it resembles what is happening in the world.

In our clinical work if we ask patients these questions we are able to clarify their answers. For example, if we ask 'How long have you had back pain?' and the patient replies 'For ages', we then clarify this, perhaps by saying 'Was it there at Christmas time?' as people can often recall a specific event and then recall if they had back pain. If we ask 'Have you had it for more than six weeks?' our patient may say 'I don't know' or do their best to answer 'yes' or 'no'. Their answer may be influenced by how they are feeling at the moment we ask, what they think we expect the answer to be, and whether they think their answer will affect what treatment we offer.

If we are going to ask questions of a large number of people, we need a simple way of doing it so that we don't need to be there to clarify the answers whilst at the same time obtaining data as close to the patient's real experience as possible. To explore how to do this we will consider each of the physiotherapist's questions. We will also consider how the overall research design, including recruitment and analysis, may make a difference to how we collect the data.

Are you an adult?

This question may seem straightforward, but we need to take a moment to consider what we really want to ask, why we want to ask it and the effect on our participants and our data of how we ask the question. We could ask 'Are you adult?', but this may mean different things to different people. People may interpret 'adult' as defined by the law of the country or 'adult' as mature in ability to make decisions about themselves. The main reason for including this question is because the physiotherapist is interested in providing the therapy for adults as defined in the research he has read. The physiotherapist may therefore define adult as in this research.

The physiotherapist could ask a question such as 'Are you over 18 years of age?' However, if the physiotherapist is collecting data from many people in a community he may want to collect more detail than this, such as age or date of birth as this may be useful for understanding the community, for example, the variation of back pain in different age groups. Some people do not like to say how old they are and so may not answer the question. Another option is to provide a list of options such as '18–25 years', 26–60 years' or 'over 60 years'. These age bands need to be chosen carefully and relate to our research focus and what we know about the world, such as age by which most people have entered employment and retire from employment. Often it is better to ask for the person's age, as this keeps open the option of changing the age bands for analysis.

Collecting date of birth makes the individual more identifiable. For example, in a community there will be many 50-year-olds but only a handful with the same date of birth (see Chapter 3).

The physiotherapist could consider finding data about age or date of birth from existing records, such as medical or administrative records, although may require the individual's consent. However, if the physiotherapist is going to recruit people for his survey via these records, then seeking consent may be relatively straightforward.

Do you have back pain?

One approach to collecting this data is to examine each individual's clinical notes. If back pain is recorded in the clinical notes, then the physiotherapist could accept that as 'having back pain', and if it is not, he could assume the patient does not have back pain. This data may not be very accurate, as people with back pain may not report it to their clinician. Back pain tends to fluctuate, so the patient may no longer have back pain.

If the physiotherapist asks people 'Do you have back pain?', he is seeking a yes/no answer from the way the question is phrased. Before answering, many questions may go through the person's mind, such as:

- Do I experience any pain in my back?

- Is it significant enough to report to a physiotherapist (who has asked the question)?

- Do I want to consider myself as suffering from back pain?

- What would others think of me if I admitted to having back pain?

- What does the physiotherapist asking the question mean by back pain?

- What might I gain or lose by saying I have back pain?

- What does the physiotherapist want to hear – if I say I have back pain, will it help them establish a new back pain treatment service?

All these considerations can affect how people answer the question. We cannot remove these influences completely, but we can minimise their effect. How we do this depends on how we define the focus of our research.

If the physiotherapist is interested in people with back pain that is severe and debilitating enough for them to seek help from a health professional, he could ask 'Do you have troublesome back pain?' This leaves it to the individual to decide if the pain troubles them. He could extend the question to 'Do you have troublesome back pain that you think needs treatment?' However, people may not respond as they do not feel expert enough to know if it needs treatment.

Asking the question 'Do you have troublesome back pain?' provides a yes/no answer. However, people may feel unsure about giving such a precise answer. For example, they may feel they have troublesome back pain sometime but not all the time, or that although it troubles them a bit they don't want to suggest that it stops them doing anything. To capture these subtle details, the physio-therapist could ask people to describe their back pain. This could be as part of a **structured interview** or a question in a questionnaire. The physiotherapist could then compare all the answers and develop categories of back pain that appeared to be similar, for example, fluctuating with severe episodes, severe and continu-ous, mild and fluctuating (Dunn et al., 2006). He would then put each individual into one of these categories and all the individuals in each category are then labelled as having the same type of back pain.

Researchers have already developed and tested ways of asking people about their back pain in ways that allows the answers to be compared. For example, there are a number of standardised questionnaires that ask a list of questions about the person's pain and ability to function, from which an overall score can be calculated. There are also pain scales where people mark the level of their pain on a graduated line from no pain to severe pain (Kopec, 2000). These questionnaires and scales have been developed and tested for their ability to give consistent results so that results from different people and different research studies can be compared. They have also been tested for their ability to detect change, for example, comparing pain before a treatment with pain after a treatment. There are similar assessment questionnaires and scales for many other specific health issues and for assessing overall health (see Further Reading). The choice can be daunting, so do seek advice. To check that they are suitable for our research it is important to read about how these questionnaires and scales were developed and what they have been used for.

If the physiotherapist uses a standardised questionnaire to assess whether a person has back pain, he will need to decide what score will count as 'having back pain' and what will not. If only interested in people with very severe back pain, he will choose one cut-off point and another if also interested in mild back pain.

Standardised questionnaires take time to fill in and people may only answer some of the questions. Asking one question tailored to the focus of the research may be a better approach as the **response rate** will be higher, if the physiotherapist does not want to compare the severity of back pain between individuals. However, it is also possible to first ask one tailored question that most people will answer followed by a standardised questionnaire.

Have you had back pain for more than six weeks?

How we remember the past is influenced by many things, including what has happened since, our current life situation, how past events are viewed by others and how we are feeling now. We also tend to forget how much time has passed since, for example, back pain started, often underestimating the time. Remembering is easier when linked to events such as holidays, family celebrations or changing seasons. If the physiotherapist asks 'Have you had the pain for more than six weeks?', people might find it difficult to think what was happening six weeks ago as that period of time is unlikely to have particular significance. It may be better to ask 'When did your back pain start?', as this allows the person to think about it in terms of their own experiences, perhaps remembering where they were when it started or what they were doing. The answers can then be converted to the best form for analysis. Back pain tends to come and go, so the physiotherapist needs to decide whether he means the current episode of back pain or the first ever experience of back pain.

There may be other questions the physiotherapist wants to ask people in his survey. For each question he needs to consider why he needs the data and then consider how to ask the question.

Collecting other forms of data

The physiotherapist may want to collect data from clinical examination or imaging technology. Although these may appear to be very different types of data, the issues to be considered are similar to those considered above. The data needs to be collected in such a way that the data resembles what is happening in the world. The data also needs to be compared, so there has to be some standard way of collecting the data. For clinical examination, the health professionals undertaking the examination may need to be trained in that particular technique and then monitored to ensure that their technique remains consistent. Equipment such as imaging equipment needs to provide images of a consistent quality, and the interpretation of the images must be consistent. If our research question focuses on what happens in the normal course of daily clinical practice, we may decide to use data collected and recorded in daily clinical practice where there may be some variation in how assessments are made or images interpreted. This is not a problem if this is the data we need for our research focus and questions. However, the nature of the data needs to be clear to people reading our research.

The design of quantitative data collection is tailored to the definition of the focus of the research but takes account of the need to compare data from lots of different people, organisations or other things. Data collection design must also dovetail with how people are identified for the study and with analysis. The next section considers the issue of identifying people for a quantitative study.

Identifying people for a quantitative study

A survey of the local population would provide data on the number of people in the local population with back pain (See Box 8.1). In this section we consider the definition of the population for such a survey and collecting data from a sample of the population. This approach to data collection is used widely in epidemiology. When we undertake research for health care practice we may use this approach to describe the local population for which we provide health care, as in this example. However, we may also consider collecting data only from those making contact with health care. This is discussed at the end of the section.

Defining the boundary of the population for our study

For a survey such as that planned by the physiotherapist (Box 8.1), we need a process of identifying who to include. The physiotherapist wants to describe how many people in the local population have chronic low back pain, but who is in the local population? To define the boundary of the local population, the physiotherapist needs to consider the overall aim of his research and his local context. He wants to provide behaviour therapy for local people with chronic back pain through his physiotherapy service, so he can restrict his study to people who could use the service if they had back pain. For example, in the UK this may be a geographical area as most health care is provided for geographically defined populations, although some people cross these boundaries. In other countries people belong to an organisation that provides medical insurance and medical services, so the boundary of who to include is defined by whether they belong to the organisation. Health services may also exclude certain groups of the population, such as children, or only include certain groups, such as those in employment. Although the structure of the health service is used to define the population for the study, the population includes people with and without back pain. A clear definition of the boundary of the population being studied is important, as the processes of data collection can exclude people. For example, if the physiotherapist was to collect data using a postal questionnaire, people with visual impairment or who read and write in a different language would have difficulty responding. If the survey involved a clinical assessment, people living in geographically remote areas may have difficulty attending. To include these people we need to make special arrangements. If this is not possible, we have to note their exclusion and take this into account when interpreting our results.

Having defined the population for the study, the next step is to plan the data collection, in particular considering whether we need to collect data from everyone in the population, as in a census, or only from a sample of the people.

Planning data collection from the defined population

Let us imagine that the physiotherapist works in a clinic serving a town of 50,000 people. Using a questionnaire he could ask every adult in the town whether, at the time of completing the questionnaire, they have back pain and if they have pain, how long they have had it. This would tell us how many people have back pain at the time of the survey. However, we know from previous studies that although back pain is a common problem, most people do not have back pain at any one particular time. This means we would be sending questionnaires to a very large number of people who, at that time, do not have any back pain. It may be more useful to know how many people have had back pain for more than six weeks in the past year. However, the question is more difficult to ask and so the data may not resemble reality as much as asking about current back pain (see previous section). There is often a trade-off between usefulness of the data and how closely the data resembles reality.

It would be excessive to send questionnaires to all the adults in the town, as we are able to answer the research question with fewer questionnaires sent to a sample of the population; however, it is useful to consider it as an ideal to be clear about the difference between this ideal and what we actually do and how the difference influences the results.

The physiotherapist can collect data from a smaller number of people who, as a group, are similar to the population of the town. The best way of ensuring that this **sample** is similar to the whole population is to choose them randomly, that is, with no pattern to how they are chosen **(random sample)**. This can be done relatively simply by giving all the potential participants an identifying number of equal length and then using a **random number** table (a list of numbers with no pattern to it) to guide the selection of the sample. It is possible to calculate the number of people the physiotherapist would need in the sample to be reasonably sure the results from the sample was similar to the result he would obtain from asking everyone. We base this calculation on what is already known about the likely number of people from previous research or a small pilot study. The data from the sample of people gives a precise description of the people in the sample. Using statistical tests it is possible to estimate how likely it is that the answers given by the people in the sample would be the same if the whole population had been asked. Details of calculating sample size, taking samples and statistical tests are found in books on epidemiology (see Further Reading at the end of Chapter 5).

The methods for describing the health of a community have been developed and refined by public health professionals, epidemiologists, social scientists and statisticians and there are excellent books to guide you in this. In consulting these guides, remember that you want to describe the health of the population. These research disciplines have also developed methods aimed at understanding the cause of disease in populations and the effect of health interventions on the health of populations. These approaches are based on the experimental method (see Chapter 1), require attention to other aspects of research design not covered in this book, and the statistics can be more complex.

A great deal of quantitative health-related research uses research designs involving taking a sample of a population for collecting data in order to describe the population. We may undertake this type of research ourselves or our colleagues may do this as part of the wider research endeavour, so we need to understand this research approach. However, when undertaking research for health care practice, we often collect data from within health care. This raises different issues, as discussed below.

Planning data collection from within health care

The overall aim of the physiotherapist's research (Box 8.1) is to find out how many people could potentially benefit from behaviour therapy, so he is particularly interested in people who seek help for their back pain. Perhaps he does not need to know about people with back pain who are not seeking help. The physiotherapist could survey people who have made contact with local health care services with back pain.

To identify these people the physiotherapist would need to know all the local health care services where people seek help. For example, in the UK people with back pain may seek help through their National Health Service (NHS) general practitioners or 'out of hours' services, and from chiropractors, osteopaths, physiotherapists and many other practitioners who are not part of the NHS. Mapping the routes by which people seek help for a particular condition can become a research project in itself and could result in a model of health services as discussed in Chapter 5. The physiotherapist can ask all the health care providers to assist him with his survey, or he may decide to limit data collection to people attending his own clinic.

There are a number of reasons why people with back pain who may benefit from behavioural therapy do not seek help and so be missed out of the physiotherapist's survey. Some people with back pain may have difficulty accessing help for a variety of reasons, including lack of knowledge of the health care service, language, disabilities including hearing, vision and mobility disability and geographical isolation. Others may not seek help as they think there is no treatment available that is likely to help, or seeking help about their back pain may be a lower priority than other health or social issues they may have. However, if as a result of the physiotherapist's research and service innovations the access to therapy changes, more people may seek help than have done so in the past. A survey within health care can quickly become out of date as the people using the health care service and the service itself change and adapt in relation to each other, a process known as **co-evolution**.

If the physiotherapist limits his survey to people attending his clinic he is likely to miss many people with back pain, but he will be able to continue data collection over time. The next section considers issues specific to collecting and using data collected over time.

Collecting data to detect change over time

To detect change over time we need to be able to compare data collected at one point in time with data collected at another point in time. Data therefore needs to be collected in a standard way, and be sensitive enough to distinguish change over the time interval.

Everything in the world is constantly changing, so however careful we are to standardise how we collect data, we will always need to consider whether we really are collecting data about the same thing and in the same way. For example, the meaning or nuance of words changes, what is considered socially acceptable changes, the level of skill in assessment or measurement changes for individuals and across groups of people or professions. Some of these changes can be very subtle and difficult to detect in the short term.

How a person, clinic or community is at one point in time influences how they are at a later point in time. However, the process of data collection can also have influence over time. This may not be a problem if there is a long interval between data collection. However if, for example, someone with back pain is asked to mark their level of pain on a pain scale every day, how they mark the scale on the second day may be influenced by how they marked it the previous day. As only one day has elapsed, they are likely to be able to remember. Asking them to complete the pain scale more frequently, such as four times a day, may reduce their ability to remember their scores, especially if the scores are hidden from them once recorded, using an electronic diary adapted for this purpose (Burton et al., 2007). Other types of data that can be collected frequently from individuals include measures such as blood glucose and blood pressure. For example, monitors are now available that record subcutaneous glucose levels (equivalent to blood glucose) every 5 minutes for 3 days. The use of such technology to record the data automatically minimises the influence of what is recorded at one point in time on what is recorded next time.

The collection of data at frequent times using technology can provide a large amount of data about one individual. Such **time series** data can be analysed for patterns of change. This requires some statistical expertise. The data from one individual can be compared with data from others, looking for similarities and differences in the patterns of change.

Every time-point has duration, however short. The duration of a glucose measurement in the data discussed above is bounded by the measurement before and afterwards. As each measurement value is about the same thing, we can make the assumption that the data are **continuous** and that the duration of each measurement is so small that its duration is irrelevant to the analysis. However, not all time-ordered data is like this. For example, we could note every action taken by a doctor or patient in a consultation in time order. We place a boundary around what we consider a discrete action when we define the data. The boundary of each action is the end of the preceding action and the start of the following action. The database will contain many different types of actions in time order. This type of data cannot be analysed in the same way as the continuous data.

Collecting data over time at relatively frequent intervals about a person, process or organisation is a relatively new field for research related to health, although other disciplines such as mathematics, physics and engineering have developed and refined ways of understanding this data. We shall consider the analysis of time-ordered data later in this book. Before considering analysis, the final section of this chapter discusses the preparation of data for analysis and data exploration.

Data management and preparation for analysis

When planning data management, we need to think through the research process from collecting the data, bringing it together in one place and keeping it in order and secure and preparing for it for analysis. A log should be kept of the whole process, including the consent process for each participant. Consent forms must be kept secure.

It is important to keep everything related to our research, including notes of meetings, notes about decisions in how to collect data and what data to collect, as well as all the original data, for example, survey forms and extracts from clinical notes. During the preparation of data for analysis and the analysis process itself it is important to keep detailed notes of every decision and every action, for example, decisions about how to enter the data into a database, how to indicate data that is missing, early exploratory analysis and our reflections on the process.

We usually analyse data collected using measurement and counting with computer software, unless there is a very small amount of data, for example, brief questionnaires to 15 people who were also interviewed. The data therefore needs to be entered into a database. For each entity studied, for example each person or event or organisation, there should be a way of identifying it (usually a number) in the first column. Each one item is represented by a row of data. What was assessed or measured will be in the columns, for example age, gender, height, weight. In this book we will mostly be considering analysis where we are looking at the rows of data, as this represents what is at the focus of our research, each person, event or organisation. When considered in this way each item of data may be referred to as an **attribute**, as it describes something about the entity being studied. When the columns of data are considered, the very same items of data may be referred to as variables, as the data in the column tells us about how this item of data varies across the group of people or events from which the data was collected. In Chapter 9, analysis focuses on using data items as attributes. However, for describing the people or events to those reading our research, we summarise the data in the columns. This is discussed in the following section.

Data entry needs to be planned carefully as it is time-consuming, so we try to avoid going back to re-enter data. I find it best to have a trial run of entering data for about 10–20 participants, as this way I learn most of the snags and can change the layout of the database. It is best to enter data in the form it was collected. For example, if we ask participants their age, then put the age in the database. For analysis we may decide to group people by age but if we change our minds we have the actual age in the database. Data that is missing because the participant didn't answer a particular question needs to be marked in an agreed way. It is best not to just leave an empty space, as this could indicate that there is data but it has not yet been put in the database. If there is text, for example the answer to a question such as 'What is your main concern about your health?', then the text, as written by the research participant, should go into the database. Later we can decide to code these answers, giving them a label that indicates which answers were similar (see Chapter 7). Often people give more than one answer to this type of question even though it is phrased in such a way that asks for one answer. It is usually best to record all the answers, making extra columns in the database to accommodate them. We then have the choice of analysing only the first answer or all the answers.

It is very easy to make errors when entering data into a database so we need to check our work. Ideally we arrange for someone else to enter at least a portion of the data onto a separate database and then compare the two databases to assess the accuracy of data entry.

Initial exploratory analysis of our quantitative data

The initial stage of analysis of quantitative data involves exploring the data to become familiar with it and checking for missing data and errors. We can also summarise the data in a way that provides a description of what we have studied, the group of people, events, organisations or other things. This section explores the exploration of quantitative data, then in Chapter 9 we consider further analysis of our data, using quantitative and qualitative data together to understand the focus of our research.

Summarising data about a group

Summaries of our quantitative data provide concise descriptions of who or what we studied at the focus of our research. Data summaries are also used to describe things in the frame of our research.

This section begins by considering methods for summarising data, as these methods are familiar to most health professionals before describing how to explore data. Summaries of data can alert us to problems with our data, as discussed below.

We will consider the example of research introduced in Box 8.1, with research data from a survey of people about back pain (see Box 8.2). The physiotherapist can consider the people who returned questionnaires as a group. For this group his main analysis is straightforward as he simply adds up the number of people with back pain. However, he may want to summarise other aspects of his data so that he and those reading his research understand more about this group.

Some data is very easily summarised. For example, data on gender can be summarise as:

Numbers of males	=	20
Number of females	=	21
Total	=	41

If the total number is large (usually over 100), this can also be expressed as a percentage to make it easier for the reader to grasp quickly, but the actual numbers should also be presented. The data can also be expressed as a **ratio**, for example male:female 20:21.

Getting started on research on chronic low back pain and behavioural therapy: quantitative data collection	**Box 8.2**

Health professional role: Physiotherapist with an interest in back pain.

Motivation: To improve the treatment of people with chronic low back pain.

Observation of difference or change: A clinical trial has demonstrated that people with chronic low back pain can benefit from a behavioural therapy.

Overall aim: To provide the behavioural therapy for local patients with low back pain who are most likely to benefit, and to evaluate the impact of this treatment.

Research issue: Behavioural therapy and low back pain.

Research focus: People with chronic low back pain.

Research aim: To describe how many people in the local population have chronic low back pain.

Research question: How many people in the local population have chronic low back pain?

Research data: Survey data from adults, including questions about back pain, gender, age, use of treatments for back pain in the past.

Data about treatments tried for back pain in the past can be summarised as:

Number with no previous treatment	=	4
Number with some previous treatment	=	34
No response to question	=	3
Total	=	41

The physiotherapist could categorise treatments, for example physiotherapy, acupuncture, chiropractor, then summarise the number of people using each treatment (Table 8.2).

As some people used more than one type of treatment, this can be summarised as the number using one, two, three or four or more different types of treatments. This summary would add to the understanding of Table 8.2. These summaries can be done by hand for small **data sets** and with spreadsheet or statistical software

Table 8.2   Number of people who have tried treatments for their back in the past

Treatment category	Number of people using treatment* (total number of people in study = 41)
Physiotherapy	10
Acupuncture	4
Chiropractor	25
No previous treatment	4
No response to question	3

Note: *Some people used more than one treatment.

for larger data sets. These summaries not only tell the reader of the research about the people, but also suggest possible future research, for example, on the combination or sequence of use of treatments by people with back pain.

Data about age can be summarised by finding the centre of the data, that is, the level around which the data is spread. We can calculate the **average** age (**mean**) by adding all the ages and dividing by the number of people: Mean = 54.7 years. However, if there are a few people who are very old or very young (known as **outliers**), the mean may not be near the centre. Instead of the average age we can calculate the **median**, where half the data is greater and half smaller. This gives an age: 38 years. The median is not affected by outliers. It is also important to describe the **range** or spread of age, for example 19–91 years. We return to how to describe the level of the data and its range or spread below, when we discuss exploring the data.

Other familiar methods of summarising data include **pie charts** and **bar graphs**. These can be useful for visualising the data, but need to be used with caution to avoid over- or under-emphasis of particular aspects of the data by making it visual.

Checking for missing data and errors

There are many reasons why data may be missing. For example, for the back pain survey there may be no data for some people because they did not return the survey. Within a returned questionnaire, only some of the questions may be answered. Data may be omitted in error when being entered into the database. When analysing data it is important to understand what is missing. For example, if data on the use of treatments for back pain in the past is missing from a high proportion of questionnaires, then it is difficult to use this data in the analysis. Missing data can be revealed through summaries of the data as described above, and then checks made to see why it is missing. Summaries of data can also reveal errors in the data or data collection. For example, the intention was to collect data from adults, so no age data should be less than 18 years.

Exploring quantitative data about a group

When we summarise data we become more familiar with the data, but there are additional ways of exploring data that stay close to the raw data. These methods may be less familiar to health professionals as they are rarely mentioned in research papers reporting quantitative research. However, they are widely used to explore data to gain an understanding of the level of the data and its spread. They also help in checking for missing data and errors, and underpin the methods of summarising data described above.

A very useful technique for looking for patterns in the data is the **stem and leaf plot**. This can be plotted quickly by hand for small numbers of people or by using a basic statistical software package for large numbers. The advantage of this plot is that it directly represents the raw data. Stem and leaf plots can be used with data such as age, height, weight, blood glucose, or the score from a questionnaire. Figure 8.1 is a stem and leaf plot of age for the group of people with back pain. The plot indicates the spread of ages, in this example from 19 to 91 years old, although most are between 28 and 77 years. The ages 28 and 77 are at the boundary of the main part of the data. The individual aged 91 is known as an outlier as there are no others near that age. Those aged 19 and 20 are also quite a lot younger than the next youngest person and so may also be considered outliers. Many of the people are in their 50s and 60s. The physiotherapist should consider if there is anything strange about the data that might indicate missing data. For example, why is there no one between age 77 and 91 years?

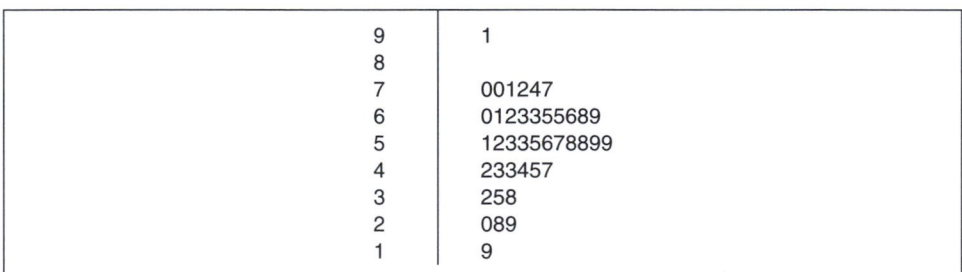

9	1
8	
7	001247
6	0123355689
5	12335678899
4	233457
3	258
2	089
1	9

The left-hand column indicates the decade of the age (20s, 30s etc.) and the right-hand column the years within the decade. A person aged 72 appears in the row with 7 in the left hand column and 2 in the right hand column. There are six people in their 70s, aged 70, 70, 71, 72, 74 and 77 years.

Figure 8.1　Stem and leaf plot of age (years)

The data presented in a stem and leaf plot can be summarised without losing too much detail. We have noted that many of the people in the group are in their 50s and 60s, with fewer in the younger and older age groups. This can be summarised as the level of the data centre or a median as discussed above. The spread of the data can be summarised as the age range of the people in the two middle quarters of the data (the quarter above the median and the quarter below): **Interquartile range** = 22. A **box plot** (see Figure 8.2) includes the median, inter-quartile range, and outliers.

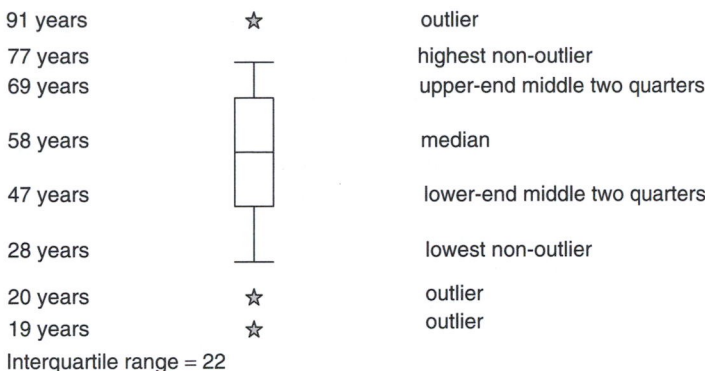

Figure 8.2 **Box plot of data on age (years) from the stem and leaf plot in Figure 8.1**

Although the box plot is a summary of the data, it closely represents the raw data as it includes information about the bunching of the data and its spread, including outliers. It provides much more information than just stating the range of the data (19–91 years). The box plot also summarises the level of the data. If the same data collection was undertaken in a different place, the box plots could be put alongside each other to compare the data without losing detail about the data.

Exploring the data in this way may suggest questions for the next stage of analysis or further research. For example, is the back pain of the 19- and 20-year-old similar to that of the people in their later 20s and older?

Exploring data collected over time

Data collected over time can most easily be explored through the use of **time-lines** or simple **graphs**. Where the data is a sequence of actions or utterances, such as in a health care consultation, each action or utterance can be marked on a timeline. The timeline indicates the direction of the sequence through time. Data from repeated measurements or assessments over time can be represented on a graph. Time is usually represented going from left to right along the horizontal axis, with what is measured at each time point on the vertical axis. For some data, time may be marked along the horizontal axis as clock time (seconds, minutes, hours) or calendar time (days, months, years), for example, for blood glucose measurements. However, we can use other ways of marking time points, such as stages of disease or stages through a process of diagnosis and treatment. Plotting out the data allows us to engage with it more easily than when it is in a database. We can familiarise ourselves with the data, including how it varies over time, and spot where data is missing or where there may be error. Data of repeated measurements or assessments for one person, organisation or other entity that is measured or assessed can also be explored and summarised, using the techniques described above for groups. With time-ordered data, the group is the group of time data points and the summary is of the data for one entity such as a single person.

Exploring quantitative data using the techniques described above helps us become familiar with the data in preparation for further analysis. As we explore the data we check it for missing data and errors, but we also reflect on the patterns in the data in preparation for further analysis.

This chapter has considered data collection using quantitative methods, from defining what the data should be for our research focus through to preparing for analysis and exploring our data. The next chapter of this book considers analysis of data in ways that have particular relevance to health care practice. Although analysis is described in a separate chapter from data collection, it needs to be considered from the very start of designing research.

References

Burton, C., Weller, D. and Sharpe, M. (2007) 'Are electronic diaries useful for symptoms research? A systematic review'. *Journal of Psychosomatic Research*, **62** (5): 553–61.

Dunn, K.M., Jordan, K. and Croft, P.R. (2006) 'Characterizing the course of low back pain: a latent class analysis'. *American Journal of Epidemiology*, **163** (8): 754–61.

Kopec, J.A. (2000) 'Measuring functional outcomes in persons with back pain: a review of back-specific questionnaires'. *Spine*, **25** (24): 3110–14.

Further reading

McColl, E., Jacoby, A., Thomas, L., Soutter, J., Bamford, C., Steen, N., Thomas, R., Harvey, E., Garratt, A. and Boud, J. (2001) 'Design and use of questionnaires: a review of best practice applicable to surveys of health staff and patients'. *Health Technology Assessment*, 5 (31). See http://www. ncchta.org/execsumm/summ531.htm

This review is from a team who have developed and used standard methods of assessing health-related issues for many years.

Erickson, B.H. and Nosanchuk, T.A. (1992) *Understanding Data*, 2nd edition. Oxford: Oxford University Press.

The first section of this book gives a particularly good introduction to exploring and comparing data, including the use of descriptive summaries, stem and leaf plots and box plots.

9   Analysing Data in Research for Health Care Practice

There are many ways of analysing data relevant to health and health care. This chapter introduces an approach to analysis which is within the expertise of health care professionals and where the results can be directly used for health care practice. Underlying the approach is the constant comparison of data both qualitative and quantitative. The approach emphasises understanding as a whole the people, events or interactions at the focus of research before considering comparison of the details in the data. The chapter cautiously goes on to explore how further analysis, requiring some expert research skills, has the potential for increasing our understanding of how to tailor health interventions for individuals in terms of the nature and timing of the intervention.

This chapter describes how to analyse our research data so that the results of our research feed as directly as possible into our health care practice. This approach to analysis draws on data of all types to understand the focus of our research. The analysis involves constant comparison of data to discern what is different and what is the same. From this we can become clearer about the nature of the focus of our research and the possible ways of **classifying** it that are recognisable to health care professionals and useful in clinical practice. The analysis can also suggest how the nature and timing of interventions can be tailored to the diversity of people, events or interactions at the focus of our research.

Clarity about the focus of our research is essential for designing our research, as discussed throughout this book. Clarity about the focus of our research remains essential when considering analysis. Our research could focus on people, events, organisations, the local community, interactions between people. For each research focus we could draw on many different types of data. Box 9.1 suggests how we get started on research for health care practice, the range of possible alternative research foci and the variety of sources of data that could be used in research about one research focus (**triangulation**).

<table>
<tr><td>

Getting started on research for health care practice, the range of possible alternative research foci and the range of sources of data for a research focus

</td><td>

Box 9.1

</td></tr>
</table>

Health professional role: Providing health advice, therapy and care to people, or planning and managing the services that provide this.

Motivation: To improve the health and wellbeing of the people in the local population served by our health care service.

Observation of difference or change: Health and wellbeing of our local population, or those who attend the health care service, or the health service itself, is different from in the past or in a different place or compared to what it could be according to research literature.

Overall aim: To understand what is happening for our patients and our health care service so we can work out how to improve the health and wellbeing of our patients and the provision of health care.

Research issue: Health and health care.

Research focus: Range of possible alternative foci:

- local community
- people attending our health care service
- the health care service
- individual patients
- pathways of care for individual patients
- interaction between individual patients and people working in the health care service
- interaction between people working in the health care service
- an event or happening

Sources of data: The variety of data sources that can be used for a research focus:

- observation
- interviews
- group data collection, such as focus groups
- existing data, such as clinical and administrative data and survey data
- surveys
- documents

This chapter initially looks at how to use our data to describe as a whole each entity at the focus of our research. For example, if our research focus is individual patients, we describe each individual patient on whom we have data. If our research focus is an event, we describe each event on which we have data. Each entity **emerges** from the interaction of many different factors within it and beyond it (**emergence**). Each is recognisable as similar to others, in that we recognise it as the same type of thing, for example, a person living with diabetes, an event such as an emergency admission to hospital or an interaction between people, such as a health care consultation. However, each one is slightly different from every other one. The process of using our data to describe each entity as a whole in relation to our research aim involves identifying what is of particular relevance to our research about each one, and what is similar or different about it compared to each of the others. The results of this analysis can reveal what is happening and why in a way that is directly relevant to health care, and the analysis provides examples of the entity, such as people, events or interactions that are recognisable to health professionals from their clinical work.

Describing each entity as a whole can be undertaken relatively easily where the number is relatively small; for example, 15 young people with diabetes or 12 emergency admissions. To understand how to tailor health care interventions for the diversity of people we encounter in clinical practice requires analysis of data from larger numbers, and is discussed in later sections of the chapter.

The approach to analysis described here differs from that described in many books on research methods but draws on the expertise of other approaches, has many processes in common and can be used alongside other approaches. The list of Further Reading at the end of this chapter and Chapters 7 and 8 includes books that discuss data analysis.

Using data to describe the focus of our research as a whole

In this section we will consider how to describe, as a whole, examples of a number of different research foci. In discussing each research focus, we will consider different issues for the analysis, but all the issues discussed have relevance for all research foci and so need to be considered whatever your research focus. The first example is perhaps the most familiar, that of an individual person. We then consider analysis of data from research focused on an event, where there is just one source of data about each event and where there is more than one source of data. The final example is analysis of data where the research focus is the interaction between people. Analysis of data about organisations as a whole has been refined within social sciences and is known as case studies (Yin, 2003). Similarly, communities can be described as case studies. Examples are not included here.

Using data where the research focus is individual people

When seeking to describe individual people as a whole, we have to make decisions about what to include in our description. The aim of the research and research question guides this. The availability of data may limit what we can include. However, the people themselves can contribute to this analysis. We will consider research focusing on young people with diabetes (Box 9.2). This is similar to that considered in Box 3.1, but here the research focus is the young people rather than the clinic.

Getting started on research focused on young people living with diabetes	**Box 9.2**

Health professional role: Nurse specialising in diabetes.

Motivation: Improve the wellbeing and life expectancy of young people living with diabetes, including reducing admissions to hospital due to diabetes being out of control by providing better health care through the diabetes clinic.

Observation of difference or change: Compared to children and older adults, more young people miss their appointments at the diabetes clinic.

Overall aim: To improve the control of diabetes among young people.

Research issue: *Young people, diabetes.*

Research focus: Young people living with diabetes.

Research aim: To understand why young people living with diabetes do not attend the clinic.

Research question: Why do young people living with diabetes fail to attend their clinic appointments?

Research data: Interviews with young people living with diabetes, data about diabetes kept by the young people, such as blood glucose measurements and insulin doses, and data from their clinic records held at the clinic and by their general practitioner.

The nurse will have prepared and coded the interviews as discussed in Chapter 7 and explored quantitative data as discussed in Chapter 8. The nurse is therefore very familiar with the data and has begun the process of comparing the data from different young people and noting her thoughts. The next step is to prepare a summary of each young person based on all the available data about that person. Each summary should be developed in a similar way so that they can be compared.

The nurse could prepare a template for a structured summary that includes what she thinks is important in relation to diabetes, including age, gender, educational attainment, who they live with, how long they have had diabetes, current treatment, level of blood glucose control and attitude to the clinic. She could then fill in the template from the data. However, what health professionals think is important may be very different from what young people think is important. The summary would more closely reflect what the young people themselves thought was important if the nurse developed the structure of the summary from reading the interview data and comparing the interviews of the young people, teasing out the issues that they have in common and where there are differences in relation to the research aim. We might have several drafts of our template before we reach a final version. Once we have identified these key issues we can then systematically go through the data for each young person again and complete the structured summary. If the nurse has designed the research to involve the young people as in action research (see Chapter 4), we could ask each teenager to collaborate on writing a summary that describes themselves, their diabetes and their clinic attendance. Through the process of developing these summaries of the individuals, the differences between them in relation to attendance at the clinic are likely to become clear. This analysis may be sufficient to answer the research question.

In the next section of this chapter we discuss further analysis, particularly if there is a large number of people in the study. The analysis could include developing a classification of the young people, a process discussed later in this section. However, we first consider the dimension of time.

The dimension of time in analysis

The young people at the focus of the research are changing all the time. The summaries are about how they are at the time of collecting data. Their past influences how they are now, and in this sense data about their past becomes data about how they are in the present time. As discussed in Chapter 5, the present time has duration, and how we define its boundaries depends on the focus, aim and design of our research. For young people living with diabetes, it may be possible to discern phases or stages in their illness. For example, from interview data it may be possible to define the present time as a phase. This may have rather unclear boundaries, or the interviewee may provide a clear time point for the boundary such as 'since I started on four times a day insulin'. Other data may also help define the present phase, for example, a change in the number of admissions to hospital for hypoglycaemia. Within the present phase the interviewee continues to change, but arguably less than the change between phases. I have found it possible to summarise the pattern of change within the current phase, based on interview data with people living with diabetes (Griffiths et al., 2007). These summaries were in terms of stability or chaos, the use of routine and the degree to which individuals tested out the effect of doing things that could upset diabetes, such as a different diet or change in routines of daily life (see Box 9.3 for examples).

<table>
<tr><td>Examples of the current pattern of change
for three individuals living with diabetes</td><td>Box 9.3</td></tr>
</table>

- Chaotic, almost no steadying effects except some use of routine.
- Stable, with almost no testing out of things that could potentially reduce stability (e.g. avoided holidays and eating out).
- Mostly stable but with ongoing testing of possibilities, occasionally leading to temporary instability (e.g. trying new restaurant, going on holiday, flexible work pattern).

The summaries of the pattern of change, or **dynamic**, drew on interview data and are limited to the present time as the data is about the present time. Later in this chapter we will consider the analysis of data where the data has a sequence over time due to the nature of the data or how it was collected. However, in this section we now consider summarising other types of research focus.

Using data where the research focus is an event with a single data source for each event

Where the focus of our research is an event, we may have data from observation, interviews and documents. Here we discuss how we can use data to describe events with a single source of data. We then consider analysis of data from many sources about a single event.

This example was discussed in Box 4.3, a study of women living with diabetes and pregnancy. Whilst undertaking the interviews, the midwife altered the focus of her research to the event of conception when living with diabetes (Box 9.4), with data about the women's lives more generally forming the frame of the research.

The interviews provide one person's perspective on the event of conception. The midwife reads the account of each event very carefully and then, staying close to the interview account, writes a summary of each event. The summary can include extracts from the text of the interviews as in Box 9.5. Data about one event is compared with other events reported by the same woman, and with events reported by other women. As the midwife makes these comparisons she considers what it is about one conception that is similar or different to other conceptions. She then attempts to classify the events based on the similarities and differences between the women that seem to be of particular relevance to the research aim. In this example, each conception event could be classified as a) one where women had taken some preparatory steps before conception, such as increasing their diabetes monitoring or taking folic acid; or b) events where there had been no preparation (Griffiths et al., 2008). Summaries of the

Box 9.4	**Getting started on research about conception for women living with diabetes: data from interviews**

Health professional role: Midwife working in hospital.

Motivation: Wanting to reduce the number of women living with diabetes who experience the distress of a serious problem with pregnancy, such as still birth or congenital malformation.

Observation of difference or change: Published evidence that women with good control of their diabetes on entering pregnancy have fewer pregnancy problems than those with less good control.

Overall aim: To improve pregnancy outcome for women living with diabetes through improved blood glucose control at conception and in early pregnancy.

Research issue: Diabetes control, conception and early pregnancy.

Research focus: Conception for women living with diabetes.

Research aim: To understand the experience of women living with diabetes at the time of conception and early pregnancy.

Research data: Interviews with women who have been or are pregnant and live with diabetes.

events for one woman are presented in Box 9.5. The second pregnancy can be classified as 'with no preparation' and the third as 'with preparation'. For her first pregnancy, the woman seems to have made some preparation, but this is not as clear as pregnancy three. The detail given in the summary is sufficient for the reader to understand this subtlety. Including extracts from the interview clarifies for the reader that the summaries are based very closely on the text. Health professionals will recognise these summaries of becoming pregnant as similar to those reported by women they encounter in clinical practice, including the summary that was difficult to classify. The classification of events as those 'with no preparation' and 'with preparation' is helpful for analysis, but we need to remember that it is a product of the research process. There is no clear boundary between the categories. Presenting summaries of events that are at the boundary of the classification is important as it enables health professionals to understand how the research relates to their clinical practice.

Summaries of the event at the focus of research: conception and pregnancy while living with diabetes	Box 9.5

Summaries of one interviewee's accounts of conception and living with diabetes

1st pregnancy: Wanted to become pregnant, came off contraceptive pill. 'Well I wanted to so I sort of planned for it but I didn't do any of the tablets or anything like that.' Felt very uncertain about what to expect. 'I think I just didn't have a clue. The first time was sort of like I was very young and I didn't even know what to expect really. I just went along with it'. No complications, blood sugars well controlled.

Outcome: Live birth.

2nd pregnancy: Wasn't using contraception. 'I think I just sort of ran out of pills and so it was my own fault.' Did not control or check sugars as much as previous pregnancy. 'It didn't go on for very long and so ... I can't remember how many weeks I was because that wasn't planned and I didn't do as much as I would have done, or I should have done probably [...] I wasn't as controlled as I was with the first pregnancy.'

Outcome: Miscarriage.

3rd pregnancy: Saw GP after decision to come off contraceptive pill to check everything was OK before becoming pregnant. 'I saw him when I first came off the pill just to sort of check that everything was alright and he did all the blood tests and that [...] so there was somebody there saying "It's alright"'. No complications with pregnancy so far. 'My sugars have been fine and I had a scan it was just a perfect weight and I know with my last one, she was three kilos, so she wasn't a big baby and so that will remain good.' Feels confident and happy with the pregnancy so far.

Note: phrases in inverted commas are quotations from interview.

(Griffiths et al., 2008)

The interview data from women living with diabetes will include a great deal of other data about themselves, how they manage their diabetes and their experience of health care. This data is about the frame of the research and not the focus. This data is used in a number of ways. Data about the women can be summarised so readers of the research know enough about them to know whether the research is likely to apply to women they see in clinical practice. This may include age, educational attainment, length of time they have had diabetes, and can be summarised as described in Chapter 8. The data can also be examined code by code to understand what might be making a difference to the events at the focus of the research. This may suggest what health care interventions may be appropriate.

Using data where the research focus is an event with many data sources for each event

To describe events that are rare or unpredictable, we can use data collected from the different participants in the event as direct observation is difficult. For example, to understand what happened when someone was suddenly taken ill, we could interview all the people involved and examine records written about it. Where a series of events occurs over a long period of time, such as consultations between a patient and their regular health professional, it is difficult to observe these interactions, but we can collect data from the different people involved, either looking back over the time period or at intervals throughout the time period. We can compare what the different data sources tell us about the events. We are not seeking to find some agreement about what happened, rather we seek the similarities and contrasts in order to understand more about the events at the focus of our research.

This approach to analysis of an event has similarities with the critical incident technique. The aim of this technique is to understand an event, usually an event when something went wrong or had the potential to go wrong, identify issues that contributed to the event and then work out how to tackle each issue so that further problematic events are avoided. The aim of the technique is to improve processes rather than to understand the event as a whole.

To explore the analysis of an event from many perspectives, we will use the example in Box 4.5 of the nurse working with people living with chronic obstructive pulmonary disease (COPD). However, as she developed and designed her research, the nurse adjusted her research focus to admission to hospital (see Box 9.6).

Box 9.6	**Developing research focused on the events leading up to admission to hospital with an exacerbation of COPD**

Health professional role: Specialist nurse working with individuals living with chronic obstructive pulmonary disease (COPD).

Motivation: To improve the life quality of those living with COPD.

Observation of difference or change: Wide variation in the number of times patients with apparently similar disease are admitted to hospital with exacerbation of their COPD.

> *Overall aim:* To reduce the amount of time those living with COPD spend in hospital with exacerbation of their disease.
>
> *Research issue:* COPD and health care services.
>
> $\downarrow$
>
> *Research focus:* The events leading up to hospital admission with an exacerbation of COPD.
>
> *Research aim:* To understand what happens leading up to a hospital admission with an exacerbation of COPD.
>
> *Research data:* Interviews with everyone who was involved in the events leading up to admission, including patient, carers and health professionals, the clinical records of the ambulance crew who transported the patient to hospital and the clinical notes in the emergency department.

All the data relating to one event or linked events is treated as a set of data. The data can be explored and coded as discussed in Chapter 7. Having become familiar with the data, the nurse summarises the accounts of what happened from the different data sources. Each of these summaries should be labelled with, for example, the role of the person from whom the data was collected, a brief summary of their involvement and the type of data (such as clinical records, interview data). As events, even short ones, have duration, data can be summarised on a timeline, marking what happened and when. The timeline should include all data about what happened: actions taken, decisions made, advice sought, the patient becoming aware of new symptoms or problems with treatment and what was happening around them. Where possible, the timeline should include the date and time of each action or event, but where this is not possible, some indication of when it was relative to other things happening. Timelines can be written during an interview, as discussed in Chapter 7.

With a timeline for each person involved in the event, the timelines can be compared, noting where they are consistent and where they are not. As we make this comparison we need to consider what the consistencies and contrasts suggest about the event and the people involved, and make a note so that we can check out these ideas in further analysis. From our comparison of timelines we can write a summary of the event that is more than any one person's perception of the event, including where there are inconsistencies in accounts. These summaries may suggest what is happening during these events that would not be revealed from the analysis of one person's account.

Similar timelines can be written for data collected about a series of events happening over a long time where the data is available. However, if the data is from interviews, for example from a doctor and their patient about their encounters over time, the interviews may not give sufficient data for a timeline. The coded data can still be compared theme by theme, looking for consistencies and inconsistencies between the two accounts.

It is tempting to think that if the nurse observed the events at the focus of her research she could provide a better description of what happened as a whole. However, it would be very difficult to collect data about everything that happened and everything that could have made a difference to what happened. For example, how someone responds to a crisis may be influenced by experiences in the past as well as immediate events. It would be difficult to know how far to go back in time and how many people and organisations to include in our data collection in our attempt to collect data about everything that directly or indirectly influenced what happened. As discussed in Chapter 5, the data collection method we use acts to place a boundary around the research focus.

The people involved in the events act as filters on the data. They may not have noticed things, may have forgotten them or not reported them because they didn't want to or because they didn't think they were significant. When writing notes or talking about an event, people reconstruct what happened for their audience. For example, clinical notes are written for other health professionals and health care administrators, and potentially for other people such as the patient or legal advisors. When people talk about an event in a research interview they reconstruct the event in the way they want to for the researcher, or think the researcher wants them to. This limits the data to some extent, but the way the data is presented tells us something about how the event was perceived. For example, someone for whom it was a crisis will talk about it very differently from someone for whom it was a relatively minor event, and different again from someone for whom it was part of routine work. The filtering of the data itself becomes data that is useful for describing and understanding the event.

Using data where the focus of the research is an interaction between people

The final example of analysis to describe as a whole the focus of the research considers interaction between people. The process of analysis is described to cover issues not discussed in the above examples.

We will discuss the example introduced in Box 2.6, of the manager interested in follow-up consultations in general practice and developed further in Box 9.7. She has now focused on the content of consultations and has video recordings for analysis. Her first step has been to look at all the consultations, immersing herself in the data. However, she has not transcribed or coded the consultations in any way.

From her own life experience, the manager knows that when she interacts with people she can characterise the interaction as a whole and that she changes through the process of interaction. For example, she may feel inspired by a stimulating conversation with a colleague or worn out after a difficult encounter with a patient. The manager could start her analysis by classifying each consultation, looking at each one as a whole including what changed for the people in

Developing research on the use of e-mail for follow-up consultations in general practice	Box 9.7

Health professional role: Manager of a general medical practice.

Motivation: For follow-up consultations in general practice, increase patient convenience and reduce doctor time.

Observation of difference or change: Reports of use of e-mail for consultations in family medicine in North America.

Overall aim: To improve the efficiency of general practice, particularly for those needing follow-up for chronic health conditions.

Research issue: Follow-up consultations and e-mail.

Research focus: Interactions between doctors and patients in follow-up consultations.

Research aim: To understand which planned follow-up consultations could be replaced by e-mail.

Research question: Which planned follow-up consultations could potentially be replaced by e-mail?

Research data: Video recordings of planned follow-up consultations between patients and doctors.

it. The classification could be: those that seem to be of a type that could be replaced by e-mail and those that could not. This would provide a way of counting how many consultations could be replaced by e-mail.

Classifying the consultations sounds easy, but needs care. When we look at data, we tend to see patterns in the data that we expect or that are familiar to us. We need to check out what we think we perceive through further examination of the data, comparing and contrasting data and asking a colleague to undertake the classification too. The manager and her colleague would initially classify a few consultations, for example five each, then discuss their classification including why they classified them as they did and resolve any differences in classification. They should keep notes of what they notice about the consultation, why they classify the consultations as they do and what they discuss about the classifications. They may change the number of categories, for example, adding a category for consultations where e-mail replacement could put patient safety at risk. Each category also needs a description which is detailed enough for other people to be able to understand the classification. Throughout this process the manager and her colleague need to keep their research question in mind. They want to distinguish consultations that could be replaced by e-mail from those that could not, rather than develop a more general classification system. Every consultation will be slightly different from every other one. Some will be difficult to classify as they seem so different from the others, and some will fall on the boundary between categories. These are important insights that are part of the analysis. The overall aim for this research is to improve the efficiency of follow up in general practice. If the analysis suggests that it is not easy to distinguish which consultations can be replaced by e-mail, the manager may have to consider other options for improvement.

The research results would consist of a description of the classification system, including the definition of each category, the classification of each consultation, including illustrations and extracts from the data (see Box 9.5) and a description of why the consultations were classified in that way. Below are two examples of category definitions.

Follow-up consultations for a 'simple' health issue that could potentially be replaced by e-mail

The agenda may or may not have been previously agreed by patient and doctor. The impact of the health issue on the patient's life is limited (e.g. acute infection). Patient knowledge about the health problem does not affect management. The doctor may or may not have seen the patient before.

Follow-up consultation for a 'complex' health issue that could potentially be replaced by e-mail

The agenda has been previously agreed by patient and doctor (e.g. impact of increased dose of medication). The impact of the health issue on the patient's life is considerable (e.g. diabetes). Patient knowledge of the health issue is considerable, and this is of importance in its management. The doctor has seen the patient recently.

By taking each consultation as a whole and classifying it, the manager has included within the classification the interactions between doctor and patient giving rise to the character of each consultation. To develop her categories the manager has noted the similarities and differences in the patterns of interaction between the doctor and patient. There may be identifiable patterns of interaction that form a small part of the whole interaction but which make a big difference to how the consultation develops overall. Identifying these key patterns might make it easier to classify consultations, and even suggest a way of predicting in advance how consultations are likely to turn out. This is considered in the next section of this chapter. However, it may be that examining the detailed patterns of interaction may not tell us more than we can discern from looking at the consultation as a whole, and could tell us less about what we want to know.

In this section we have considered how to describe the focus of our research as a whole through comparing and contrasting people, events or interactions, or comparing and contrasting different accounts of an event. Through this process of analysis it is possible to develop new classifications directly relevant to the research aim, focus and questions and recognisable to health professionals. The analysis provides clues as to what is happening that was not apparent before. This may also suggest how to tailor health care interventions for individuals. However, taking this further requires comparison of larger numbers of entities, as discussed in the next section.

Analysis for understanding the tailoring of health care interventions

In this section we consider the comparison of large numbers of entities. We will consider the study of young people living with diabetes which was presented Box 9.2. As an interview study, this is likely to involve small numbers of people. We now discuss how to include larger numbers of young people whilst using a similar approach to analysis.

In the process of developing the summaries of the young people, as described above, the nurse identified the aspects of these young people that seem to make a difference to their clinic attendance. This may include characteristics of the young people themselves, how they relate to their family or how they relate to the health care service, particularly the clinic. Each of these is then coded in the interview data. The nurse then takes the coded data about each of these key aspects from all the young people and through comparison develops a classification. For example, one key aspect may be the way young people describe how they relate to their doctor. By comparing these descriptions she may find they can be categorised in three groups, each with a different style of relationship: 'faith with doubt', 'unengaged' or 'partnership' (Griffiths et al., 2007). The nurse then classifies each young person. Each key aspect that is developed into a classification is known as an attribute of the individual. The same process can be used for all key aspects the nurse has noted, so each young person ends up with a number of attributes. These attributes are another way of summarising what we know from the data about each young person. A young person's attributes should convey similar information as their structured summary, but the attributes have been defined. The process of defining the attributes, so that there is a limited number of categories, means detail is lost; for example, detail of where an aspect is difficult to classify. An example of attributes and their categories is given in Table 9.1.

Table 9.1   Attributes of people in relation to diabetes and attribute categories (Griffiths et al., 2007)

	Attribute categories (numbers refer to category numbers used in the rows about the six individuals in Table 9.2)			
Attributes (numbers refer to numbers in top row of Table 9.2)	0	1	2	3
1 Sense of control over diet	Absent	Present		
2 Knowledge of diabetes	Poor	Good		
3 Type of relationship with health professional	Unengaged	Faith with doubt	Partnership	
4 Confidence and contentment about medication and health professional	Uneasy	Moderately confident and content	Confident and content	
5 Use of routine to control diet with loss of other things requiring flexibility	Little	Moderate	High	
6 Sense of support	Sense of being alone	Some support but not enough	Sense of being supported	
7 Style of use of information	Erratic	Conservative	Consistent	Experimental

It is important to keep detailed notes of each step of this analysis and to review whether the analysis stays true to the data. It is also important to include only key aspects that the data suggests make a difference to at least some young people. Attributes can include other data such as age, gender, education, income, occupation, and data from sources other than interviews such as questionnaire scores or laboratory test results if these are relevant to the focus of the research. The nurse has to judge whether the attribute is important for the research based on the data. Interview data can assist her in deciding whether data from other sources may be relevant as the young person may mention how they perceive and use this information. If we want to include large numbers of young people in our study, we can develop questions for a survey based on the attributes developed from an interview study. Researchers using surveys for other approaches to analysis, such as epidemiology, undertake qualitative data collection to inform the development of their survey.

The pattern of attributes for each teenager can be compared to that for each other teenager. As an example, Table 9.2 presents the attributes of six people living with diabetes from a published study (Griffiths et al., 2007).

All the participants have a different combination of attribute categories, which is not surprising given the small number of participants. If there were large numbers of people there may be participants with the same pattern of attributes. However, there are interesting differences and similarities between the participants:

• Participant A is different from the other participants for all but two attributes (5 and 7).

• For the remaining participants, attributes 1 and 2 are the same and so do not help distinguish between participants.

- Participants B and C have attributes 3 and 4 in common, but differ on attributes 5, 6 and 7.

- Participants D, E and F have attributes 3, 4 and 6 in common, but differ on attributes 5 and 7.

Table 9.2   Comparison of attributes of people living with diabetes (Griffiths et al., 2007)

id	1	2	3	4	5	6	7
A	0	0	0	0	1	0	0
B	1	1	1	1	2	0	1
C	1	1	1	1	1	1	2
D	1	1	2	2	0	2	3
E	1	1	2	2	1	2	2
F	1	1	2	2	2	2	0

id: participant A–F

If these patterns of attributes can be related to an outcome relevant to the focus of the research, it may reveal that people reach the same outcome but with different patterns of attributes. For example, consider that participants B, C and F have outcome X and participant D and E have outcome Y and outcome X is the preferred outcome. This suggests that people can have very different patterns of attributes and have the same outcome, as although participants B and C have some common attributes, F has a very different pattern of attributes (apart from attributes 1 and 2).

Studying the patterns may suggest how interventions can be tailored to different people. For example, for D and E to be more like one of the participants with outcome X, they would each change only two attributes to be like participant F. However, D and E would need to change three or more attributes to become like participants B or C. The intervention needed for participants D and E for their attributes to become more like those of B and C would be very different to one aimed at making them more like F. There is also participant A to consider, who seems very different from the rest of the group and would perhaps benefit from a very different approach in health care.

With larger numbers of participants, we may find a group of participants with very similar attributes relevant to the research focus where an intervention is likely to be useful, and another group with a different pattern of attributes who may benefit from a different intervention to achieve the same outcome. The comparisons can be undertaken by hand when there are small numbers of individuals. However, analysis of large numbers in this way would benefit from computer analysis using appropriate software. There is no consensus yet on the best way of doing this, but **cluster analysis** is a method that may be appropriate and is available with many of the common statistical packages. Cluster analysis compares each of the rows of data in a data set with each other row and groups together in a cluster those that are most like each other. 'Qualitative Comparative Analysis' is the term used for this analysis approach for relatively small numbers of individuals (see Resources). The analysis software undertakes the comparisons, but we have to decide what data is relevant for the analysis and interpret the results. These judgements are based on what we already know about the research focus and what the data suggests is important.

When using computer analysis, it is tempting to include a large number of attributes. However, this is unlikely to reveal patterns of similarity and difference relevant to the research aim, focus and question. The comparative method described above is only appropriate when the data used is of relevance to a carefully refined research focus.

As discussed in Chapter 8, the items of data we have referred to as the attributes of each person are the same items of data that can be used as variables if the nurse wanted to explore the data about the whole group of young people. There are also methods for comparing the pattern of variables across the group with outcome, as discussed in Chapter 5. Some of these methods lose the detail about the diversity of pathways to the same outcome although innovative statistical methods are able to include this.

Analysis for understanding the timing of health care interventions

This section considers the analysis of data with a particular focus on the dimension of time. To explore this we will consider the analysis of health care consultations in terms of the sequence of actions or utterances. We will then consider how this analysis could be used for other types of time-ordered data. This approach aims to understand how the timing of interventions impacts on what then happens and has the potential to clarify how the timing of interventions could be tailored to improve health outcome.

We will consider the example presented in Box 9.8. The research data is video recordings of consultations collected by an educator of general practitioners. The research aim is to understand how to improve the effectiveness of consultations in general practice for patients with chronic illness. The educator has coded and explored the data as described in Box 9.8 and discussed in Chapter 8. In this section we consider the analysis in terms of the sequence of items of data on the timeline.

The educator is interested in how the time ordering of different types of utterance or action in the interaction between doctor and patient influences how the interaction develops, for example, who initiates the interaction and the type of initial response.

The codes for actions and utterances could be used as attributes to characterise individual consultations, as described earlier in this chapter, in order to identify the combination of actions and utterances in a consultation that leads to enabling

<table>
<tr><td colspan="1">Analysing data from recordings of follow-up consultations in general practice</td><td>Box 9.8</td></tr>
</table>

Health professional role: Educator of general medical practitioners.

Motivation: Increase patient's confidence in their ability to manage their chronic illness; increase patient convenience and reduce doctor time.

Observation of difference or change: Some health care consultations enable people to manage their health problems more than others (Howie et al., 1999).

Overall aim: To improve the effectiveness of general practice, particularly for those with chronic health conditions.

Research issue: Consultations for chronic health conditions.

Research focus: The timing of doctor talk or actions in consultations with patients for chronic health conditions.

Research aim: To understand how the timing of doctor talk or communication can be improved for more effective consultations.

Research question: How does the timing of doctor's talk or actions impact on the development of the consultation?

Research data: Video recordings of consultations between patients with chronic health conditions and their doctors.

Research data coding and exploratory analysis: Each action or utterance in the consultation is coded. Each code has a standard definition. Types of codes include greetings, type of question asked (open or closed), communication of empathy, giving information, technical skill used, prescribing, closing the consultation. The timing of each utterance or action is noted (Roter and Larson 2002). The actions and utterances are then displayed on a timeline in the order in which they occur.

For each consultation, the patient has scored how enabled they feel from the consultation (Howie et al., 1999). This score is used to classify the consultations as effective or not effective in enabling patients to manage their chronic illness.

consultations and those that do not. However, the codes for actions and utterances have a sequence, so analysis could explore the order in which the codes occur, not just whether or not they occur. To explore this approach further, let us consider a simplified example of coding. Imagine the educator has used five codes, A B C D and E, in coding his data. A consultation could be represented by: B D C D A D E. Table 9.3 shows four consultations coded in this way, along with their classification as enabling or not.

The example in Table 9.3 is very simplified in terms of the number of different codes and the number of coded sections in each consultation. Notice that every consultation has one B and one E. If B is a greeting and E is a farewell, we would expect to see them in just about every consultation, so these codes do not help us distinguish between consultation patterns.

Table 9.4 shows the same set of data simplified. With so little data, removing B and E makes little difference to seeing patterns in the data by eye. However, in a real data set with hundreds of codes for each consultation, removing codes that are not contributing to distinguishing between consultations can make analysis much easier. Removing codes, however, should be undertaken after careful consideration of the research question, what the codes represent, what is already known about the research issue and an initial analysis of at least part of the data.

Table 9.3 Example of coding and classification of four simplified doctor–patient consultations

	Codes	Classification
1	B D C D A D E	Enabling
2	B C C D C A E	Not enabling
3	B D C A C A E	Enabling
4	B A C D C A E	Not enabling

Table 9.4 Codes and classification of four simplified doctor–patient consultations: codes of the same type and position in the sequence have been removed

	Codes	Classification
1	D C D A D	Enabling
2	C C D C A	Not enabling
3	D C A C A	Enabling
4	A C D C A	Not enabling

In each of the four consultations in Table 9.4 there is a combination of codes D C and A. By comparing consultations, both by the codes they contain and by the sequence of the codes, we can see one difference between the consultations that are enabling and those that are not. Only enabling consultations have D in the first position and C in the second position of the sequence of codes. The other consultations include D and C, but not in this position in the sequence. This finding would suggest that doctors should consider ensuring the actions or utterances D and C occur after the greetings in a consultation. This pattern can be spotted by eye in our simplified data. With large data sets this requires computer software that can sift through the data looking for sequences that are the same.

The analysis process looking for similar sequences was initially developed and used for the analysis of genetic code. It can be used in an undirected way, sorting through the data looking for any sequences that are the same. The analysis software identifies the sequences but doesn't tell us what they mean. If we are interested in particular sequences, the analysis can be directed to look for these sequences or those that are similar. The use of **sequence analysis** in health science and social science is too new to be sure how useful it will be. It may reveal nothing more than we can discern by looking at each consultation as a whole, or it might bring novel understanding about the timing of what we do as health care professionals.

Our simplified consultations all appear to be the same length, but in reality they would vary. We have also not considered the duration of each of the coded sections (D lasting 5 seconds may have a different impact from D lasting 30 seconds – I have not suggested what D represents). This detail could potentially be included in the coding of actions and utterances if this was thought to be important. For example, each code could have sub-codes for short, medium and long duration. However, the more different codes and sub-codes there are, the more difficult the analysis and the less likely we are to find any patterns in common. There is a balance to be found between trying to incorporate details in the coding and keeping it relatively simple for analysis. These judgements can only be made based on what we already know about the focus of the research and what seems to be important, based on our exploration of the data.

Time-ordered data about one aspect of a person such as blood glucose, can be analysed for patterns of change. Although each data item is about the same thing, the value varies across time and so analysis focuses on the sequence of these values. From what we know about glucose metabolism, we would expect the glucose value at one time point to have some influence on the value of glucose at the next time point. As the length of time between the time points increases, we would expect the influence to be less. However, the pattern of change over a number of preceding measurements may have more influence on a particular glucose value than the value of one preceding measurement. As blood glucose is continuously changing, any particular glucose value soon becomes part of the pattern of measurements preceding a future value. Understanding how the evolving pattern of change of blood glucose influences subsequent blood glucose levels, and the impact of diet, exercise and insulin doses, has the potential to inform the tailoring and timing of decisions made by people living with diabetes in controlling their blood sugar (Holt, 2002).

The approaches to analysis discussed in this section are relatively new to health-related research, but they have the potential to help us understand how the timing or sequence of interventions may influence health outcome.

Conclusion

When we think of analysis we tend to think of teasing out the details of our data, hoping that the closer we look the more we will find out. However, by looking at the details we may miss seeing what emerges from the details. The approach to analysis suggested in this chapter starts with what emerges from the details, the person as a whole, an event as a whole, or the whole of an interaction between people. Through describing each example of what we are studying while comparing it to others, we can gain new understanding. The process of describing while comparing also enables us to develop classifications that are directly relevant to our research aim and recognisable to other health care professionals. This approach to analysis can be undertaken by health care professionals who bring to the analysis a critical mind but does not require the expertise of specialist researchers. In research for health care practice, this may be as far as we need to go with analysis as the implications for health care practice may be clear.

This chapter has also considered analysis that looks at the details of our data, as these methods of analysis have the potential for increasing our understanding of how to tailor health interventions for individuals in terms of their nature and timing. These methods of analysis are not easy to implement and may require specialist research expertise. However, they also require an understanding of the research focus and an ability to explore the data and stay close to the data in analysis. Health professionals can offer these skills to an interdisciplinary research team, and leave the specialist analysis skills to other experts. It is not yet clear what will be gained by this approach to analysis, but increasing our understanding of how to tailor health care interventions to individuals will allow patients and health professionals to make better use of evidence from clinical trials.

References

Griffiths, F., Anton, N., Chow, E., van Royen, P. and Bastiaens, H. (2007) 'Understanding the diversity and dynamics of living with diabetes: a feasibility study focusing on the case'. *Chronic Illness*, 3: 29–45.

Griffiths. F., Lowe, P., Boardman, F., Ayre, C. and Gadsby, R. (2008) 'Becoming pregnant: exploring the perspectives of women living with diabetes'. *British Journal of General Practice*, 58: 184–90.

Holt, T. (2002) 'A chaotic model for tight diabetes control'. *Diabetic Medicine*. 19 (4): 274–8.

Howie, J., Heaney, D., Maxwell, M., Walker, J., Freeman, G. and Rai, H. (1999) 'Quality at general practice consultations: cross-sectional survey'. *BMJ*, 319: 738–43.

Roter, D. and Larson, S. (2002) 'The Roter Interaction Analysis System (RIAS): utility and flexibility for the analysis of medical interactions'. *Patient Education and Counselling*, 46: 243–51.

Yin, R.K. (2003) *Case Study Research: Design and methods*. London: Sage

Further reading

For understanding more about emergence, see the books on complexity listed at the end of Chapter 1.

For other approaches to analysis of data, see books on research and evaluation in Further Reading at the end of Chapter 1, and the books listed in Further Reading at the end of Chapters 5, 6 and 7. In addition, the following book covers the whole range of approaches to research and analysis used in health-related research.

Bowling, A. (2002) *Research Methods in Health*, 2nd edition. Buckingham: Open University Press.

Resources

The following provide guidance on 'qualitative camparative analysis':

Rihoux, B. and Ragin, C.C. (2008) *Configurational Comparative Methods, Qualitative Comparative Analysis (QCA) and Related Techniques*. London: Sage.

Website: Comparative methods for the advancement of systematic cross-case analysis and smaller studies. www.compasss.org.

Conclusion

Research can be undertaken by health care professionals within their own health care context that directly informs their own clinical practice and generates new knowledge for the wider world. Research can become part of everyday health care practice involving users of health care, health professionals and health service managers, planners and policy makers. Research forms one part of an ongoing spiral of investigation and implementation in innovative, evidence-based clinical practice. Local research for health care practice generates knowledge for the locality and knowledge that can be transferred to other similar contexts; it also illuminates the mechanisms underlying what we perceive as happening in the world. This is a small but important contribution to the global research enterprise of understanding how our world works.

Research for health care practice draws on the experience and expertise of many research disciplines, but refines their approach for generating results that are meaningful to health care professionals and that feed directly in to health care practice. This book has mapped out how research for health care practice relates to other research approaches. The early chapters have much in common with other research approaches, but the distinctive nature of research for health care practice is clarified throughout the book.

The basics for all research apply to research for health care practice. Research aims to understand what is not obvious about how the world works by building on current knowledge and using research methods and skills, a way of reasoning and, where necessary, special equipment. Research for health care practice is different from a great deal of health-related research in using abduction as the way of reasoning. This distinguishes it from research using experimental research methods such as clinical trials. Abduction is a way of reasoning that can admit the constantly changing nature of the world and a diversity of mechanisms underlying similar events in the world. The complexity of the world makes it difficult to predict what will happen when we intervene to try to change it, but research can suggest what is likely to happen, although it is ultimately uncertain.

The basic skills for undertaking research for health care practice are similar to those used in clinical practice. These can be summarised as observation, comparison and asking questions. Observation involves taking note of all the available data of whatever form. Constant comparison, which underlies the research approach, involves comparison of what we notice with what we expect, with what others have found and with what we notice elsewhere or at different times. Asking questions includes being critical of what we think we already know and questioning what we think our data suggests is happening. These skills of observation, comparison and asking questions are used at every stage of research for health care practice and have been a recurring theme throughout the book.

Research for health care practice demands time and care in the early stages of developing the research. This includes clarifying what the research is about, ensuring that it is undertaken ethically, and involving people who have an interest in the research, including health care users. These preparations are common to all health-related research. However, research for health care practice requires greater emphasis on certain aspects of these activities. Clarity about the focus of the research is essential; that is, what the research is investigating. This differs in emphasis from other research approaches where clarity about the research question is essential. With a clear research focus, decisions about how the research is undertaken become relatively straightforward, although it often takes several attempts and false starts before the focus becomes clear. Research for health care practice uses the same ethical principles that apply to all research involving people, but particular care is needed in considering the consequences of the local nature of the research. Its local nature makes the involvement of users both relatively easy and essential for the success of the research. The research has clear relevance for health care users, those that provide or plan for services and the wider public locally, but it needs the active support of these people for it to succeed and for its results to be used to benefit health care. The inclusion of previously unheard voices within research for health care practice has the potential for illuminating aspects of the world that are difficult for health professionals to understand.

Defining the focus of the research in terms of its substance, what it is, and in terms of time or duration, goes hand in hand with designing the research. The way data is collected often defines the boundary of what the research investigates. Data collection methods can also place data from beyond the boundary onto the focus of the research; for example, for research focused on individual people, how each person relates to their family becomes data about the individuals. These problems of defining boundaries are common to many research approaches but can become hidden beneath their research methods. Keeping these issues in the foreground of research enables it to stay closer to the reality of the world. Results from research for health care practice which describe unclear boundaries and uncertainty in how things are categorised will be recognised by health professionals as reflecting what it is really like working in health care.

Research for health care practice occupies a domain bounded by many other research approaches. This domain is recognisable and has been described in this book. However, the domain has indistinct boundaries, with a great deal of exchange of knowledge and skills across boundaries. Into the domain of research for health care practice flow the skills of data collection and analysis developed in disciplines such as epidemiology, psychology and the social sciences. For example, the skills of collecting data from a population can be used to collect data from a group of patients in research for health care practice. The analysis of data about a population or community may be important for understanding the frame around the focus of research for health care practice. The skills involved in collecting data by observation or interview are used in collecting data from health care practice. Out of the domain of research for health care practice flows expertise in understanding health care and people in relation to their health that can assist other approaches to research. For example, understanding the variation in how health care is delivered to a group of patients can assist in the development of new health interventions. Understanding how people themselves change over time in relation to their health problems can inform the design of research evaluating health interventions.

Research for health care practice is most distinctive at the stage of data analysis. The principles underlying analysis are basic to analysis in many research disciplines: constant comparison and the development of classification. These are used in relation to the defined research focus in order to understand more about the research focus. This should lead to finding answers for our research questions, and has the potential for finding answers to questions we had not thought to ask. By seeking to understand the focus of our research we remain open to what we find out about it. However, this requires clarity about what is the focus of research, otherwise we get lost in the complexity of the world. Our investigation is driven by our motivation and aims, which also help to contain our exploration, although research for health care practice demands constant questioning of what is driving and containing it, otherwise we may only discover what is already obvious.

Health professionals have the skills to undertake analysis of data using constant comparison and classification, and this is sufficient for a great deal of research for health care practice. There is potential for using research skills from other disciplines, such as statistics, computer science and complexity science, to develop this approach to analysis further. This is an area of ongoing research and development. However, even with further developments of the methods for research for health care practice, the principles underlying this approach, as set out in this book, will remain the same.

Glossary

This glossary aims to give you a notion of the meaning of words used in research but does not provide formal definitions. The precise way the words are used changes all the time. Some words encapsulate concepts which have been debated for centuries and will continue to be debated. Where a glossary entry consists of more than one word such as 'research diary' or 'non-participant observation' there is one entry in the glossary under one of the words such as 'diary (research diary)' or 'observation (non-participant)'.

Abduction – the analysis and thinking process that aims to develop theory about how and why the world works as it does from data about the world. The theory describes the essential elements of how and why it works, so is a simplified model of what actually happens in the world.

Abstraction – isolating an essential aspect of a phenomenon under study, e.g. gender, socio-economic status, depression, tuberculosis. This is done in order to develop theory.

Action research – research closely linked to development where people who are affected by the research and development are involved with the research and there is a commitment to valuing the perspectives offered by everyone.

Aggregate data – where information about individuals is put together, e.g. the total number of patients in a practice with asthma and the number of these who smoke.

Aim (research aim) – refers to where our research is leading, what we hope it will achieve. Research for health care practice often has an aim linked with improving health care or the health status of patients. However, we may undertake research with the aim of improving how we measure health status or helping health professionals to understand the meaning of illness for patients.

Analysis – the process of examining research data to help us understand what is happening in the world that is not obvious.

Anonymity – where the identity of a particular person is not apparent from the data available.

Attribute – data that tells us something about the person, event, organisation or other entity we are studying. The same item of data is known as a 'variable' if it is used to describe the variation across a population of people, events, organisation or other entities.

Audit – is a way of reviewing and improving a process. For example, in health care audit involves collecting and reviewing data about a process of care, deciding what needs changing to improve care, implementing the change and then collecting and reviewing further data to see if the change has led to the desired improvement in care.

Average – also known as 'the mean', summarises the level of the centre of continuous data (e.g. for age of a group of people, average age = total of all ages/number people).

Behavioural sciences – the group of academic/research disciplines that study behaviour. This includes psychology.

Box plot – represents a set of data including its level and spread. It is a method for summarising raw data without losing detail about the data and can be used to compare sets of data.

Case – a particular person, family, household, organisation, community or society that is being studied. The term is used in research and in clinical practice, e.g. a case of multiple sclerosis in clinical practice is taken to mean a particular person who has the illness multiple sclerosis.

Case study – the study of a particular case as a whole. A case study of living with multiple sclerosis would study a particular person with multiple sclerosis. A case study of a particular hospital would be research seeking to understand how the hospital works.

Census – refers to the collection of data from every individual in a population. Many countries have a national census, e.g. in the UK there is a national census every 10 years when every household completes a questionnaire about the household members.

Classify/Classification – comparing two entities and deciding if they are similar enough to be described as the same type of thing and so put in the same category.

Clinical trial – the evaluation of a treatment, to work out whether or not it is successful.

Cluster analysis – a statistical analysis method for finding things that are similar within a large data set. The analysis process involves comparing every row of data in a data set with every other row in a data set, finding the rows that are most similar and identifying these as a group or cluster. There are a number of different statistical methods for cluster analysis and these are being developed and refined. Cluster analysis is one statistical method within a group of methods known as 'data mining', as they are used to see what is in the data rather than to test predetermined hypotheses.

Coding – giving a label to something, e.g. a section of text in an interview, that summarises what it is about. Different sections of text about the same thing are coded in the same way.

This allows them to be identified easily for comparing them. Clinical notes may be coded, sometimes at the time they are written, e.g. using standard diagnostic codes.

Co-evolution – describes how change in one aspect of the world influences change in another and vice-versa, e.g. the provision of health care changes how a community perceives and deals with health issues, which in turn influences how health care is delivered, which again influences how the community perceives and deals with health issues, and so on.

Cohort – a group of people or other entities that are followed up over time. The people or entities in the group are the same people or entities at the start of the study and throughout the study.

Collaboration (research collaboration) – a research team working together. The team may involve people with different roles, e.g. health professionals, academics or other professional researchers and research users.

Comparison – underlies a great deal of research as by comparing two things we work our whether and how they are different, and this may give clues as to why they are different.

Complexity – has an everyday meaning and is also used with reference to complexity science. Complexity science investigates the world as complex: there are many components interacting in the world; interaction makes predicting what will happen difficult; from interaction emerge phenomena that have characteristics that are not reducible to the component parts.

Confidentiality – allowing information to be known only by certain people, e.g. a health care team or a research team.

Consent (to research) – formal agreement to participate in research.

Cost-effective – describes a treatment or health service when there is evidence that it improves health and is no more costly than other treatments or services with the same impact on health.

Critical realism – an approach to research where we assume that there is a real world which exists even when we are not aware of it, and we can research it, but we need to be cautious about the assumptions we make, in particular the assumption that we can prove beyond dispute what causes what, or that it is possible, at least in theory, to know everything about the world.

Cross-sectional – research that looks at an issue at one point in time.

Data – the information we collect about the aspect of the world we are studying. It represents something about the world. Examples of data from clinical practice and research are height, weight, age, blood glucose, patient descriptions of how they feel, recordings of clinical consultations, photographs.

Data (categorical) – when the data about something is in terms of the category into which it fits, e.g. categories of people in terms of gender are male and female.

Data (continuous) – refers to data such as measurement of height, weight, age, seconds. Compared to the length of the scale used for measuring, the differences between the points on the scale for measurement are very small.

Data extraction – is when data is taken from one source for use in another form, e.g. from text into a spreadsheet or.

Data (ordinal) – is data that has some order to it. The term is usually used for categorical data where there is an order to the categories, e.g. indicating strength of opinion.

Data protection – keeping confidential any data about identifiable people, including storing it securely and destroying it so it cannot be retrieved. Many countries have laws about access to, use of and storage of personal data.

Data saturation – the point at which, when collecting qualitative data, no new information about the focus of the research is revealed.

Data set – all the data for a study.

Deduction – the way of reasoning used in disciplines such as mathematics and philosophy that demonstrates the truth of a proposition by a sequence of logical arguments.

Delphi method – a process of developing ideas and forming a consensus about an issue among a group of people without them being in contact with each other.

Design (research design) – the detailed planning of how the research will be undertaken, including how to collect and analyse data.

Diary (research diary) – the document all researchers are advised to keep where they note what they do, what they think, discussions with people about their research, reflections on the research and changes they make to the research process. The form of the research diary varies (formal or informal, paper or computer-based, individual or team). It is often in several forms, e.g. a diary of activities such as during data collection or analysis, a project blog for reflecting on the research and discussing with colleagues, and notes of research team meetings or research supervisions.

Dissemination – telling others about your research, particularly the research results, conclusions and implications for health care practice.

Diversity – the range of differences between things (people, organisations, etc); e.g. there is a diversity in how people understand their illness, which means that most people have a slightly different way of understanding their illness. Diversity of ethnicity in a population means that the population includes people of a number of different ethnicities. Diversity can also be called 'variation'.

Dynamic – the pace and pattern of change over time.

Emancipatory research – action research where the research process enables voices that have previously not been heard, or have been ignored, to influence the research and development.

Emerges/Emergence – when used in the context of complexity science, refers to phenomena which result from the interaction of many components but have characteristics that are not reducible to the components and their interaction. Temperature is an emergent phenomenon; an ecology such as a woodland is emergent as emerges from the co-existence and interaction of many plants and animals.

Epidemiology – the study of health of populations.

Epistemology – questioning and understanding how we know what we know.

Ethics (research ethics) – the value system currently held to be the norm in our society for how research is undertaken. Ethical principles and the details of what is considered ethical research is constantly being debated, adjusted and refined.

Ethical approval – formal approval that proposed research is ethical. The process for gaining this varies between countries. In the UK research in the NHS has to be approved by a Research Ethics Committee.

Evaluation – the assessment of whether something works in the way it is expected to work and has the impact that was intended, such as a new treatment or health care service.

Exclusion criteria – attributes of people or other entities that mean they are not included, e.g. individuals excluded from a study, or research papers excluded from a literature review.

Feasibility study – a small study undertaken early in research to check whether it will be possible to do the research in the way it is planned, i.e. is it feasible?

Field notes – notes taken during the process of research. For data collection using observation, what is observed is recorded in field notes: the notes are made in the research field.

Focus (research) – used in this book for what it is we want to investigate. It is a non-technical usage of the word focus.

Focus group – a research method where a group of people are asked to discuss an issue. It is particularly used for research seeking to understand how people discuss, debate and develop ideas about an issue.

Frame – the context of research in terms of time, place and what is happening.

Framing – is a term that has a technical meaning in research. It refers to how the context in which data is collected influences the data results; e.g. if people are to be interviewed about their experience of health care, they may say very different things while in hospital than if asked when fit and well interviewed when out shopping. The term can also refer to the ordering of questions in an interview or questionnaire, as one question may influence how later questions are answered.

Generalise – moving from understanding something about particular people, organisations, events and so on, to saying the same understanding applies more generally. The term is also used in a more technical way when describing how what is known about a sample of people, organisations, events and so on can be applied to the whole population from which the sample was drawn. The term can be used in both qualitative and quantitative methods where a sample is taken.

Generation effect – the difference in experience of people of different generations.

Graph – a method of summarising data to make it easily visualised. The nature of the data determines which type of graph is appropriate.

Graph (bar) – suitable for visualising data where there are relevant categories; e.g. the number of people in a population in five-year age bands (0–4 years, 5–9 years, 10–14 years etc.).

Group dynamics – how people respond to each other in a group. This needs to be taken into account in focus groups and group interviews. There are many studies of group dynamics.

Hypothesis (research hypothesis) – is a way of formulating what we think might be happening in the world, which we then test through our research. Hypotheses are often associated with using research techniques such as statistical modelling and experimental methods. However, we can also develop hypotheses when we are using other research approaches, e.g. during analysis of interview data we may develop a hypothesis about people's attitudes to a health issue, then test our hypothesis by looking for data that does and does not support it.

Incidence – describes the number of people in a population who develop a disease expressed as a rate (e.g. number per 1,000 people in the population). It is usually described for the time period of one year, but a different timeframe can be used. The incidence of diabetes in a population would be the number of people being diagnosed as having diabetes in a year, expressed as a rate.

Inclusion criteria – attributes of people or other entities that mean they are included, e.g. individuals included in a study, or research papers included in a literature review.

Induction – a way of reasoning used in research where a general statement about how the world works is made based on the observation of a relatively small number of occurrences of something happening.

Information science – the knowledge and skills of storing, retrieving and analysing information. Librarians have training in information science.

Interview – a method of collecting data through communication with a person or people.

Interview (group) – an interview with more than one person at the same time, e.g. a family or team.

Interview (key informant) – an interview with someone who has knowledge and expertise about an issue.

Interview (semi-structured) – where the interview is focused on particular topics, but allows the interviewee to talk about them as they want.

Interview (structured) – an interview with a tight structure similar to that of a questionnaire.

Iteration – in research this refers to going through a process such as thinking through a research question, collecting initial data or undertaking first stage analysis, then going back to what seems like the start to see what needs to be changed in the light of our new understanding following this process; e.g. changing a research question after reviewing the literature, changing a recruitment process after the first few participants have been recruited, changing an interview schedule after the first few interviews. There is movement forward, like a spiral, as we develop our understanding.

Literature (research) – the written reports of research, often published in research journals.

Literature review – reading and analysing published research (see systematic review).

Longitudinal – research that follows a research issue over time.

Mean – also known as 'average', summarises the level of the centre of continuous data (e.g. for a group of people, average age = total of all ages/number of people).

Median – the centre of a set of data, where half the data is larger and half smaller.

Methodology – the theory of research methods, how and why research methods work.

Mixed methods – studies or literature reviews where more than one type of method is used – qualitative, quantitative or experimental. It is a term used particularly in health sciences where these different approaches may be used in relation to the same health issue.

Model – a simplified version of what we think is happening in the world (usually a model deals with the small part or aspect of the world we are interested in).

Narrative analysis – an approach to the analysis of stories that has become popular in health research in the last decade. The analysis seeks meaning and purpose in the telling of the story and takes account of its structure and audience.

Nominal Group Technique – a method of engaging a group of people in generating ideas about an issue and then reaching a consensus.

Objective (research objective) – what each task in a research project is intended to achieve. When all research objectives are achieved, we should be in a position to answer our research questions.

Observation (non-participant) – observing a situation when not actually part of what is happening, e.g. observing a health care consultation but not taking part in it.

Observation (participant) – observing a situation while also taking an active role in what is happening, e.g. observing the reception area of a health care clinic while working as a receptionist.

Ontology – questioning and understanding the nature of things, the world, life, e.g. Does the entity we are studying really exist?

Outlier – a data point that is a long way from any other data point, e.g. on a box plot.

Participant (research) – a person taking part in a research project, e.g. by providing data about themselves.

Participatory research – where the public, stakeholders and users are all involved in the research process. The research can include a whole community. The terms participatory research, emancipatory research and action research refer to very similar research approaches. The terms have been developed in different disciplines and contexts with varying political aims.

Pie chart – a visual method of representing data about one aspect of the people or other entities studied.

Pilot study – a small study undertaken early in research that guides the design of the research.

Population – commonly used to describe people, but can describe any collection of cases where the individual cases are similar. The population is all the cases in a defined place and time, e.g. population served by a health clinic, population of London, population of Canada, population of bacteria in a bucket of water.

Prevalence – the number of people in a population living with an illness at a particular time, e.g. the prevalence of asthma in a community is the number of people who have asthma at the time when the count is undertaken.

Probability – the likelihood that something will happen in certain circumstances. This is often expressed as a ratio, e.g. the probability of a woman consistently taking the oral contraceptive pill for a year becoming pregnant is less than one in one hundred (1:100); so of one hundred women taking the pill for a year, one (or less) women will become pregnant.

Qualitative – research methods such as interviews, focus groups and observation.

Qualitative Comparative Analysis – comparison of cases by comparing the pattern of attributes of each case to that of other cases.

Quantitative – research methods involving counting and measurement such as surveys and cohort studies.

Question (closed) – phrased to offer a limited choice of answers, e.g. How old are you? Do you attend the clinic?

Question (leading) – one that suggests what might be an acceptable answer.

Question (open) – the respondent decides how to answer.

Question (research question) – a way of formulating what we want to understand about the world through our research. For all research it is important to clarify the research question. The research question can also be expressed as a 'hypothesis'.

Questionnaire – a list of questions designed for collecting research data.

Questionnaire (standardised) – a list of questions for collecting research data that have been tested for their ability to collect comparable data in different research studies or from different groups of people or in different settings.

Randomised controlled trial – an experimental research method used for testing the effectiveness of health interventions. It is a particularly rigorous type of clinical trial, where participants are allocated randomly to the intervention or control group.

Random numbers – are numbers with no pattern to them.

Random sample – is a sample where there is no pattern to how the members of the sample are identified. Every case in the population from which the sample is taken has the same chance of being included in the sample.

Range – the two extremes of data in a data set.

Range (interquartile) – the range of the data that includes a quarter of all data points either side of the median.

Rate – a way of describing events or occurrences in a standardised way for comparison, e.g. the incidence of disease is described as a rate, such as the number of people developing the disease per 1,000 people per year.

Ratio – the relationship of size, e.g. if there are 100 people in a group, 60 men and 40 women, the ratio of men to women is 60:40 or 3:2.

Recruitment – the process of inviting people or organisations to participate in research.

Recruitment (snowball) – when people or organisations participating in research are asked to suggest other people or organisations who are then invited to participate (also known as 'snowball sampling').

Reductionism – the idea that it is possible to understand how the world works by looking at the details, e.g. a molecular biologist may seek to understand how the world functions in terms of all the molecules that make up the world and how they interact.

Reflexivity – the process of reviewing research plans, research data, data collection processes and data analysis, reflecting on what has influenced the data or process, being critical of the data or process and limiting interpretation to what the data can support.

Response rate – the number of people responding (e.g. to an invitation to take part in research or to a questionnaire) divided by the number of people asked.

Sample – the cases chosen to be studied from a larger population.

Sampling (for diversity) – choosing people or organisations that represent a range of characteristics based on what is known about the population and the aims of the study; e.g. a study of people with back pain may recruit people with very little back pain, moderate back pain and severe back pain and people who are young, middle-aged and old.

Sampling (purposive) – choosing people or organisations for a study who are most likely to provide the data needed for the aim of the study.

Sampling (snowball) – when people or organisations participating in research are asked to suggest other people or organisations who are then invited to participate (also known as 'snowball recruitment').

Scoping the literature – examining the range of literature on a topic.

Search engines (literature search systems) – computer-based systems available to assist in finding literature on a particular topic.

Secondary analysis – analysis of data that was collected for some other purpose (e.g. clinical records, hospital administrative data) or data collected for a different research project.

Secular trend – change observed over time. Used in research to distinguish changes in the wider world from changes related to an intervention being evaluated.

Sequence analysis – looks for repeated patterns in the sequence of data.

Social science – the group of research/academic disciplines that study the social world, including how society works, culture and meaning, organisations and how they function. The academic disciplines include anthropology, sociology, politics, economics, business studies and legal studies.

Stakeholder – someone with a particular interest in an issue because of their role or occupation.

Standardised – uniform comparison to ensure that we indicate real differences rather than differences due to the way the things have been observed or measured; e.g. measuring equipment is standardised so we can compare measurement made on different people (height, weight, blood cholesterol etc.). The way questions are asked in surveys can be standardised so that they elicit comparable information. Data collected from many people or many communities can be standardised for comparison, e.g. death rates from heart disease in communities are standardised to take account of the age of people in the communities (a community with lots of young people will tend to have a lower number of deaths, but the rate of death for older people may be the same as in communities with few young people).

Statistics – the research discipline expert in methods for the analysis of numerical data.

Stem and leaf plot – a method of exploring raw data for its pattern and spread without summarising the data.

Survey – collecting data from across a population (or sample of the population) to understand the variation across the population.

Synthesis – bringing together theory and knowledge from various sources and from this, developing new theory and knowledge.

Systematic review – the process of reviewing research literature in a way that other people can follow and if repeated by them would lead them to similar conclusions.

A systematic review can use all types of research literature. The term is sometimes used as shorthand for the Cochrane style of systematic review, which is a particular style of review for assessing the effectiveness of health interventions.

Theory – an understanding about how and why things happen in the world that is currently the best understanding we have but that may change as science progresses. Theory is tested and improved through research.

Time series – data about an aspect of something that is collected at frequent time points.

Timeframe – a particular period of time in which we are interested, for example the period of time a person has a disease or the period of time a health care team works together.

Timeline – a line indicating direction in time along which data can be plotted.

Transferability – is a term used in contrast to 'generalisability'. If the results of research in one place and time are likely to be relevant to another place and time, then they are considered transferable.

Transparency – in research means the same as in common usage, that something is see-through. The term is used to indicate that nothing is hidden about the way research is done so the whole process is open to scrutiny.

Triangulation – the use of different sources of data or different research methods for one research question.

User (research user) – people who have an interest in what research is undertaken, how it is done and the results of the research, through their role or occupation. Users of health-related research include people with health problems, health care professionals, health service managers and policy makers and the public.

Validity – refers to how closely what we describe, assess or measure in our research resembles what is in the world or happening in the world.

Variable – an aspect of the entity we are studying (patient, organisation, etc.) which is different or varies between the patients, organisations and so on; e.g. age describes something about patients, it varies between patients, so age can be called a variable. The difference or variation can also be over time, e.g. blood glucose changes in the same patient over time, so blood glucose can be called a variable.

Variable (confounding) – a term used in analysis for example, when analysing survey data, where one variable appears to relate to another variable although there is no relationship. This can occur if a third variable relates to them both.

Variation – the differences between things, e.g. differences between patients with diabetes or between hospitals. This type of variation can be called 'diversity'. Variation can also refer to change over time, difference detected in the same thing over time.

Variation (random) – the observation that events or variation have no pattern when looked at overall. However, the events or variation can have what appears to be a pattern over a limited space/time. If our research is undertaken within a limited space/time, then we can confuse these patterns within the random variation with patterns that are caused by something happening in the world. Making this distinction is what underpins many statistical methods.

Write and draw – a method of collecting data, particularly from children where they are asked to draw and write something about the research issue.

Index

Research Methods Books from SAGE

Read sample chapters online now!

Basics of QUALITATIVE RESEARCH 3e

Juliet Corbin
Anselm Strauss

The Mixed Methods Reader

Vicki L. Plano Clark • John W. Creswell

DOING QUALITATIVE RESEARCH USING YOUR COMPUTER

A PRACTICAL GUIDE

CHRIS HAHN

SECOND EDITION
INTERVIEWS
Learning the Craft of Qualitative Research Interviewing

Steinar Kvale
Svend Brinkmann

DISCOVERING STATISTICS USING SPSS THIRD EDITION

ANDY FIELD

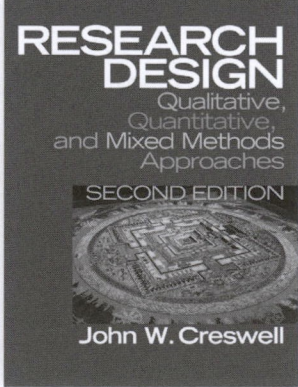

RESEARCH DESIGN
Qualitative, Quantitative, and Mixed Methods Approaches
SECOND EDITION

John W. Creswell

www.sagepub.co.uk

The Qualitative Research Kit

Edited by Uwe Flick

Read sample chapters online now!

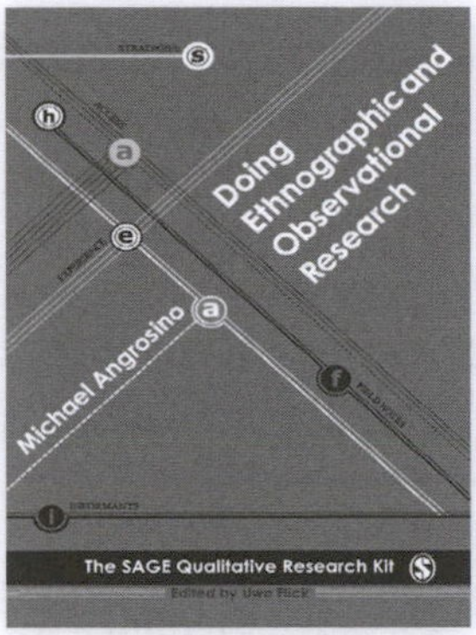

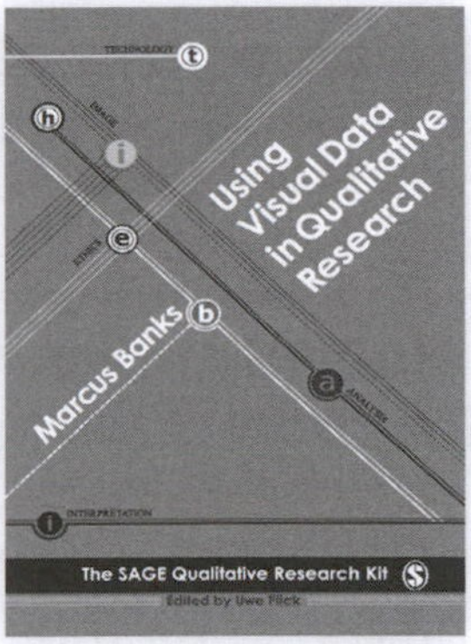

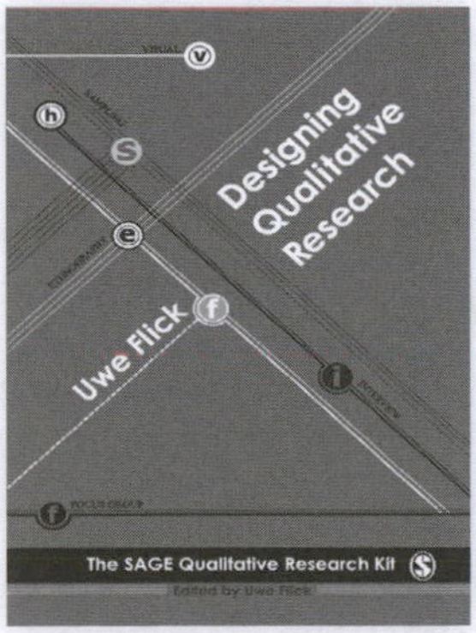

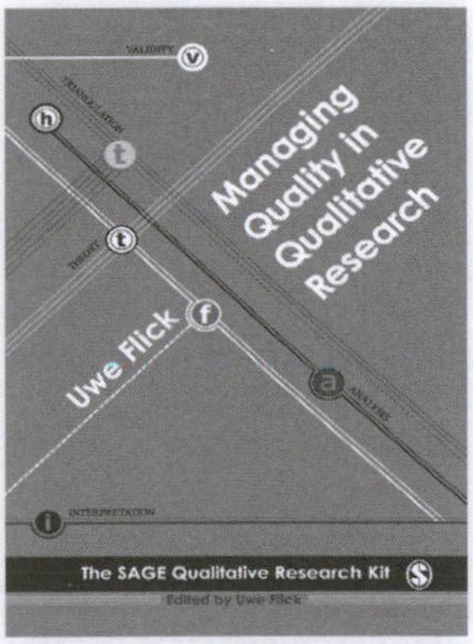

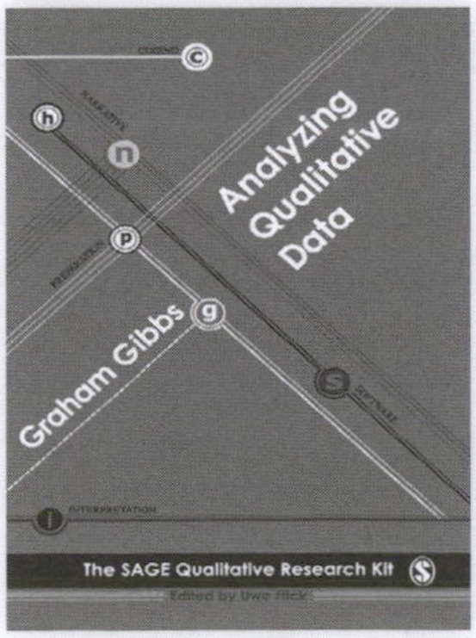

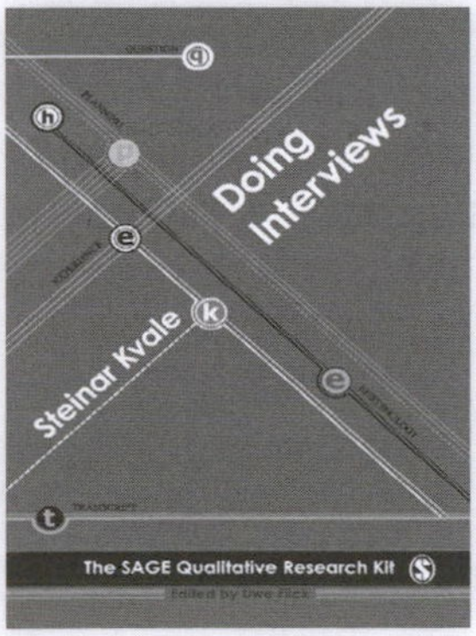

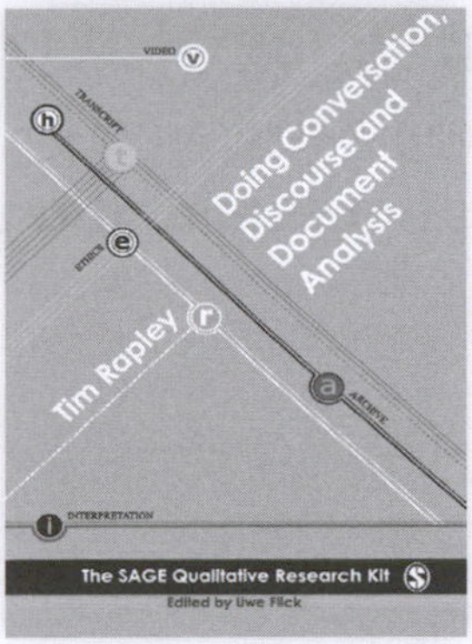

Doing Ethnographic and Observational Research — Michael Angrosino — The SAGE Qualitative Research Kit — Edited by Uwe Flick

Using Visual Data in Qualitative Research — Marcus Banks — The SAGE Qualitative Research Kit — Edited by Uwe Flick

Doing Focus Groups — Rosaline Barbour — The SAGE Qualitative Research Kit

Designing Qualitative Research — Uwe Flick — The SAGE Qualitative Research Kit — Edited by Uwe Flick

Managing Quality in Qualitative Research — Uwe Flick — The SAGE Qualitative Research Kit — Edited by Uwe Flick

Analyzing Qualitative Data — Graham Gibbs — The SAGE Qualitative Research Kit — Edited by Uwe Flick

Doing Interviews — Steinar Kvale — The SAGE Qualitative Research Kit — Edited by Uwe Flick

Doing Conversation, Discourse and Document Analysis — Tim Rapley — The SAGE Qualitative Research Kit — Edited by Uwe Flick

www.sagepub.co.uk

Supporting researchers for more than forty years

Research methods have always been at the core of SAGE's publishing. Sara Miller McCune founded SAGE in 1965 and soon after, she published SAGE's first methods book, *Public Policy Evaluation*. A few years later, she launched the Quantitative Applications in the Social Sciences series – affectionately known as the 'little green books'.

Always at the forefront of developing and supporting new approaches in methods, SAGE published early groundbreaking texts and journals in the fields of qualitative methods and evaluation.

Today, more than forty years and two million little green books later, SAGE continues to push the boundaries with a growing list of more than 1,200 research methods books, journals, and reference works across the social, behavioural, and health sciences.

From qualitative, quantitative and mixed methods to evaluation, SAGE is the essential resource for academics and practitioners looking for the latest in methods by leading scholars.

www.sagepublications.com